individual personality. Two other papers that involve SRM techniques focus on gender differences in peer reputation (Card, Hodges, Little, & Hawley, 2005) and gender differences in parent–sibling relationships (Martin & Ross, 2005). The specifics of the statistical procedures differ, but both may be conceptualised as variants on a familiar analysis of variance theme with reports of participant behaviour as dependent variables and either gender and age as independent variables or gender of nominator and gender of target as independent variables.

Interdependence in family and friend relationships

APIM and SRM techniques are a means to an end, not an end unto themselves. The truism bears repeating: Statistical procedures are only as valuable as the data to which they are applied. The data presented in this Special Issue reflect a social world that is complicated and sometimes messy, where statistical nonindependence is a fact of life. APIM and SRM procedures were designed specifically for this purpose, which not only makes them more accurate and more robust than their predecessors but also more practical and more flexible. This should be welcome news for scholars of close relationships who have long struggled to adapt experimental practices to a world in which everything seems to be correlated. Scholars contributing to this Special Issue have taken full advantage of these new analytic techniques, providing a detailed glimpse into the inner workings of family and peer relationships.

Family relationships are the focus of four papers in this special issue. Cook and Kenny (2005) describe how mother and adolescent child perceptions of attachment security are stable over time yet also responsive to bidirectional influence processes. Ross and colleagues (2005) reveal that despite the generally positive views that parents and school-aged children hold for one another, participants maintain distinct perspectives of relationships that are more consistent within generations than between generations. Branje and colleagues (2005) report that individual agreeableness is positively associated with perceived support in all family relationships for all participants except mothers, who are considered supportive regardless of their personality. Martin and Ross (2005) describe findings indicating that as young children grow older, parents are more likely to prohibit mild physical aggression by and toward daughters and are more likely to tolerate mild physical aggression by sons.

Peer relationships are the focus of four other papers. Adams et al. (2005) report that reciprocated friendship moderates the stability of aggression during early adolescence, such that aggression declines for aggressive youth with nonaggressive friends but not for other aggressive youth. Burk and Laursen (2005) describe data indicating that adolescent friendship negativity is associated with poorer school grades, self- and friend reports of difficulties managing conflict, and self- and mother reports of heightened behaviour problems. Cillessen and colleagues (2005) report that self- and peer reports of adolescent aggression and prosocial behaviour are linked to the perceptions that friends share about conflict, closeness, companionship, helping, and security in their relationship. Card and colleagues (2005) identify gender differences in peer nominations of relational aggression and social status such that early adolescent girls offer more nominations (but are not necessarily nominated more often) than boys.

Two themes are [...] [...] The first theme is that close relationships matter. Most scholars will find reassurance on this point. We thought we knew that parents and friends made important contributions to developmental outcomes, but prior studies have tended to rely on statistical techniques that were inappropriate for nonindependent data. Several studies in this special issue confirm that individual outcomes are strongly linked to specific characteristics as well as to the overall quality of relationships with parents and friends. The second theme is that perspectives on relationships matter. This point may be uncomfortable for some scholars. Concordant views on relationships and individuals are common, but not compulsory. APIM analyses confirm that actor effects are more prevalent than partner effects, which raises questions about the extent to which prior studies may have overestimated the significance of close relationships. One conclusion is certain: Overly simplistic views of influence processes must necessarily be revised in the face of findings indicating that outcomes vary as a function of the shared and independent perspectives of relationship participants.

Implications for development

Procedures for analysing interdependent data were developed by social psychologists and social psychologists remain the primary beneficiaries of these techniques (Kashy & Kenny, 2000). Developmental scholars have been slow to adopt these new analytic methods and slow to adapt them to their needs. Perhaps this is because their developmental implications are not readily apparent. Indeed, a review of the literature reveals few developmental applications of either procedure. To be sure, developmental journals include a small number of empirical studies that employ SRM and APIM analyses, but invariably these involve associations among concurrent data points that do not address the fundamental developmental issue of change over time in relationships or groups.

It should be clear from the papers in this Special Issue that APIM procedures can be readily applied to developmental data. Cook and Kenny (2005) provide an elegant tutorial on the use of longitudinal dyadic data to assess relationship stability. The central premise of this paper cannot be overstated: Bidirectional influences are inherent in most close relationships and APIM procedures are uniquely suited to address issues of relationship stability and change. Novel applications of APIM procedures to longitudinal data are also detailed in papers by Adams et al. (2005) and by Martin and Ross (2005). Each describes change from one time period to the next in individual behaviour as a function of participation in different relationship constellations. Put simply, identical assessments were obtained from both participants in a relationship at two consecutive times, thus permitting the stability of a construct to be compared across friend and sibling relationships. Admittedly, two time points do not a developmental trajectory make, but there is no reason why similar analytic procedures cannot be adapted to accommodate additional time points. Developmental scholars can and should move quickly to apply APIM procedures to longitudinal data that address issues of long-term stability and change in close relationships.

APIM procedures also ought to be amenable to delineating pathways of individual adjustment. Two papers in this Special Issue (Burk & Laursen, 2005; Cillessen et al., 2005) apply

APIM techniques to concurrent data in order to explore associations between relationship characteristics and individual outcomes. It should not take much imagination to modify the design of these studies to accommodate longitudinal data; assessments of prior adjustment could be added to the model as predictor variables and subsequent outcomes could be substituted for concurrent outcomes. Again, models that incorporated multiple time points have yet to be articulated, but this should not prove to be an insurmountable obstacle.

Developmental applications of SRM procedures are less obvious. As noted by Little and Card (2005), SRM modelling of longitudinal processes is virtually uncharted territory. The papers in this Special Issue that employed SRM techniques were consistent in their exclusive focus on concurrent patterns of association. Branje and colleagues (2005), however, offer a glimpse into a future where SRM techniques are applied to longitudinal data. In their paper, concurrent assessments of SRM components of support and SRM components of agreeableness were found to be related. One could imagine expanding the model to incorporate similar associations between variables over time. No doubt this will prove to be a modest initial step toward the goal of expanding SRM procedures to address issues of developmental change.

Conclusion

The study of close relationships is rapidly emerging as one of the unifying themes in contemporary behavioural science (Hartup & Laursen, 1999). Interest in the topic has fostered methodological advances on several fronts. It is now standard practice to collect data that reflect the experience and perspectives of all participants in a relationship or a group. But collecting more and better data creates new challenges. What to do with all of this information? The papers in this Special Issue highlight analytic techniques that will enable developmental scholars to take full advantage of the rich and nuanced data that characterise contemporary research on close relationships.

References

Adams, R. E., Bukowski, W. M., & Bagwell, C. (2005). Stability of aggression in early adolescence as moderated by reciprocated friendship status and friend's aggression. *International Journal of Behavioral Development, 29*, 139–145.

Baumeister, R. F., & Leary, M. R. (1995). The need to belong: Desire for interpersonal attachments as a fundamental human motivation. *Psychological Bulletin, 117*, 497–529.

Branje, S. J. T., Van Lieshout, C. F. M., & Van Aken, M. A. G. (2005). Relations between Agreeableness and perceived support in family relationships: Why nice people are not always supportive. *International Journal of Behavioral Development, 29*, 120–128.

Burk, W. J., & Laursen, B. (2005). Adolescent perceptions of friendship and their associations with individual adjustment. *International Journal of Behavioral Development, 29*, 156–164.

Card, N. A., Hodges, E. V. E., Little, T. D., & Hawley, P. H. (2005). Gender effects in peer nominations for aggression and social status. *International Journal of Behavioral Development, 29*, 146–155.

Cillessen, A. H. N., Jiang, X. L., West, T. V., & Laszkowski, D. K. (2005). Predictors of dyadic friendship quality in adolescence. *International Journal of Behavioral Development, 29*, 165–172.

Cook, W. L., & Kenny, D. A. (2005). The Actor–Partner Interdependence Model: A model of bidirectional effects in developmental studies. *International Journal of Behavioral Development, 29*, 101–109.

Hartup, W. W., & Laursen, B. (1999). Relationships as developmental contexts: Retrospective themes and contemporary issues. In W. A. Collins & B. Laursen (Eds), *The Minnesota Symposia on Child Psychology: Vol. 30. Relationships as developmental contexts* (pp. 13–35). Mahwah, NJ: Lawrence Erlbaum Associates Inc.

Kashy, D. A., & Kenny, D. A. (2000). The analysis of data from dyads and groups. In H. Reis & C. M. Judd (Eds.), *Handbook of research methods in social and personality psychology* (pp. 451–477). New York: Cambridge University Press.

Kelly, H. H., Berscheid, E., Christensen, A., Harvey, J. H., Huston, T. L., Levinger, G., McClintock, E., Peplau, L. A., & Peterson, D. R. (1983). *Close relationships*. New York: Freeman.

Kenny, D. A. (1995). Design and analysis issues in dyadic research. *Review of Personality and Social Psychology, 11*, 164–184.

Kenny, D. A., & La Voie, L. (1985). Separating individual and group effects. *Journal of Personality and Social Psychology, 48*, 339–348.

Laursen, B., & Bukowski, W. M. (1997). A developmental guide to the organisation of close relationships. *International Journal of Behavioral Development, 21*, 747–770.

Little, T. D., & Card, N. A. (2005). On the use of Social Relations and Actor-Partner Interdependence Models in developmental research. *International Journal of Behavioral Development, 29*, 173–179.

Martin, J. L., & Ross, H. S. (2005). Sibling aggression: Sex differences and parents' reactions. *International Journal of Behavioral Development, 29*, 129–138.

Reis, H. T., Collins, W. A., & Berscheid, E. (2000). The relationship context of human behavior and development. *Psychological Bulletin, 126*, 844–872.

Ross, H., Stein, N., Trabasso, T., Woody, E., & Ross, M. (2005). The quality of family relationships within and across generations. A social relations analysis. *International Journal of Behavioral Development, 29*, 110–119.

International Journal of Behavioral Development
2005, 29 (2), 97–100

http://www.tandf.co.uk/journals/pp/01650244.html

Ψ Psychology Press
Taylor & Francis Group

© 2005 The International Society for the
Study of Behavioural Development

DOI: 10.1080/01650250444000450

Dyadic and group perspectives on close relationships

Brett Laursen

Florida Atlantic University, Fort Lauderdale, FL, USA

Recent advances in the study of close relationships hold the potential for new insights into the significance of interdependence and the mechanism of relationship influence. The papers in this special issue apply two new data analytic techniques to the study of family and friend relationships. The Actor–Partner Interdependence Model incorporates the perspectives of both participants in a dyad into analyses that describe shared and unique views of the relationship. The Social Relations Model incorporates the perspectives of all members of a group into analyses that ascribe views unique to ... al applications of ... with the aim of ...

Interdependence ca... study interpersonal ... terises close affiliati... dent relationship c... interconnections. F... interdependence de... variables that lack ... variables are modera... incongruous constr... devoted to dyadic ... ships. A distinguish... for papers with an ... into family and frie... recent advances i... interdependence.

influence that participants exert on ... ...elings, and behaviours. Affective ... al to many close relationships, but ... ...ary such that particular emotional ... in all affiliations.

...temporary scholars have devoted to ...ships, it may come as a surprise to ... ...ce is often the first casualty in ... the topic. Data from all participants ... ...up are a prerequisite for assaying ... ...se, shared perceptions and mutual ... ...urmised. Yet all too often scholars ... ...ce and assume (or hope) that this will ... ...avour of the relationship or group. ... ...pproach is not just that individual ... ...rate or systematically biased. Mutual ... ...esented if the behaviours or percep- ... ...recorded. Participants in a group or ... ...ch other and, in turn, jointly and ... ...ividual and relationship outcomes. ... ...oning variance is impossible if there ... ...ation. Some scholars have attempted ... ...lem by controlling the input from ... ...get participant through the use of ... ...cal scenarios. Success in minimising ... to interdependence gives rise to a ... ...use the strength and influence of ... ...onstant from one relationship to the ... ...compromised as variation attributed ... ...ines.

The sign...

Close relationships ... human culture; fam... transmit lessons a... across generations ... dependence is so e... postulated to be pa... participate in close ... Research on close ... family members, ... dependent relation... contribution to d... kowski, 1997). Ce... close relationships are built upon bidirectional social interactions: Frequent, strong and diverse interconnections between participants in a close relationship are maintained over an extended period of time (Kelley et al., 1983). Interdependence

all participants in a relationship is a ...ient condition for addressing inter- dependence. Appropriate analytic models must be adopted that permit the unique partitioning of variance to the different sources. Most conventional statistical approaches fail to capture the richness of relationship experiences. The common

Correspondence should be sent to Brett Laursen, Department of Psychology, Florida Atlantic University, 2912 College Avenue, Fort Lauderdale FL 33314, USA; e-mail: laursen@fau.edu.

Support for the preparation of this article was provided by a grant from the US National Institute of Mental Health (MH058116). Special thanks to Todd Little, Noel Card, William Cook, and William Graziano for reviewing the manuscripts in this special issue and to Bill Bukowski for providing comments on a previous draft of this paper.

strategy of summing or averaging reports across participants in a relationship or group reduces multiple data points to a single score, but it does so by eliminating all traces of variation that may be attributed to individuals. It also masks considerable heterogeneity among groups or dyads that share the same score. Despite identical means, couples that report similar moderate levels of relationship satisfaction bear little resemblance to those in which one person is happy and the other is miserable.

Another common approach is to deny statistical nonindependence and treat correlated dyadic data as if they were independent data. Some conventional parametric statistics (e.g., analyses of variance) are built upon the assumption that independent variables are uncorrelated. Violation of the independence assumption introduces systematic bias into significance tests. The type of error depends upon the direction (positive or negative) of the correlation and the type of independent variable (Kenny, 1995). One common problem involves inflating Type II error (concluding that there is no effect when there really is an effect) because positively correlated scores from two or more different sources (e.g., friends or parents and children) are treated as independent variables. Should these scores be negatively correlated, Type I error (concluding that there is an effect when there really is not) is inflated. Collinearity analyses may identify biased significance tests but the problem remains that variance attributable to mutual influences cannot be readily disentangled from that attributed to individuals.

Lamentations about the lack of statistical tools to deal with interdependent data are out-of-date; the analytic capabilities available to scholars are more than adequate for most research designs. Instead, obstacles tend to be conceptual and paradigmatic. After all, the implications of interdependence are unsettling: Most of what we think we know about relationships and groups is predicated on research employing inadequate designs and inappropriate statistics. There is some comfort in the knowledge that experimental manipulations are largely immune to concerns about interdependence and that robust effects are resilient to all but the most egregious violations of independence. Still, we must acknowledge that as a consequence of prior research practices, our understanding of close relationships is quite limited; effects currently attributed to unique constructs will decline as variance is apportioned among different sources and as the statistical power to detect differences increases the number of higher order interactions.

Statistical analyses with interdependent data

This Special Issue highlights two analytic strategies designed specifically for nonindependent data. The Actor–Partner Interdependence Model (APIM: Kashy & Kenny, 2000) is designed to describe dyads. Each person in the study contributes data for only one relationship and scores from both participants describe the same independent variables and the same outcome variables. *Individual-level measures* contain separate scores for each participant. *Dyad-level measures* contain a single summary score that includes data contributed by both participants in a relationship. The specifics of the model differ depending on whether the participants in a dyad are distinguishable (e.g., parent and child, husband and wife) or interchangeable (same-sex friends). Regardless of the particulars, two effects are estimated: *Actor effects* describe

the association between a person's score on an independent variable and their own score on an outcome variable. *Partner effects* describe the association between a person's score on an independent variable and the partner's score on an outcome variable. These unique effects include adjustments for the correlation between participant scores on the independent variable and the correlation between the unexplained variance of each participant's outcome score. Actor–partner interaction effects may also be estimated.

APIM analyses are designed to shed light on individuals and relationships. Three of the papers in this Special Issue that employ APIM procedures involve exchangeable cases, namely same-sex friendships (Adams, Bukowski, & Bagwell, 2005; Burk & Laursen, 2005; Cillessen, Jiang, Laszkowski, & West, 2005). In each case, statistical nonindependence was observed between friend reports. In some studies the independent variables described individual-level measures of participants, such as aggression and prosocial behaviour, whereas in other studies the independent variables described dyad-level measures of the friendship, such as perceptions of positive and negative relationship qualities. Participants also provided information about outcome variables, some pertaining to individual-level measures describing the adjustment of one of the participants and others describing dyad-level measures of characteristics of the friendship. One of the papers in this special issue employs APIM procedures that involve distinguishable cases, namely mother–child dyads (Cook & Kenny, 2005). As might be expected, statistical nonindependence characterises mother and child perceptions of attachment security. Individual-level reports about the relationship at different time points served as predictor and outcome variables.

The Social Relations Model (SRM: Kenny & La Voie, 1984) is designed for use with groups in which each person participates in multiple dyads and generates a score for each relationship. These scores may be *individual-level measures* about specific participants, *dyad-level measures* about specific relationships, or *group-level measures* that describe the entire collective. As Little and Card (2005) emphasise in their discussion, actor and partner effects refer to latent variables in SRM analyses. Here, the terms carry a different meaning from their APIM counterparts. *Actor effects* describe the perceptions that an individual holds about other people in general, whereas *partner effects* describe the perceptions that others hold about the individual. *Relationship effects* describe perceptions that two participants in a relationship hold that are unique to their relationship, and *group effects* describe perceptions shared by all members of the collective. As is evident from the studies in this Special Issue, SRM analyses partition variance into a large number of categories. At a minimum, four participants who provide data on one construct will yield 42 distinct effects; the number of effects escalates dramatically with each incremental increase in participants or variables.

SRM analyses are designed to shed light on the interplay between individuals, relationships, and groups. Two of the papers in this Special Issue apply structural equation modelling techniques to SRM analyses of four-person families (Branje, Van Lieshout, & Van Aken, 2005; Ross, Stein, Trabasso, Woody, & Ross, 2005). In each case, mothers, fathers, older siblings, and younger siblings described their relationships with each other family member. Actor, partner, relationship, and group effects identified unique patterns of relationship quality as well as associations between relationship support and

International Journal of Behavioral Development
2005, 29 (2), 101–109
http://www.tandf.co.uk/journals/pp/01650244.html

Ψ Psychology Press
Taylor & Francis Group

© 2005 The International Society for the
Study of Behavioural Development
DOI: 10.1080/01650250444000405

The Actor–Partner Interdependence Model: A model of bidirectional effects in developmental studies

William L. Cook
Maine Medical Center, Portland, ME, USA

David A. Kenny
University of Connecticut, Storrs, CT, USA

The actor–partner interdependence model (APIM) is a model of dyadic relationships that integrates a conceptual view of interdependence with the appropriate statistical techniques for measuring and testing it. In this article we present the APIM as a general, longitudinal model for measuring bidirectional effects in interpersonal relationships. We also present three different approaches to testing the model. The statistical analysis of the APIM is illustrated using longitudinal data on relationship specific attachment security from 203 mother–adolescent dyads. The results support the view that interpersonal influence on attachment security is bidirectional. Moreover, consistent with a hypothesis from attachment theory, the degree to which a child's attachment security is influenced by his or her primary caregiver is found to diminish with age.

The Actor–Partner Interdependence Model (APIM: Kashy & Kenny, 1999; Kenny, 1996a) is a model of dyadic relationships that integrates a conceptual view of interdependence in two-person relationships with the appropriate statistical techniques for measuring and testing it. The APIM is being increasingly used in the social sciences; for example, in studies of emotion (Butler, Egloff, Wilhelm, Smith, Erickson, & Gross, 2003), health (Butterfield, 2001), leisure activities (Berg, Trost, Schneider, & Allison, 2001), communication competence (Lakey & Canary, 2002), personality (Robins, Caspi, & Moffitt, 2000), and attachment style (Campbell, Simpson, Kashy, & Rholes, 2001). Additionally, the model has been recommended in the area of the study of families (Rayens & Svavardottir, 2003), close relationships (Campbell & Kashy, 2002), small groups (Bonito, 2002), and as a framework for evaluating treatment outcomes in couple therapy (Cook, 1998; Cook & Snyder, in press). The purpose of this article is to describe the APIM and discuss one key use of the model: to assess bidirectional effects within longitudinal designs. We begin with an explication of interdependence in relationships from conceptual and statistical perspectives. This necessarily involves a discussion of measurement issues in relationship research. Next we use a path diagram to elucidate the components of APIM. Three different statistical approaches for testing the parameters of this path diagram are provided and the advantages and disadvantages of each are discussed. We then illustrate the application of the APIM by investigating processes of interpersonal influence in the attachment security of mothers and their adolescent children.

Interdependence and the assumption of independent observations

As the name suggests, the APIM is designed to measure interdependence within interpersonal relationships. There is interdependence in a relationship when one person's emotion, cognition, or behaviour affects the emotion, cognition, or behaviour of a partner (Kelley & Thibaut, 1978; Kelley, Holmes, Kerr, Reis, Rusbult, & Van Lange, 2003). A consequence of interdependence is that observations of two individuals are linked or correlated such that knowledge of one person's score provides information about the other person's score. For example, the marital satisfaction scores of husbands and wives tend to be positively correlated. This linkage of scores is more generally referred to as *nonindependence of observations*. Other processes by which nonindependent observations may arise in dyad scores are discussed elsewhere (Cook, 1998; Kenny, 1996a; Kenny & Cook, 1999). Commonly used statistical procedures (e.g., ANOVA and multiple regression) assume independent (uncorrelated) observations in the dependent variable. Consequently, the scores of two "linked" individuals would be treated as if they were completely independent observations, when in fact the correlation would indicate that they are not independent observations. When the assumption of independence is violated, the test statistic (e.g., t or F) and the degrees of freedom for the test statistic are inaccurate, and its statistical significance (i.e., the p value) is biased (Kenny, 1995; Kenny & Judd, 1986; Kenny, Kashy, & Bolger, 1998). Thus, whenever there are nonindependent observations, it is necessary to treat the dyad (or group) rather than the individual as the unit of analysis (see Kenny, 1995; Kenny & Judd, 1986).

The presence of nonindependence is determined by measuring the association between the scores of the dyad members. Different measures are used depending on the type of dyad. For dyads with distinguishable members (e.g., husbands and wives or older and younger siblings), nonindependence can be measured with the Pearson product–moment correlation. For indistinguishable dyad members (e.g., identical twins or same-sex couples), nonindependence is measured with the intraclass correlation (Kenny, 1995). According to

Correspondence should be sent to William L. Cook, Center for Psychiatric Research, Maine Medical Center, 22 Bramhall Street, Portland, ME 04102-3175, USA; e-mail: cookw@mmc.org.

The research was supported in part by a grant from the National Science Foundation (DBS-9307949).

Myers (1979), a liberal test ($p = .20$, two-tailed) should be used in testing whether there is nonindependence because the failure to detect nonindependence could lead to bias in significance tests. If the independence of observations is supported statistically, then one could, in principal, treat the individual rather than the dyad as the unit of analysis. The larger N would generally result in greater power for testing hypotheses. Additional information on the measurement of nonindependence as well as the effects on power of using the dyad rather than the individual as the unit of analysis can be found in Kenny et al. (1998) and Gonzalez and Griffin (2001).

Measurement and the meaning of interdependence

What does it mean to treat the dyad rather than the individual as the unit of analysis? It means that the sample size for the analysis is based on the number of pairs of participants (parent–child, siblings, or married couples), rather than the number of individuals. This requirement begs another question. How can the scores of two individuals be analysed as if they are one? One of the early solutions to this problem was to take the sum or the average of the two individual scores and treat it as a "dyad score" in the analysis. This solution had some appeal because it seemed, on the surface at least, to imply that a "higher-order" phenomenon was being measured, something truly "dyadic". Baucom (1983) recognised that there are conceptual problems with such measures when he criticised the practice of summing husband and wife scores on marital satisfaction measures to create a dyad-level variable. Christensen and Arrington (1987) have re-articulated this complaint:

> For instance, a summing (or averaging) procedure could produce results that would equate a couple in which one spouse is very satisfied and the other unsatisfied with a couple in which both partners are moderately satisfied (the average marital satisfaction score would be the same). Most clinicians and researchers would conceptualize these two cases in very different ways, and the unit resulting from an averaging procedure would not capture these distinctions (pp. 268–269).

Thus, regardless of the type of dyad (e.g., husband–wife, father–child, brother–sister), summed or averaged scores may well create a *mis*-measure of the dyad. This may also be the case when ratings are made of dyadic or group characteristics such as cohesion (Cook & Kenny, 2004).

The actor–partner interdependence model

As an alternative to combining the scores of dyad members to manage nonindependent observations, a generally more informative approach is to retain the individual unit measures but treat them as being nested within the dyad. As will be seen, this approach allows for the estimation of both individual and dyadic factors. For purposes of illustration, suppose we are interested in the development of relationship-specific attachment security in mother–adolescent relationships (Cook, 2000). By relationship-specific attachment security, we mean how secure each person feels in relationship to the other and not the more global measure of attachment style. For brevity, these measures are referred to as *attachment security*. A unidirectional, social-mould theory would predict that the

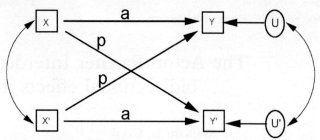

Figure 1. The actor–partner interdependence model (APIM). $X =$ data for person A, Time 1; X' data for person B, Time 1; $Y =$ data for person A, Time 2; $Y' =$ data for person B, Time 2; $U =$ residual (unexplained) portion of person A's Time 2 score; $U' =$ residual for person B's Time 2 score. Single-headed arrows indicate causal or predictive paths. Double-headed arrows indicate correlated variables. Paths labelled as a indicate actor effects and paths labelled as p indicate partner effects.

adolescent's attachment security would be predicted by characteristics of the mother. A more contemporary, bidirectional view would predict that each person influences the other (Kobak & Hazan, 1991; Lollis & Kuczinski, 1997; Kuczinski, 2003).

Figure 1 presents the path diagram for the essential version of the APIM. There are four variables in this model. The two dependent or outcome variables are labelled Y and Y' and stand for the outcomes for persons A (e.g., mother's attachment security or Y) and B (e.g., child's attachment security or Y'), respectively. The X and X' variables are the measures of Person A and Person B, respectively, that are expected to predict Y and Y'. In the most basic longitudinal model, the model of focus in this article, they would be based on the same measurement instrument as the Y variables but measured at some earlier point in time. For example, earlier measures of the mother's attachment security (X) and the child's attachment security (X') are expected to predict mother's (Y) and child's (Y') attachment security at a later point in time.

The two most central components of the APIM are the actor effects and the partner effects. In longitudinal terms, an *actor effect* measures how much a person's current behaviour is predicted by his or her own past behaviour. In Figure 1, the actor effects are represented by the two paths labelled a. The actor effect is a measure of the *stability* of mother's attachment security in relationship to the child (X to Y) and the *stability* of the child's attachment security in relationship to the mother (X' to Y'). Developmental researchers have long understood that the prediction of development (i.e., change) must occur within the context of having statistically controlled for the stability of the outcome variable. Thus, the inclusion of actor effects in longitudinal models has a long history, although these stability effects have not been typically labelled as actor effects until recently (Cook, 1998). What may not be as well understood is that actor effects, to be measured accurately, should be estimated while controlling for partner effects. *Partner effects* measure how much one person is influenced by a partner and are represented in Figure 1 by the diagonal paths labelled p.[1] For example, the path from X to Y' might measure the mother to adolescent partner effect (how much her prior attachment security predicts her child's later attachment security) and the path from X' to Y would measure the

---

[1] Although we use the term *influence*, an actor or partner path in the model may simply indicate a predictive relation, not necessarily a causal one.

adolescent to mother partner effect (i.e., how much the child's prior attachment security predicts his or her mother's later attachment security). Partner effects measure a form of interdependence. Consequently, they cannot be measured within individuals; they are by definition dyadic. Because the APIM is not limited to longitudinal designs, actor effects can more generally be defined as the effects of a person's own characteristics on his or her own outcomes, and partner effects are defined as the effects of a partner's characteristics on a person's outcome.

There are two additional features of the APIM to consider, correlations between the independent variables and correlations between residual variables: The correlation between the independent variables is indicated by the curved, double-headed arrow between X and X'. There is an important statistical role for this correlation. It ensures that if either of the X variables predicts a Y variable, it is done while controlling for the other X variable. Thus, actor effects are estimated controlling for partner effects, and partner effects are estimated controlling for actor effects.

It is unlikely that the X variables explain all the variance in the dependent variables. The extent to which the Y variables are not explained by either of the X variables is represented in Figure 1 by U and U'; the residual or error terms for Y and Y', respectively. If the actor and partner effects are the only reason for the correlation between Y and Y' (i.e., the only source of nonindependence), when the variance in Y and Y' due to partner effects is removed, Y and Y' should no longer be correlated. However, there may be other reasons for the correlation between Y and Y'. For example, if the two individuals come from the same family, a family-level factor may cause their scores to covary. The curved, double-headed arrow connecting U and U' indicates that the unexplained

variance in the dependent variables is correlated, even after the covariance due to partner effects has been removed. Specification of a correlation between the residuals controls for additional sources of nonindependence such as family effects.

It should be clear from Figure 1 that when one tests for bidirectionality, one is not testing a single hypothesis but rather two hypotheses. Bidirectionality is supported only if X predicts Y' *and* X' predicts Y (i.e., both partner effects are statistically significant). Typically, theory would suggest the inclusion of additional variables into the model. If the added variables measure characteristics of the individuals in the dyad, their effects on the dependent variables would also be either actor or partner effects. For example, in Figure 2 child age and gender have been added to the model for mother's and child's attachment security. If child age or child gender predicts the child's own attachment security, it is a child actor effect. If child age or child gender predicts the mother's security in relationship to the child, it is a partner effect. Note that there would be bidirectional effects if mothers feel more secure in relationship to older children (a child partner effect for age) and if children feel more secure if they have been raised by secure mothers (a partner effect for mother's attachment security). Thus, the two partner effects do not have to be defined over the same variable to conclude that there is bidirectional influence.

Interaction effects

In the language of the analysis of variance (ANOVA), actor and partner effects are main effects, i.e., the direct effects of the independent variables on the dependent variables. The standard ANOVA model also tests whether *combinations* of

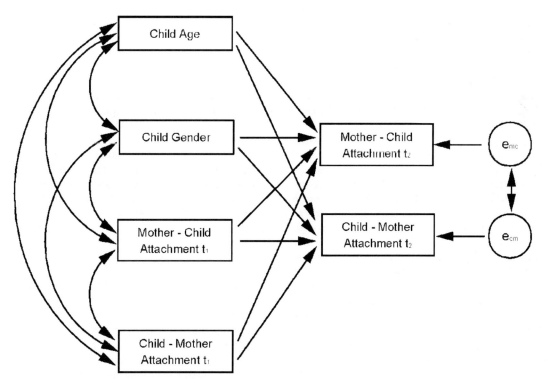

Figure 2. The actor–partner interdependence model including child age and gender variables. Child age, child gender, security of child's attachment to mother, and security of mother's attachment to child at time t_1 predict security in child's attachment to mother and security in the mother's attachment to child at time t_2. Single-headed arrows indicate causal or predictive paths. Double-headed arrows indicate correlated variables.

the independent variables have an effect on the outcome, interaction effects. In terms of parent–child relationships, interaction effects can be important determinants of child outcomes. Sameroff (1975; Sameroff & Chandler, 1975) coined the term *interactional model* to describe the investigation of child outcomes that are affected by the crossing of parent and child characteristics. The interactional model has also been referred to as the "goodness of fit" model because it assumes that developmental outcomes depend on the extent to which parent and child characteristics match or fit together (Lerner, 1993; Thomas & Chess, 1977).

In an interactional model, one of the independent variables, called the *moderator* variable, affects the size of the effect of another independent variable on the outcome variable. Of particular importance are partner characteristics that moderate the effect of actor characteristics, or actor–partner interactions. As an example of actor–partner interaction, suppose that temperamentally easy children are relatively compliant to low power-oriented parental demands and temperamentally difficult children are relatively compliant to high power-oriented parental demands. In this case, the main effects (parental power orientation and child temperament) would not be predictive of child compliance. Rather, it is the combination or goodness-of-fit of parent and child characteristics that determines child compliance. The interaction of actor and partner characteristics can also be used to model synergy or reciprocity. If reciprocity of negativity is characteristic of their relationship, the product of parent and child negativity scores at one point in time would be predictive of their negativity scores at a later point in time, independent of the main effects (i.e., actor or partner effects). That there is often conceptual overlap in the nature of the data (i.e., *interpersonal* interactions) and analytic terminology (i.e., *statistical* interaction) no doubt has led to confusion in the use of the term *interactional* in research studies.

Sometimes the size of an actor or partner effect can be different depending on the value of a third variable. For example, if a parent has been very responsive to the child, the probability that the child will comply with a subsequent parental request (a partner effect) may be greater than in parent–child relationships of unresponsive parents (Parpal & Maccoby, 1985). This would constitute a *partner-moderated partner effect* because parental responsiveness (a partner characteristic) moderates a partner effect (i.e., the probability that the child will comply with a parental request). If we look for a more proximal cause, we may find that children in a positive mood or who, more generally, have warm feelings for their parents, are more compliant (see Lay, Waters, & Park, 1989). This would constitute an *actor-moderated partner effect* because the child's attitude toward the parent (a child characteristic) moderates the probability of his or her being compliant with a parental request (a partner effect). An interaction like this is what is meant when it is said that relationships are contexts for interaction (Hinde & Stevenson-Hinde, 1987; Lollis & Kuczinski, 1997). The relationship as constituted by the enduring attitudes and expectations of one person toward another (e.g., the child's positive attitude toward the parent) moderates how that person responds to the other at any given moment.

Age as a moderator of actor and partner effects. In the previous example, relationships (and attitudes toward others) were proposed as moderators of interpersonal processes affecting child compliance. Given the importance of parent–child relationships to child development, developmental researchers are naturally interested in the development of relationships. In this regard, we do not simply mean the processes of influence that unfold over time, but how the age and development of the participants affects these processes (Hartup & Laursen, 1999). Stated differently, the interest is in how development may affect actor and partner effects.

As noted earlier, one type of actor effect is that the person's past score on a variable will predict his or her future score on the same variable. For example, a child's attachment security at age 15 would tend to be a strong predictor of his or her attachment security at age 16. According to attachment theory (Bowlby, 1973), the strength of this relationship should change over time. As the child ages, working models of relationships (i.e., over-learned expectations or schemas) should become increasingly stable and influential psychological factors. Consequently, the degree to which an 11-year-old's attachment security predicts his or her attachment security at age 12 should not be as strong as the degree to which a 17-year-old's attachment security predicts his or her attachment security at age 18. In other words, the child's age moderates the child's actor effect, revealing that the stability of internal working models of relationships is developmental. Such would constitute an *actor-moderated actor effect*.

The child's age might also moderate the parent partner effect in this example. It could be that the more the child's expectations are predicted by intrapersonal processes (i.e., by internal working models), the less they would be predicted by interpersonal processes (i.e., the parent's actual behaviour). If true, we may find that the older the child, the less the influence of the parent's attachment security on the child's attachment security. Such would constitute an *actor-moderated partner effect*.

The statistical analysis of the APIM

In this section, we provide general guidance for the analysis of the APIM using three statistical techniques: ordinary regression analysis, structural equation modelling (SEM), and multilevel modelling (MLM). The methods presented here apply to dyads in which two persons are distinguishable by their role (e.g., mother and child) or some other characteristic (e.g., birth order of siblings). The methods for the analysis of dyads in which the members are indistinguishable (e.g., identical twins, gay couples) are detailed elsewhere (Griffin & Gonzalez, 1995; Kenny 1996a; Kenny, Kashy, & Cook, in press).

Ordinary regression analysis

The simplest, but least general approach to the assessment of bidirectional influence in longitudinal research with dyads is via a pair of separate multiple regression analyses, one each for predicting the outcome of the two partners. In one analysis, the mother outcome variable (i.e., the variable measured at time t_2) would be regressed on the child and mother predictor variables measured at time t_1. In the other analysis, the child outcome variable would be regressed on the child and mother predictor variables measured at time t_1. (The order of these two analyses does not matter.) Couple is the unit of analysis (i.e., the N being the number of dyads, not the number of individuals), so the independence assumption is not violated. The interests are the magnitude of actor and partner effects in each analysis and their statistical significance. The actor effect estimating the stability of the variable over time would almost always be present, but other actor effects (e.g., age or other measures of actor characteristics) may not be. If any of the partner effects are present, the inference can be that there is interpersonal influence or interdependence. A partner effect for each partner must be statistically significant to support the hypothesis that influence is bidirectional. Additionally, the model may also include contextual variables or other factors that are not personal characteristics of either partner.

There are drawbacks to this ordinary least squares approach. First, this method of analysis does not allow a test of differences between the two actor effects or between the two partner effects of the dyad members. So if a researcher were interested, for example, in whether children influence their mothers more than mothers influence their children, this approach cannot address the question. Second, it cannot address the question of whether for either individual the actor or partner effect is the larger effect. Third, it also does not allow one to pool effects across dyad members. For example, it may be that the partner effect for neither mothers nor children is statistically significant when evaluated separately, but when the two partner effects are pooled, the combined partner effect is significantly different from zero. Thus, one would conclude that there is interdependence, but it is not role-specific. Tests of pooled effects generally have more power than do tests of separate effects (Kenny & Cook, 1999).

Structural equation modelling (SEM)

The SEM approach has several advantages over the ordinary regression analysis approach to testing the APIM. With respect to the APIM, key features of SEM are (1) that more than one equation can be estimated and tested simultaneously and (2) the relations between parameters in different equations can be specified. This allows a direct translation of the model in Figure 1 into one model to be estimated and tested using a *SEM* statistical program (e.g., LISREL, EQS, AMOS). The dyad is the unit of analysis (i.e., the N is equal to the number of dyads) and the model is estimated from the covariance matrix of all the independent and dependent variables. Unless latent variables are used, the sample size requirements are no different than for ordinary regression analysis (Kenny & Cook, 1999).

Different SEM software programs have different languages and procedures for estimating the components in the model, but all require the same general specifications. In the basic model, there are two equations, one for each of the dependent variables. So for an analysis of mother–child dyads, there would be one equation written for the mother outcome at time t_2 and another for the child outcome at t_2. The mother and child variables at time t_1 would be the predictor variables in this equation. The regression coefficient for the mother's time t_1 variable would estimate the actor effect for mothers and the regression coefficient for the child's time t_1 variable would estimate the partner effect for the child on the mother. The child outcome at time t_2 would be the dependent variable in the second equation and, again, the predictor variables would be the mother and child variables measured at time t_1. In this case, the regression coefficient for the mother variable would estimate the partner effect of the mother on the child and the

regression coefficient for the child variable would estimate the child actor effect. There is a residual variance for each equation, representing the effect of all the other predictor variables that have not been included in the equation plus errors of measurement. The residual effects from the mother and child equations would be allowed to correlate, as noted earlier, to control for other sources of nonindependence. The independent variables (mother's and child's scores at time t_1) would also be allowed to correlate so that partner effects would be estimated while controlling for actor effects and vice versa. Some software programs now have graphical interface tools that can be used to draw a path model like that of Figure 1. The software translates the drawing into the corresponding specifications.

A powerful feature of SEM is that it is possible to compare and statistically evaluate the size of parameters within the model, something that cannot be done within least squares. For example, one can test whether the mother partner effect is equal to the child partner effect, which answers the question of who has more influence in the relationship. One can test whether actor effects, partner effects, and residual variances are equal across time, thus testing whether the data have stationarity. Finally, one can compare parameters within a given role (e.g., just the mothers); for example, whether the actor effect for mothers is equal to the partner effect for mothers. To compare the size of two parameters, one compares the chi-square goodness-of-fit value for a model with the two parameters forced to be equal to the chi-square goodness-of-fit value for the same model but without the parameters set to be equal. If the difference between the two chi-square values is statistically significant, then forcing the parameters to be equal has significantly worsened the fit of the model. Thus, it is inferred that the parameters are not equal. This procedure, referred to as the chi-square difference test, is described in any text or manual for structural equation modelling.

Multilevel modelling (MLM)

The analysis of the APIM using multilevel modelling procedures, compared to SEM methods, requires a considerable shift in thinking about the organisation of data and the estimation of effects. Whereas there are two equations in the SEM version of the APIM, one for each member of the dyad, MLM estimates all the parameters of the model within a single equation and so implies a very different data structure. Table 1 presents an example of the data for three dyads organised for a MLM analysis. There are several ways to model dyadic processes within MLM. We illustrate what is called the "two-intercept" approach that was introduced by Raudenbush, Brennan, and Barnett (1995).

The first two variables in Table 1 are dyad ID and the person number. Note that for every dyad there is a record for person 1 (e.g., mother) and a record for person 2 (e.g., child) and always in that order (or always in the order of child followed by the mother). This ordering reflects the nested structure of the data; person nested within dyad. The data must be organised according to the appropriate nesting structure for most MLM programs. The next variable in Table 1 is the dependent variable (DV) or outcome score. The value of the dependent variable is typically different for each member of the dyad. That each person occupies a separate record gives the appearance that the individual is the unit of analysis, but

Table 1

Organisation of data for multilevel modelling

ID	Person	DV	M_dum	C_dum	M_act	C_act	M_prt	C_prt
3	1	3.8	1	0	5.0	0	0	3.5
3	2	3.7	0	1	0	3.5	5.0	0
5	1	4.4	1	0	3.7	0	0	3.5
5	2	3.4	0	1	0	3.5	3.7	0
6	1	4.7	1	0	4.3	0	0	2.8
6	2	3.0	0	1	0	2.8	4.3	0

DV = dependent variable; M_dum = dummy code identifying records where mother is the actor; C_dum = dummy code identifying records where child is the actor; M_act = mother actor variable; C_act = child actor variable; M_prt = mother partner variable; and C_prt = child partner variable.

this is not the case. MLM programs take into account the nesting of individuals within dyads and the concomitant nonindependence of observations this entails.

As in any regression analysis, the predictor variables must be on the same record as the outcome variable. This introduces a complexity into the data organisation, because the identity of the actor and the identity of the partner shift with each record. For record 1, the actor is mother (her outcome is the Y variable) and the partner is child. For record 2, the actor is the child (his or her outcome is the Y variable) and the partner is mother. To ensure that the appropriate actor and partner variables are used in predicting a particular outcome, the following procedure can be used.

First, in the two-intercept approach, two dummy variables are created to identify whose outcome the Y variable refers to for that particular record. The mother dummy variable, labelled M_dum in Table 1, is scored as 1 for records in which mother's outcome is the Y variable and 0 if the child's outcome is the Y variable. The child dummy variable, labelled C_dum in Table 1, is scored as 1 for records in which the child's outcome is the Y variable and 0 if the mother's outcome is the Y variable. These dummy codes are used to create the predictor variables that measure and test for actor and partner effects. Recall that the original predictor variables are the mother and child scores at time t_1. These two scores are multiplied by the two dummy variables, as if to create moderator variables. Multiplying the mother dummy variable by the mother time t_1 variable reproduces the mother's time t_1 variable for records where the mother's outcome is the Y variable and she is the actor, but it produces a zero for records where the child's outcome is the Y variable. This new variable is the mother actor variable (M_act). Multiplying the mother dummy variable by the child's time t_1 variable reproduces the child's time t_1 score for records where the mother's outcome is the Y variable (and so the child is the partner) and a zero otherwise. This new variable is therefore the child partner variable (C_part). Now, for all the records in which the mother's outcome is the Y variable, the mother's time t_1 score is the mother actor variable and the child's time t_1 score is the child's partner variable. Otherwise, these variables are scored with zeros.

Creation of the child actor variable and the mother partner variable uses the same procedure as above, but now the predictor variables are multiplied by the child dummy variable. When the child dummy variable is multiplied by the child's time t_1 score, this creates the child actor variable (C_act), which will be the child's time t_1 score for records where the child's outcome is the Y variable and the child is the actor.

When the child dummy variable is multiplied by the mother's time t_1 score, it reproduces the mother's time t_1 score on records where the child's outcome is the Y variable and the mother is in the partner role (M_prt). In summary, four variables are created; a mother actor variable, a mother partner variable, a child actor variable and a child partner variable. These variables have values for every record, but they have non-zero values only for those records where the appropriate dyad member's outcome is the Y variable. Thus, they are predictor variables only for the outcomes that they are supposed to predict.

Specifications

After the data file has been created and read into the multilevel modelling program, the details of the analysis must be specified. It is necessary to indicate number of levels (of nesting) in the data. For the APIM, the outcome variable (e.g., attachment security at time t_2) has two levels; dyad and individual. The dyadic level is identified by the ID variable, and the individual level is identified by the person variable. Next, one specifies the independent variables, indicating for each whether it has fixed and/or random components, and if it has a random component, at what level (individual or dyadic) it varies. There are a total of six independent variables in the simplest version of the APIM. The model has no ordinary error term. Rather M_dum and C_dum variables are used as intercept variables for mother and child, respectively, instead of the usual common intercept. The intercept variables will each have a fixed component, which is the intercept, and a random component. The correlation between random components for M_dum and C_dum models the residual covariance in Figure 1. Not all MLM programs (e.g., SAS and SPSS[2]) allow for the multiple intercepts and zero error variance needed to replicate precisely the SEM approach, but several programs do (e.g., HLM and MLwiN).

The other four variables in the model are the two actor variables and the two partner variables. Estimation of these coefficients is the primary goal of the analysis. Most multilevel modelling programs also allow for the comparison of effects (e.g., whether mother or child has the larger partner effect) using a procedure comparable to the chi-square difference test. Thus, it shares an important advantage with SEM.

---

[2] SPSS and SAS can be used to estimate a version of the two-intercept model but space precludes a complete description of these models.

Illustration

Returning to the example of attachment security in mother–adolescent dyads, we said that the bidirectional view would predict that each person influences the other. We can test this using the APIM. Our outcome variables are mother's comfort depending on the adolescent (Y) and the adolescent's comfort depending on the mother (Y'), both obtained at time t_2. Our predictor variables are mother's comfort depending on the adolescent (X) and the adolescent's comfort depending on mother (X') at time t_1, approximately a year earlier. These data are from a larger study of attachment security in family relationships (Cook, 2000). That study investigated the interdependence of attachment security using the social relations model (SRM: Cook, 1994; Kenny & La Voie, 1984). The SRM analysis (Cook, 2000) was cross-sectional, but provided information on whether one person's attachment security in relationship to another family member was due to family, actor, partner, or unique relationship effects.[3] We will focus here only on the variable "relationship specific comfort depending on others", which we refer to as *attachment security*.

Participants

The data involve 203 mother–adolescent pairs who provided data at both of two waves of sampling, approximately 1 year apart. The average age at time 1 of the mothers was 46 years ($SD = 3.36$), and the average age of the adolescent was 16 years ($SD = 2.15$). There were 96 boys and 106 girls in the adolescent sample.

Analysis and results

We first examine the APIM with only main effects included, which corresponds to the path diagram presented in Figure 2. We also test for the equality of the actor and partner effects within each role; that is, whether a person's actor effect is equal to his or her own partner effect. The purpose of this test is primarily to illustrate the technique of testing equality constraints. Finally, we test whether age of the adolescent moderates the actor or partner effects of the mothers and adolescents. We performed all tests using the SEM approach because for distinguishable dyads it offers the simplest and most direct way to perform the analysis. The EQS program is used for all SEM analyses.

Actor effects. The question of whether characteristics of the person predict his or her own outcome over time is measured and tested by the actor effects. The results are presented in the first four rows of Table 2. For both mothers and adolescents, the actor effects for attachment security are large, positive, and statistically significant, indicating that there is reliable stability in the degree to which they feel comfortable depending on each other. We do note that as predicted, the actor effect for the mother is more stable than it is for the child. Two additional actor effects were tested for the child; whether the child's

---

[3] The actor and partner effects of the APIM should not be confused with similarly named effects from the social relations model (Kenny & La Voie, 1984). In the social relations model analysis, actor and partner effects are components in a measurement model (i.e., latent variables or factors) rather than causal variables. In the APIM the actor and partner effects reflect causal or predictive effects.

Table 2

APIM of mother–child dynamics (N = 203 dyads)

APIM parameters	Estimate	Z
Actor effects		
$C_1 \rightarrow C_2$	.663*	11.40
$M_1 \rightarrow M_2$	.789*	16.18
Child age$_1 \rightarrow C_2$	.037	1.86
Child gender$_1 \rightarrow C_2$	−.045	−0.51
Partner effects		
$C_1 \rightarrow M_2$	.155*	3.07
$M_1 \rightarrow C_2$	.127*	2.26
Child age$_1 \rightarrow M_2$	.013	0.77
Child gender$_1 \rightarrow M_2$	.139+	1.82
Interaction effects		
Child age*$M_1 \rightarrow M_2$	−.017	−0.827
Child age*$C_1 \rightarrow C_2$	.056+	1.891
Child age*$M_1 \rightarrow C_2$	−.052*	−2.167
Child age*$C_1 \rightarrow M_2$	−.027	−1.043

The estimates are unstandardised regression coefficients. M_1 = mother's attachment security, time t_1; C_1 = child's attachment security, time t_1; M_2 = mother's attachment security, time t_2; C_2 = child's attachment security, time t_2. An asterisk between two variables indicates an interaction effect. Interaction effects were tested within a model that included all the main effects.

* $p < .05$; + $p < .10$.

gender and age predict changes in the child's attachment security. Neither of these actor effects was statistically significant.

Partner effects. The question of whether characteristics of the mother or the child predict each other's attachment security is measured and tested by the partner effects. The results are presented in the middle section of Table 2. Both of the partner effects for attachment security are positive and statistically significant. These results indicate that the mother's prior level of attachment security influences the child's later level of attachment security, and that the child's prior level of attachment security influences the mother's later level of attachment security. In other words, the influence process is bidirectional.

In many cases an interesting question might be: Who has more influence on whom? As seen in Table 2, the effect of child on the mother is slightly larger than the effect of the mother on the child, but the difference is very small and not very meaningful theoretically. For these data, a more interesting comparison is between the actor and the partner effects predicting a given person's outcomes. For the adolescent the comparison is between the adolescent actor effect (an intrapsychic variable) and the mother partner effect (an interpersonal variable). For mother outcomes, this comparison is between the mother actor effect and the adolescent partner effect. These comparisons are made using the chi-square difference test, which was described earlier. Because the basic APIM is a saturated model and so has zero degrees of freedom, the chi-square for goodness of fit for the model is zero. If we constrain the adolescent's actor effect ($b = .663$) and the mother partner effect ($b = .127$) to be equal, we gain a degree of freedom and the chi-square will be non-zero. If the chi-square were statistically significant, we would reject the null hypothesis that the two covariances are equal. For this test, we find χ^2 ($N = 203$, df = 1) = 33.23, $p < .001$, indicating that the two effects cannot be treated as equal without seriously worsening the fit of the model. The adolescent's outcome is affected more by his or her own prior level of attachment security than by the mother's influence over the course of a year. The comparison of the predictors of mother's outcomes yields a similar result. The mother actor effect ($b = .789$) is significantly larger than the child partner effect ($b = .155$), $\chi^2 (1, N = 203) = 58.27, p < .001$.

Interaction effects. Lastly we tested whether child age moderated the actor and partner effects for attachment security in mother–adolescent dyads. This involved creating two interaction variables; (1) the product of mother's attachment security by child age, and (2) the product of child's attachment security by child age. Prior to performing these multiplications, we centred each of the variables (Aiken & West, 1991). Centring involves subtracting out the mean of each variable in the interaction. It has the important role of reducing multi-collinearity due to high correlations between interaction terms and the independent variables from which they are created, and it increases the interpretability of the main effects. In the case of dyadic measures, the centring variable (or mean) that is subtracted out should be the mean of the partners' scores taken together (Kenny & Cook, 1999; Kenny et al., in press). In other words, one does not subtract the mean for mothers from the mother score and the mean for adolescents from the adolescent score; rather, one subtracts the mean of their combined score from both of their scores.

The interaction terms were included as independent variables, along with the actor and partner main effects, in a new model predicting mother and child attachment security (time t_2) outcomes. The results of this analysis are presented in the bottom third of Table 2. The first two rows of the table present the effects of child's age as a moderator of the actor effects. Age does not moderate the mother actor effect or the child actor effect at conventionally accepted levels of statistical significance. The last two rows in Table 2 present the effects of child's age as a moderator of the partner effects. The results indicate that the child's age moderates the mother partner effect, but not the child partner effect. The attachment security of younger adolescents is affected more by their mothers than that of older adolescents, $b = -.052, Z = -2.167, p < .05$. This result is consistent with the hypothesis from attachment theory that the internal working models of younger adolescents, compared to older adolescents, are affected more by recent relationships with significant others (Bowlby, 1973). It also demonstrates how the APIM can be used to test hypotheses on the development of relationships.[4]

feelings, or behaviour of another person. Bidirectional effects are present when the partner effects for both members of a dyad are present and statistically significant. Although the APIM has often been presented within the context of cross-sectional data analysis (Berg et al., 2001; Butler et al., 2003; Butterfield, 2001; Campbell et al., 2001; Lakey & Canary, 2002), we hope we have demonstrated that it is equally applicable to longitudinal data analysis.

There are other models of dyadic relationships that correspond to other forms of dyadic nonindependence. These include the common fate model, in which group effects (or couple effects) are distinguished from individual effects, and the dyadic feedback or mutual influence model, in which each person's outcomes affect the other's outcomes (Cook, 1998; Kenny, 1996a). Of all these models, the APIM has been—and is likely to continue to be—favoured by researchers. As we hope this article has shown, the APIM corresponds to patterns of interpersonal processes that are of considerable interest to family and developmental researchers.

As a conceptual model of interdependence, the APIM is applicable to a variety of analytic situations. For example, in time-series analyses of dyadic interaction such as sequential analysis and cross-lagged regression analysis, the conceptualisation of actor–partner interdependence is the same as presented in Figure 1. The only difference is that the unit of analysis is time (or event) rather than dyad. In this context, the autocontingency or autocorrelation effects are actor effects and the measures of reciprocity (i.e., cross-lagged contingencies) are partner effects (Cook, 2002). The APIM has also been used in complex analyses of growth in relationships. For instance, Raudenbush et al. (1995) tested whether growth (or decline) in a partner's job-role quality predicted growth (or decline) in own or partner's marital satisfaction. Kurdek (1998) has also published analyses that integrate the APIM with growth curve modelling. He found that growth in a person's depressive symptoms was associated with decline in own marital satisfaction (an actor effect) but was not associated with decline in partner's marital satisfaction.

In summary, the APIM is a method of estimating interdependence in naturalistic studies of close relationships. It is particularly well-suited to developmental research in areas where experimentation is not appropriate. Finally, the APIM is not a model that is in competition with other methods of analysis such as sequential analysis or growth curve analysis. Rather, it is a general model that is complementary to these other methods. The integration of the APIM with other analytic methods has the potential to address important and complex questions about human development.

Conclusion

This article has presented and illustrated the APIM as a means of conceptualising and measuring interdependence in close relationships, with a special focus on the assessment of bidirectional effects. Interdependence is measured by the APIM partner effect, the extent to which one person's thoughts, feelings, or behaviour influence the thoughts,

References

Aiken, L. S., & West, S. J. (1991). *Multiple regression: Testing and interpreting interactions.* Newbury Park, CA: Sage.

Baucom, D. H. (1983). Conceptual and psychometric issues in evaluating the effectiveness of behavioral marital therapy. *Advances in Family Intervention, Assessment and Theory, 3,* 91–117.

Berg, E. C., Trost, M., Schneider, I. E., & Allison, M. T. (2001). Dyadic exploration of the relationship of leisure satisfaction, leisure time, and gender to relationship satisfaction. *Leisure Sciences, 23,* 35–46.

Bonito, J. A. (2002). The analysis of participation in small groups. Methodological and conceptual issues related to interdependence. *Small Group Research, 33,* 412–438.

Bowlby, J. (1973). *Attachment and loss: Vol. 2. Separation.* New York: Basic Books.

---

[4] We also tested whether child gender moderated the actor and partner effects in this model, and it did not.

Butler, E. A., Egloff, B., Wilhelm, F. H., Smith, N. C., Erickson, E. A., & Gross, J. J. (2003). The social consequences of expressive suppression. *Emotion, 3*, 48–67.

Butterfield, R. M. (2001). Health related social control and marital power: A test of two models. *Dissertation Abstracts International: Section B: The Sciences and Engineering, 61*(12-B), 6757.

Campbell, L., & Kashy, D. A. (2002). Estimating actor, partner, and interaction effects for dyadic data using PROC MIXED and HLM: A user-friendly guide. *Personal Relationships, 9*, 327–342.

Campbell, L., Simpson, J. A., Kashy, D. A., & Rholes, W. S. (2001). Attachment orientations, dependence, and behavior in a stressful situation: An application of the actor–partner interdependence model. *Journal of Social and Personal Relationships, 18*, 821–843.

Christensen, A., & Arrington, A. (1987). Research issues and strategies. In T. Jacob (Ed.), *Family interaction and psychopathology: Theories, methods, and findings* (pp. 259–296). New York: Plenum Press.

Cook, W. L. (1994). A structural equation model of dyadic relationships within the family system. *Journal of Consulting and Clinical Psychology, 62*, 500–509.

Cook, W. L. (1998). Integrating models of interdependence with treatment evaluations in marital therapy research. *Journal of Family Psychology, 12*, 529–542.

Cook, W. L. (2000). Understanding attachment security in family context. *Journal of Personality and Social Psychology, 78*, 285–294.

Cook, W. L. (2002). Quantitative methods for deductive (theory testing) research on parent–child dynamics. In L. Kuczynski (Ed.), *Handbook of dynamics in parent–child relations* (pp. 347–372). Thousand Oaks, CA: Sage.

Cook, W. L., & Kenny, D. A. (2004). *A critique of contemporary self-report assessments of family functioning.* Unpublished manuscript. Maine Medical Center, Portland, ME.

Cook, W. L., & Snyder, D. K. (in press). Analyzing nonindependent treatment outcomes in couple therapy using the actor–partner interdependence model. *Journal of Family Psychology.*

Gonzalez, R., & Griffin, D. (2001). A statistical framework for modeling homogeneity and interdependence in groups. In G. J. O. Fletcher & M. S. Clark (Eds.), *Blackwell handbook of social psychology: Interpersonal processes* (pp. 505–534). Malden, MA: Blackwell Publishers.

Gottman, J. M. (1979). *Marital interaction: Experimental investigations.* New York: Academic Press.

Griffin, D., & Gonzalez, R. (1995). Correlational analysis of dyad-level data in the exchangeable case. *Psychological Bulletin, 118*, 430–439.

Hartup, W. W., & Laursen, B. (1999). Relationships as developmental contexts: Retrospective themes and contemporary issues. In W. A. Collins & B. Laursen (Eds.), *Relationships as developmental contexts: The Minnesota symposia on child psychology*, Vol. 30 (pp. 13–35). Mahwah, NJ: Lawrence Erlbaum Associates, Inc.

Hinde, R. A., & Stevenson-Hinde, J. (1987). Interpersonal relationships and child development. *Developmental Review, 7*, 1–21.

Kashy, D. A., & Kenny, D. A. (1999). The analysis of data from dyads and groups. In H. T. Reis & C. M. Judd (Eds.), *Handbook of research methods in social psychology.* New York: Cambridge University Press.

Kelley, H. H., Holmes, J. G., Kerr, N. L., Reis, H. T., Rusbult, C. E., & Van Lange, P. A. M. (2003). *An atlas of interpersonal situations.* New York: Cambridge University Press.

Kelley, H. H., & Thibaut, J. W. (1978). *Interpersonal relations: A theory of interdependence.* New York: Wiley.

Kenny, D. A. (1995). The effect of nonindependence on significance testing in dyadic research. *Personal Relationships, 2*, 67–75.

Kenny, D. A. (1996a). Models of nonindependence in dyadic research. *Journal of Social and Personal Relationships, 13*, 279–294.

Kenny, D. A. (1996b). The design and analysis of social-interaction research. *Annual Review of Psychology, 47*, 59–86.

Kenny, D. A., & Cook, W. L. (1999). Partner effects in relationship research: Conceptual issues, analytic difficulties, and illustrations. *Personal Relationships, 6*, 433–448.

Kenny, D. A., & Judd, C. A. (1986). Consequences of violating the independence assumption in analysis of variance. *Psychological Bulletin, 99*, 422–431.

Kenny, D. A., Kashy, D. A., & Bolger, N. (1998). Data analysis in social psychology. In D. Gilbert, S. Fiske, & G. Lindzey (Eds.), *Handbook of social psychology* (vol. 1, 4th ed., pp. 233–265). Boston: McGraw-Hill.

Kenny, D. A., Kashy, D. A., & Cook, W. L. (in press). *Dyadic data analysis.* New York: Guilford Press.

Kenny, D. A., & La Voie, L. (1984). The social relations model. In L. Berkowitz (Ed.), *Advances in experimental social psychology*, Vol. 18 (pp. 142–182). Orlando, FL: Academic Press.

Kobak, R. R., & Hazan, C. (1991). Attachment in marriage: Effects of security and accuracy of working models. *Journal of Personality and Social Psychology, 60*, 861–869.

Kuczinski, L. (2003). *Handbook of dynamics in parent–child relations.* Thousand Oaks, CA: Sage.

Kurdek, L. A. (1998). The nature and predictors of the trajectory of change in marital quality over the first 4 years of marriage for first-married husbands and wives. *Journal of Family Psychology, 12*, 494–510.

Lakey, S. G., & Canary, D. J. (2002). Actor goal achievement and sensitivity to partner as critical factors in understanding interpersonal communication competence and conflict strategies. *Communication Monographs, 69*, 217–235.

Lay, K., Waters, E., & Park, K. A. (1989). Maternal responsiveness and child compliance: The role of mood as a mediator. *Child Development, 60*, 1505–1511.

Lerner, J. V. (1993). The influence of child temperamental characteristics on parent behaviors. In T. Luster & L. Okagaki (Eds.), *Parenting: An ecological perspective* (pp. 101–120). Hillsdale, NJ: Lawrence Erlbaum Associates, Inc.

Lollis, S., & Kuczinski, L. (1997). Beyond one hand clapping: Seeing bidirectionality in parent–child relations. *Journal of Social and Personal Relationships, 14*, 441–461.

Myers, J. L. (1979). *Fundamentals of experimental design* (3rd ed.). Boston: Allyn & Bacon.

Parpal, M., & Maccoby, E. E. (1985). Maternal responsiveness and subsequent child compliance. *Child Development, 56*, 1326–1334.

Raudenbush, S. W., Brennan, R. T., & Barnett, R. C. (1995). A multivariate hierarchical model for studying psychological change in married couples. *Journal of Family Psychology, 9*, 161–174.

Rayens, M. K., & Svavardottir, E. K. (2003). A new methodological approach in nursing research: An actor, partner, and interaction effect model for family outcomes. *Research in Nursing and Health, 26*, 409–419.

Robins, R. W., Caspi, A., & Moffitt, T. (2000). Two personalities, one relationship: Both partners' personality traits shape the quality of a relationship. *Journal of Personality and Social Psychology, 79*, 251–259.

Sameroff, A. J. (1975). Early influence on development: Fact or fancy. *Merrill-Palmer Quarterly, 21*, 267–294.

Sameroff, A. J., & Chandler, M. (1975). Reproductive risk and the continuum of caretaking casualty. In F. D. Horowitz (Ed.), *Review of child development research*, Vol. 4 (pp. 187–244). Chicago: University of Chicago Press.

Thomas, A., & Chess, S. (1977). *Temperament and development.* New York: Bruner-Mazel.

International Journal of Behavioral Development
2005, 29 (2), 110–119

http://www.tandf.co.uk/journals/pp/01650244.html

Ψ Psychology Press
Taylor & Francis Group

© 2005 The International Society for the
Study of Behavioural Development

DOI: 10.1080/01650250444000351

The quality of family relationships within and across generations: A social relations analysis

Hildy Ross[a], Nancy Stein[b], Tom Trabasso[b], Erik Woody[a], Michael Ross[a]

Parents and two children (average ages: 8½ and 5½ years) in 76 families each appraised the quality of their relationships with one another. Family members described generally positive relationships, both from their own perspectives (e.g., "I am often nice to my mother") and from the perspectives of their relationship partners (e.g., "My mother is often nice to me"). Sibling relationships were rated less positively than other family relationships. The Social Relations Model was utilised to examine the patterning of family relationships. Actor effects, indicating consistent relationship qualities for each individual family member, were found, especially for ratings of self. Partner effects, indicating consistency in relationships as assessed by others in the family, were present for ratings of the children as relationship partners. Relationship effects were pervasive, indicating that specific family relationships had distinct qualities. Participants' own ratings suggested that reciprocity would characterise all family relationships, in that strong correlations were found between each person's rating of self and other, but only the marital and the sibling relationship evidenced relational reciprocity, as assessed by correlations between relationship effects found for relationship partners.

Introduction

In the last decade, researchers have advanced the study of family processes by taking seriously the metaphor of the family as a dynamic system of interacting, adapting relationships (e.g., Cox & Paley, 2003). There is compelling evidence that healthy family and child development is fostered by a system of strong, affectionate relationships among family members (e.g., Cummings, Davies, & Campbell, 2000). The evidence is less clear, however, with respect to how affection is organised in the family, and the importance of the qualities of individual family members, of the family as a whole, and of the specific relationships within the family. Much of the relevant research has focused on the influences of the parents on other family members. For example, research has established that positive co-parenting processes promote children's adjustment (McHale & Rasmussen, 1998), that parental conflict is detrimental to children's well-being (e.g., Cummings & Davies, 1995), that parents who especially favour one child foster dissatisfaction in the sibling relationship (e.g., Brody, Stoneman, & McCoy, 1992), and that parental coalitions thwart effective family problem solving (Vuchinich, Vuchinich, & Wood, 1993). Although these concepts have enriched the study of families by focusing on the interplay of relationships among family members, the study of family relationships has emphasised the influence of parents, with children relegated to a more passive role.

In the current study of family relationships, we give more equal status to the perspectives of young family members. We do this in two ways: first, we asked children as well as parents to assess their relationships with other family members by answering the same set of questions; second, we employed the Social Relations Model (Kashy & Kenny, 1990; Kenny & LaVoie, 1984) to examine the dynamic organisation of relationships within families.

Young children's assessments of the quality of family relationships

Although many researchers have examined adolescents' and pre-adolescents' assessments of their relationships with their parents (e.g., Cook, 2000, 2001; Devereux et al., 1974; Furman & Buhrmester, 1985; Laursen, Wilder, Noack, & Williams, 2002; Stemmler & Peterson, 2000), few researchers have asked children under 10 years of age to provide similar information. Researchers have sometimes asked younger children for indirect assessments of family relationships. For example, children have been asked to respond to hypothetical parent–child scenarios (e.g., Burks & Parke, 1996; MacKinnon-Lewis, Volling, Lamb, Dechman, Rabiner, & Curtner, 1994), to produce hypothetical narratives concerning conflict in families with "children about your age" (Fisher & Johnson, 1990), and to portray family relationships in abstract diagrams (Mostkoff & Lazarus, 1983). In the most direct assessment of children's perspectives on their relationships with parents, Buhrmester and Furman (1987) asked children, including 2nd grade children, to rate the frequency of companionship and intimacy interactions with family members, friends, and teachers. They generally found that the youngest children didn't differentiate among close family members, but did

---

[a] University of Waterloo, Canada; [b]University of Chicago, USA.

Correspondence should be addressed to Hildy Ross, Department of Psychology, University of Waterloo, Waterloo, ON, Canada, N2L 3G1; e-mail: Hross@uwaterloo.ca.

This research was supported by a Grant HD38895 from the National Institute of Child Health and Human Development. We thank the families who generously participated in this study, Marc Hernandez who coordinated the data collection, William Cook, David Kenny, and Todd Little, who advised us on the statistical procedures, and Alex North and Michael Trink, who assisted with data analysis.

distinguish between close family and others in their social networks. One exception was that girls reported greater intimacy with parents than with siblings. Gleason (2002) simplified this procedure and asked 4-year-olds to make binary choices between parents, siblings, friends, and imaginary friends with respect to what each provided in the relationship. With this procedure, children generally chose parents more often as offering help and exerting power, and siblings as sources of conflict, thus differentiating between parents and siblings.

In contrast, young children are more often asked to appraise their relationships with their siblings (Mendelson, Aboud, & Lanthier, 1994; Ross, Woody, Smith, & Lollis, 2000; Stromshak, Ballanti, Bierman, & CPPRG, 1996). Children as young as 4 years of age can provide assessments of sibling relationships that are related to their mothers' assessments of the same relationships, and that are as reliable and valid as the appraisals provided by their older sisters and brothers. Moreover, Ross et al. (2000) assessed sibling relationships both from the perspective of the self ("I like my brother") and other ("My brother likes me"), and found that young children were able to respond reliably from both standpoints. The children regarded their own qualities as slightly but consistently more positive than those of their siblings.

In the current research we have adapted this same scale for use in all family relationships. The use of the same measuring instrument also gives equal weight and respect to the views of young children and the views of their parents. This does not mean that we expect the same patterns to emerge regardless of the assessor or relationship. However, we require that individuals use the same instrument to determine both consistencies and differences in partners' assessments of family relationships.

Using the Social Relations Model (SRM) to examine the dynamics of family relationships

Developed by David Kenny, the Social Relations Model was modified for application to families by William Cook (Cook & Dreyer, 1984; Kashy & Kenny, 1990; Kenny & LaVoie, 1984). The model enables researchers to examine interactions and appraisals of family members as a network of interconnected individuals. As the data from the present study consist of family members' (two parents and two children) appraisals of each of their relationships, we outline the features of the model with this in mind. When one family member appraises his or her relationship with another family member, there are a number of influences on that appraisal that can be assessed separately within the SRM. First, there are the characteristics of the person doing the ratings (actor effects). A mother might rate all of her family relationships (with spouse and both children) favourably in comparison with other mothers. Second, appraisals reflect the general influence of the other person in the relationship (partner effects). If the oldest son is generally agreeable, then others, including the mother, might assess their relationship with him positively. Third, a relationship can have unique characteristics (relationship effects). A particularly close relationship between a mother and her oldest child will be appraised as more positive by the mother than would be predicted by the mother's characteristic ratings of family members (actor effects), or the typical ratings of relationships with the eldest child according to all family members (partner effects). Relationship effects are directional, in that estimates of relationship effects are assessed for each individual within each relationship. Fourth, the family members, as a group, might be especially content or fractious with one another. These total family characteristics (family effects) can also be assessed within the SRM.

The degree of reciprocity in relationship effects is another important variable assessed in the SRM. One can ask whether qualities of relationships are particularly positive or negative according to one member of the dyad, and whether the other dyad member shares the same sentiments about the specific relationship. Finally, reciprocity can also be assessed in relation to the characteristics of individual family members. If the mother is especially enthusiastic about all of her relationships with others in her family (a positive actor score), do other family members (as a group) share the same opinion of their relationships with the mother?

With the separation of family, actor, partner, relationship, and reciprocity effects, one can ask questions about family processes that are not otherwise possible. For example, the presence of only very strong actor effects for parents might indicate a lack of sensitivity to individual differences that might exist among other family members. Strong partner effects, for example, of the children, would indicate the consistent influence that the younger generation exerts on how family relationships are appraised by others. Relationship effects are possibly the most interesting of all, indicating that particular family members elicit unique characteristics in one another. If relationship effects are reciprocal within some but not all family dyads, we find further evidence of the dynamic processes that contribute to associations among family members.

Many of the strengths of the Social Relations Model have been demonstrated in previous research on family relationships. In an early application of the SRM to family processes, Stevenson, Leavitt, Thompson, and Roach (1988) found relationship effects in observations of parent–child and parent–infant play. Both parents and children made unique and generally reciprocal adjustments in their play behaviour that depended on the particular partner. More recently, Cook (1993, 1994, 2001) obtained family effects for family members' beliefs that they coerced each other, but not for their beliefs that they effectively influenced one another. He also obtained strong actor effects for coercion, but not for influence. Thus, the presence or absence of coercion seems to be more characteristic of families and their members than does the capacity to exert influence. Cook, Kenny, and Goldstein (1991) found that adolescents elicit negativity and overt criticism from their parents (a partner effect), which puts them at risk for psychopathology. A second finding, of no actor effect for mothers, suggested that mothers were not themselves negative, but were responsive to the characteristics of their offspring. Cook (2000) also examined adult attachment security in the network of relationships in families with two parents and two adolescent children. In those analyses, relational reciprocity was evident for the marital relationship and the relationship between the two adolescent children. With one exception (mothers' and older siblings' judgments of depending on one another), parent–child attachment was not reciprocal. A similar finding of relational reciprocity within, but not between, generations was reported for adolescents' and parents' perceptions of support (Branje, Van Aken, & Van Lieshout, 2002). Apparently a different dynamic governs relationships between from those within generations.

Although the Social Relations Model has become an important tool for researchers of family dynamics, previous researchers have not examined young children's perspectives on the set of family relationships. In the current study we examine whether young children's assessments will reflect the dynamics of family relationships in social relations analyses.

The current study

Affectionate relationships are central components of the family as a dynamically organised system. We adapted the Quality of Relationships Scale (QRS), used by Ross et al. (2000) to assess sibling appraisals, for all family relationships. It consists of affectively-toned items phrased from the perspective of the individual completing the scale (e.g., "How often are you nice to your mother?") and identical items from the perspective of the other person in the relationship (e.g., "How often is your mother nice to you?"). Family members assessed their relationships with every other family member on this scale.

Despite a systemic view, we enter the family system at the level of dyadic relationships. Specifically, we ask questions about each individual's relationship with each other family member, and not about the more general characteristics of the person or about the family as a cohesive or disorganised system in itself. In the SRM, total family characteristics are revealed when all members of the family share views about all of their relationships.

How might patterns of family affective relationships be organised within families with young children? Robert Hinde (1988) envisioned a set of dialectic links among individuals, relationships, families, and the larger culture in which families participate. Relationships bring individuals together and the qualities of relationships reflect the ways in which individuals respond to one another as they interact together. Histories of interaction determine relationships, and memories of past emotional events are important aspects of close personal relationships (Stein, Trabasso, & Liwag, 1994). Relationships, such as those between parents and children, are embedded within larger social systems of the family, and families are part of, and influenced by, the norms and standards of larger social groups. In most cultures there are strong constraints on the roles of mothers and fathers to love, nurture, and support their offspring (e.g., Branje et al., 2002; Sroufe & Fleeson, 1988). Children, in turn, are characteristically dependent upon and normatively attached to their parents, especially when parents are responsive to their needs (e.g., Stevenson-Hinde & Verchueren, 2002). Although critical for the whole family, marital affection is less certain. It depends more on mutual respect between equal partners and can be influenced by a host of factors (e.g., Branje et al., 2002; Gottman, 1994). Finally, the sibling relationship is normatively expected to vary greatly in quality, depending on a mix of rivalries and affection (Dunn & Kendrick, 1982; Parker & Stimpson, 2002).

Thus affectionate relationships among family members are constrained to different degrees. These constraints may lead to different normative patterns of assessment on the QRS, such that parent–child relationships would be evaluated relatively positively and sibling relationships relatively negatively. Also, normative constraints imply different degrees of variability between families (within-generation relationships would be most variable, between-generations relationships would be least variable). Since variability among families produces relationship effects, we would expect stronger relationship effects within than between generations. Moreover, the relative absence of strong social imperatives with respect to affection within generations should make relationship-specific processes more important. Affection directed to a spouse or sibling should grow to the extent that it is returned in kind, and thus processes of reciprocal affection or dissatisfaction (i.e., relational reciprocity) should characterise within-generation relationships to a greater extent than relationships between parents and children (Branje et al., 2002; Cook, 2000).

In the current study we ask each family member to assess their relationships from two perspectives: they appraise their own qualities in each relationship as well as the qualities of other family members in the same relationship. Because of these different points of view, we can examine whether family members evaluate themselves more positively than they evaluate others, the extent to which their perceptions of self and other indicate relationships that are inherently reciprocal, and the degree of agreement between participants on the qualities of each individual within a relationship. We also explore SRM patterns for self and other appraisals. Stronger actor effects would be anticipated in self ratings, when family members focus attention on their own qualities, and stronger partner effects would be anticipated in appraisals of others, if family members agreed on the qualities that others bring to their various family relationships.

Method

The entire study included multiple visits to each family's home (14 sessions in total), interview and observational data, conflict negotiations, and conflict training in some families. Families were compensated at a rate of $330 for their participation in 14 sessions across the entire study.

Participants

Families were recruited through the school system in the Chicago Metropolitan area. After securing school or district approval, we sent letters to all families who had children enrolled in kindergarten through the 4th grade in 20 largely middle-class, ethnically diverse schools (5 in Chicago City, 5 in Oswego suburb, and 10 in Oak Park suburb). Initially, 132 families returned a slip indicating interest in the study to the school and were contacted by telephone to determine their eligibility for participation. Eligibility criteria were that one or two parents and two children between the ages of 4 and 12 lived together in the family home, that no serious developmental delays or ongoing physical or mental health problems existed in the family, and that all family members were willing to participate. Of those families initially interested, 36 did not meet the eligibility criteria. For those who were eligible, a researcher visited the family home, the study was fully discussed (without assignment to groups), final agreement obtained, and permission forms signed. At this point, 11 families decided not to participate, generally due to the time requirements of the study. Of the 85 families that did participate, 9 single-parent families of mothers and two children could not be included in the current analyses because of the requirements of the SRM.

Seventy-six families with four family members (mother, father, older child, and younger child) provide data for the current report. Older siblings were 8.8 years of age on average

($SD = 1.23$, range = 5.3–12.3) and included 37 boys and 39 girls. Younger siblings were 5.8 years of age ($SD = 1.14$, range = 3.7–9.7 years) and included 48 boys and 28 girls. Parent ages averaged 39 years for mothers ($SD = 4.2$, range = 29–50) and 40 years for fathers ($SD = 5.1$, range = 30–56). The 76 families included 65 Caucasian, 3 African American, 3 Latino, and 4 families with mixed ethnicity. The average family income was over \$75,000. Two families reported incomes under \$30,000, 9 reported incomes between \$30,000 and \$50,000, 23 reported incomes between \$50,000 and \$75,000 and 41 reported incomes over \$75,000. Parents were fairly well educated; 7 parents had only high-school education, 30 had some college (up to 2 years), and 51 parents were college graduates. An additional 62 parents had some graduate or professional training beyond the bachelor level. Eighty-three per cent of the mothers and 99% of the fathers held full- or part-time jobs outside the home. Their occupations included: professionals (58, including police officers, lawyers, therapists, architects, physicians, and carpenters), educators (26 including teachers, daycare workers, and librarians), business people (52 including marketing, sales, construction managers, executive recruiters, public relations personnel), and homemakers (13). One father described himself as unemployed and income, education, and occupation information was missing in one family.

Measure

The data included in the current report was part of the pre-test phase of the study. To the point of this data collection all families had been treated identically. During the second and third visits to the homes, family members completed the Quality of Relationship Scale (QRS) with respect to each of their family relationships. The order of completing the QRS for different relationships was counterbalanced across families.

The QRS consists of eight items phrased from the perspective of the individual completing the scale (e.g., How often are you nice toward your sibling?) and 8 identical items from the perspective of the other person in the relationship (e.g., How often is your sibling nice to you?). One item asked how much one family member liked the other, and this item was scored on a 4-point scale from *not at all* to *a lot*. The seven remaining items concerned how often family members were nice, liked to do things together, fought (reverse-scored), shared, helped, were mean (reverse-scored), and tried to hurt the other (reverse-scored). Family members responded on a 4-point scale indicating whether the described behaviour occurred *never*, *sometimes*, *most of the time*, or *all of the time*. Identical items were completed in a paper and pencil version by the parents and in an interview by the children. For the children, the researcher read each question and recorded the child's response. As the data consists of each family member's ratings of self and other for each relationship (24 individual data points per family), Cronbach's alphas were computed for each separate scale (Table 1). These were generally in the moderate but acceptable range (.59–.81) and did not appear to depend on which family member was doing the ratings or on whether participants rated self or other.

Evaluating the Social Relations Model

The SRM is tested with a structural equation model that is essentially a confirmatory factor analysis in which factors that

are initially tested consist of a family effect, actor effects for each family member, partner effects for each family member, and relationship effects for each of six family relationships (Figure 1). By examining the total set of ratings that four family members make of their relationships with one another (six relationships in total for a four-person family), the SRM can attribute variance in the ratings to actor, partner, relationship, and family effects. Additionally, actor and partner effects can be specified in terms of particular family members (mother actor and partner, father actor and partner, older or younger child actor and partner), and relationship effects can be specified in terms of the particular relationship assessed (mother to father relationship effect, older to younger child relationship effect, etc.).

Figure 1 displays a simplified diagram of the model tested. Family, actor, partner, and relationship effects are latent variables estimated within the model. The measured variables are the ratings that individual family members make within the context of their specific relationships. To estimate latent variables independently of error, more than one measured variable must contribute to each latent variable. Since our 8-item scale provides only a single measure of each relationship, we have divided the scale into two 4-item split scales, attempting to balance the content of the items on each scale. Ratings by a single family member measure that individual's actor effects; ratings by others of a single relationship partner (e.g., mothers' and both children's ratings with respect to their relationships with the father) contribute to that family member's partner effect, and ratings by one family member of his or her relationship with another family member (e.g., father's ratings with respect to his relationship with his older child) measure the directional (Father→Older) relationship effect. All measured variables contribute to the family effect. In the SRM, initial weightings of all measured variables on relevant latent variables are set to 1.0, so that the remaining degrees of freedom will be sufficient to estimate SRM effects. Associations between actor and partner effects (for example, do fathers both give and receive consistent ratings from others in the family?) and between individual raters of the same relationship (for example, do older and younger children rate the sibling relationships similarly?) are assessed as individual and relational reciprocity respectively. Figure 1 does not depict error terms (latent variables), which are associated with each measured variable and allow error to be separated from other SRM effects. Additionally, because individuals might display some consistent idiosyncrasies in how they interpret particular items, we allowed the error terms for each half scale score to be correlated within each rater.

The model estimates the strength (variance associated with) of family, actor, partner, and relationship effects, and these are divided by the associated standard errors to create z-statistics whose significance can be determined (with a 1-tailed test, since variances must always be positive). In addition, the significance of the reciprocity effects can also be assessed as z-statistics using a 2-tailed test, since negative relationships can exist between variables.

Missing data

In 14 families there was missing data on scattered scale items, usually of one item (but in four cases between two and six items). These data were imputed using the EM algorithm within SPSS, and scale scores as well as split scale scores were computed that include the imputed data. In seven additional families, data were missing completely on all items of one or more of the scales for one or more respondents. Missing scale data consisted largely of ratings by younger siblings (one younger child didn't complete any relationship measures, five others did not respond concerning either mother or father, or both parents), but included mothers (one mother whose younger children's data were missing also had missing data on both of her children), and both parents (in one family no data was provided on the spousal relationship). As with the item data, scale data were imputed with the SPSS EM procedure for the preliminary analyses of family members' ratings. Amos 5.0 (Arbuckle & Wothke, 1999), which was used to evaluate the Social Relations Model, has its own solution for missing data (FIML; see Arbuckle, 1996), and so data with missing scale scores were entered into Amos. In a total data set that included 24 scales for each of 76 families, a total of 26 scales were missing across all families.

Results

Preliminary analyses: Self-evaluations and evaluations of relationship partners

We summed participants' responses to the self questions and to the questions concerning the other dyad member for each relationship. We thus obtained two scores from all participants for each of their family relationships, with higher numbers indicating more favourable evaluations. Family members reported, on average, quite favourable appraisals of their relationships with one another (Tables 1 and 2). Of a possible 32 points, participants averaged scores greater than 26 for the marital and parent–child relationships. As anticipated the sibling relationship received lower ratings, $Ms = 23.2$ for self and 20.5 for other.

ANOVAs assessed how individuals evaluated themselves in comparison to their partners in each family relationship (Table

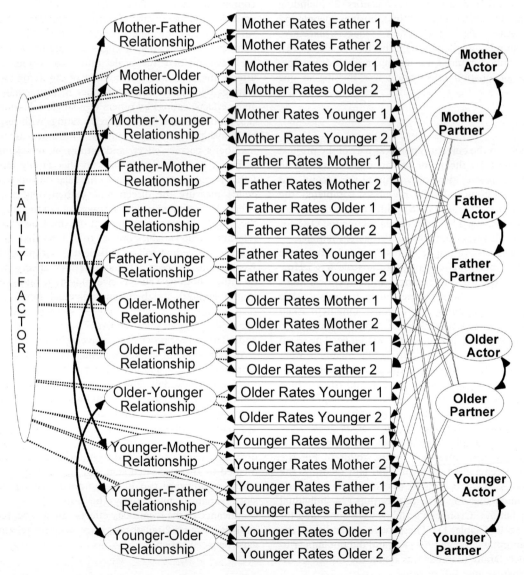

Figure 1.   The Social Relations Model of the quality of family relationships. Measured variables are in the rectangles in the centre of the diagram; latent variables are actor and partner effects on the right, relationship effects on the left, and family effects on the far left. Arrows linking latent to measured variables indicate which measured variables contribute to each latent variable, and weights were uniformly set at 1.0. Double-headed arrows indicate reciprocity correlations that were estimated within the SRM. Although not depicted in Figure 1, each measured variable has an associated error term, and error terms for each rater and covariances between error terms for each half scale for each rater were estimated. The fit of this model is evaluated separately for ratings of self and rating of others.

Table 1

Family members' ratings, means (and SDs), of self and other within each relationship

Rater	Relationship partner	Self-ratings	α[a]	Ratings of others	α	Ratings of self vs. other by each family member	
						Comparisons $t(75) =$	Correlations $r(75) =$
Mother	Father	26.6 (2.19)	.69	27.2 (2.34)	.70	−2.46*	.63***
	Older	26.7 (2.26)	.70	25.8 (2.66)	.79	3.39***	.58***
	Younger	27.2 (2.03)	.68	26.3 (2.31)	.71	3.64***	.58***
Father	Mother	26.4 (1.84)	.62	26.5 (2.35)	.72	n.s.	.63***
	Older	27.2 (1.92)	.65	26.5 (2.35)	.68	2.67**	.51***
	Younger	27.5 (1.89)	.59	26.6 (2.41)	.71	3.60***	.55***
Older child	Mother	26.8 (2.57)	.64	27.3 (2.99)	.71	n.s.	.67***
	Father	26.8 (2.78)	.72	27.2 (2.71)	.67	n.s.	.61***
	Younger	22.8 (3.65)	.74	20.8 (4.43)	.81	4.45***	.55***
Younger child	Mother	27.6 (3.23)	.66	26.4 (3.30)	.59	3.78***	.62***
	Father	27.3 (3.14)	.61	26.3 (3.52)	.66	3.58**	.74***
	Older	23.6 (4.05)	.67	20.2 (4.66)	.77	6.53***	.47***

[a] The N for the reliability analysis was the 69 families in which all family members provided information on each of the scales.

*$p < .05$, **$p < .01$, ***$p < .001$.

1). In general, participants report that they bring more to their relationships than do their partners. A 2 (target: self versus other ratings) × 12 (relationship: ratings of each relationship by each family member) ANOVA resulted in significant main effects for target, $F(1, 75) = 51.59$, $p < .001$, and relationship, $F(11, 65) = 23.11$, $p < .001$, as well as a target × relationship interaction, $F(11, 65) = 12.03$, $p < .001$. The tendency to rate self higher than relationship partners was most evident among younger children, who rated themselves as superior to each of their partners. Comparisons of ratings of self versus other revealed only one significant reversal; mothers rated themselves less favourably than they rated their spouses. Additionally, there were no differences in fathers' ratings of self and mother, and older children's ratings of self and each parent (Table 1). Finally, the children rated both themselves and their siblings significantly less favourably in the sibling relationship than they or other family members rated participants in all other relationships, $ts(75) \geq 5.51$, $ps < .001$.

The correlations among ratings are also presented in Table 1. In general, family members' ratings of others in each dyad were highly associated with their self ratings. The lowest correlation was for younger children's ratings of self and sibling, which were still quite strongly related. Thus, individual ratings of self and other indicated reciprocity in all family members' perceptions of their relationships.

Comparisons were also made based on the ratings each individual received within a particular relationship. Each family member's ratings of self were compared with the evaluations provided by their relationship partners (Table 2). Thus, for example, the mother's rating of herself was compared with the father's rating of the mother within the marital relationship. A 2 (rater: ratings by self versus other) × 12 (relationship) ANOVA resulted in effects for rater, $F(1, 75) = 51.54$, $p < .001$, for relationship, $F(11, 65) = 21.44$, $p < .001$, and an interaction between rater and relationship, $F(11, 65) = 14.11$, $p < .001$. Follow-up t-test comparisons between raters (Table 2) indicated that each of the children rated themselves more positively than either their siblings or their mothers rated them. Younger children also rated their parents less favourably than parents rated themselves. In contrast,

fathers' ratings of self were less positive than mothers' ratings of fathers. Finally, in other family relationships (fathers' ratings of mothers, older children's ratings of both parents, and father's ratings of both children) self-ratings did not differ systematically from ratings provided by relationship partners.

Correlations were computed for both partners' assessments of the qualities of each person within their relationship. These correlations reflect agreement between partners concerning their appraisals of each family member within a relationship. As is evident from Table 2, agreement between raters was found more often within than between generations; mothers and fathers agreed with one another with respect to the characteristics each brought to their relationship and the children also agreed with each other with respect to the sibling relationship. Additionally, within mother–child relationships, children and mothers agreed with one another on ratings of the mothers, but no significant associations were found on ratings of the children.

Evaluating the Social Relation Model

Self-ratings. For family members' ratings of themselves, the initial model tested (Figure 1) encountered some admissibility problems (i.e., occasional estimated variances with slightly negative values). Since Mother partner effects and Father→Older relationship effects were negligible, these were set to zero, and the model was tested again. With one additional modification (removing the covariance between error terms for older children's ratings of mother and sibling in part 2 of the split scale), the Social Relations Model provided an admissible solution which fit the data well, χ^2 (226, $N = 76$) $= 279.54$, $p < .01$, RMSEA $= .056$, CFI $= .929$, IFI $= .936$. Actor effects were significant for all family members; relationship effects were found for all family relationships with the exceptions of Mother→Younger, Father→Younger, Father→Older (set to zero) and Younger→Father (Table 3). The family effect was not significant, and no partner effects appeared in any of the ratings.

Reciprocity was estimated for individual effects (e.g., the covariance between mother actor by mother partner) and for

Table 2

Family members' ratings, means (and SDs),[a] *of each individual within each relationship*

Family member rated	Relationship partner	Self-ratings by family member	Ratings by relationship partner	Comparisons t (75) =	Correlations r (75) =
Mother	Father	26.6 (2.19)	26.5 (2.35)	n.s.	.40***
	Older	26.7 (2.26)	27.3 (2.99)	n.s.	.37***
	Younger	27.2 (2.03)	26.4 (3.30)	2.10*	.26*
Father	Mother	26.4 (1.84)	27.2 (2.34)	−2.73**	.34**
	Older	27.2 (1.92)	27.2 (2.71)	n.s.	.16
	Younger	27.5 (1.89)	26.3 (3.52)	2.80**	.11
Older child	Mother	26.8 (2.57)	25.8 (2.66)	2.44*	.08
	Father	26.8 (2.78)	26.5 (2.35)	n.s.	.12
	Younger	22.8 (3.65)	20.2 (4.66)	4.65***	.30**
Younger child	Mother	27.6 (3.23)	26.3 (2.31)	3.01**	.17
	Father	27.3 (3.14)	26.6 (2.41)	n.s.	.20
	Older	23.6 (4.05)	20.8 (4.43)	4.84***	.33**

The header above "Comparisons" and "Correlations" reads: *Ratings of each family member by self and relationship partner*

[a] Means and standard deviations in this table are identical to those in Table 1, but re-arranged to facilitate comparisons between each family member's ratings of self within each relationship (e.g., mother's rating of self within the marital relationship) with the relationship partner's rating of the same individual (e.g., father's rating of mother).

*p < .05, **p < .01, ***p < .001.

relationships (e.g., the covariance between Mother→Father and Father→Mother). Given the absence of partner effects, one would not expect significant correlations between actor and partner effects, and none was found. For relationship effects, reciprocity was obtained only for the marital relationship: Husbands and wives who showed particular affection (or the lack thereof) in relation to one another, have that affection returned in kind.

Ratings of others. As was the case for self-ratings, the initial model for family members' ratings of others produced some fairly minor admissibility problems. When the covariance between error terms for older children's ratings of mothers and their ratings of fathers and siblings on part 2 of the scale

were omitted, the SRM provided an admissible solution with good fit for the data, χ^2 (224, N = 76) = 286.19, p < .01, RMSEA = .061, CFI = .887, IFI = .900. When family members rated their relationship partners, actor effects were found only for mothers, and this effect did not appear to be as strong as its counterpart in self-ratings. Partner effects were found for the two children, but were negligible for their parents. As with the self-ratings, most relationship effects were significant. The exceptions were for the Father→Younger relationship, the Mother→Older and Mother→Younger relationships and the Older→Father relationship, although in the latter three cases marginal effects (p < .10) were found. Unlike in the self-ratings, a family effect was obtained as well (Table 3).

Table 3

Social relations analysis of family appraisals

SRM individual effects[a]		Ratings of self	Ratings of others	SRM relationship effects	Ratings of self — Relationship effect[a]	Ratings of self — Relational reciprocity[b]	Ratings of others — Relationship effect[a]	Ratings of others — Relational reciprocity[b]
Actor	Mother	0.49***	0.25*	Mother→Father	0.60***	0.22*	0.77**	0.36*
	Father	0.29**	0.17	Father→Mother	0.33*		0.72***	
	Older	0.57**	0.21	Older→Younger	2.03***	0.42	2.99***	1.25*
	Younger	0.94**	0.27	Younger→Older	1.88***		3.51***	
Partner	Mother	set to 0.0	0.05	Mother→Older	0.19*	0.09	0.54	−0.01
	Father	0.08	0.04	Older→Mother	0.39*		1.05***	
	Older	0.04	0.28*	Mother→Younger	0.06	−0.16	0.33	0.02
	Younger	0.04	0.33**	Younger→Mother	0.95**		1.30**	
Family		0.08	0.15*	Father→Older	set to 0.0	not estimated[c]	0.38*	0.02
				Older→Father	0.48**		0.54	
				Father→Younger	0.07	−0.04	0.23	0.34
				Younger→Father	0.41		1.73***	

[a] Estimated variances are reported to assess all SRM effects.

[b] Estimated covariances are reported to assess relational reciprocity.

[c] Because Father→Older relationship variance was set to 0.0, the covariance between these two variables could not be estimated.

*p < .05, **p < .01, ***p < .001.

Once again, reciprocity was not found for individual effects, which is consistent with the absence of a combination of both actor and partner effects for any individual family member. For ratings of others, relational reciprocity was obtained within, but not between, generations. Within both the marital and the sibling relationships, specific levels of affection were reciprocated within the dyad.

Discussion

Family members appraised their relationships with each other quite favourably. Children reported the greatest degree of differentiations among their family relationships. They rated parent–child relationships consistently higher than relationships with their siblings. Although sibling relationships received the lowest ratings, the means indicated that brothers and sisters were fairly content with one another. Branje et al. (2002) also reported that adolescents perceived less support in their sibling relationships than in parent–child relationships; indeed, perceived sibling support was lower than in any other family relationship.

Two types of comparisons emerged from relationship appraisals. Individuals' self ratings were contrasted to their ratings of their relationship partners and to the ratings that they received from their partners. Younger children evaluated themselves more favourably than they assessed all of their relationship partners; also younger children were more impressed with themselves than were their relationship partners, although the difference was not significant for fathers. Older children rated themselves as superior to only their younger siblings. Older children evaluated themselves more favourably than they were appraised by either their sibling or mother. Mothers, in turn, rated themselves more favourably than either child but less favourably than their spouse. Mothers' self-ratings did not differ from the evaluations they received from their relationship partners, with one exception: Mothers evaluated themselves more favourably than they were rated by their younger child. Fathers' self-ratings exceeded their ratings of both children, but did not differ from their ratings of their spouse. Finally fathers' self-ratings were lower than the ratings they received from their spouses, but higher than the ratings they received from their younger child.

Three trends are most evident in the appraisal data. First, younger children appreciate themselves more than they appreciate their relationship partners. They consider themselves to be better brothers and sisters than their siblings are, and to be better to their parents than their parents are to them. Not surprisingly, perhaps, younger children's relationship partners (with the exception of fathers) are less impressed. Second, both older and younger children's ratings were most self-enhancing with respect to their sibling relationships, replicating the findings of Ross et al. (2000). Children consistently reported that they are better brothers and sisters than their siblings are. Finally, there was more variability within the parent–child relationships. Parents rated themselves somewhat more favourably than they rated their children. In contrast, parents evidenced no tendency to favour themselves when rating the spousal relationship; indeed mothers rated their spouses' contributions to their relationship more favourably than they rated their own.

We also examined the degree of reciprocity in participants' appraisals of self and others at the correlational level. Parents and children both reported considerable consistency concerning their own qualities and the qualities that others brought to the same relationships (e.g., mother rated self and father as spouses). However, partners' appraisals of the same person within a relationship (e.g., mothers' appraisals of self as a spouse and fathers' appraisals of mother as a spouse) evidenced considerably less agreement. Family members tended to agree more closely in their assessments within than across generations. In within-generation relationships, roles allow for greater discretion and spouses and siblings seemed to agree, to some extent, on the qualities of each relationship partner. Also, both children's appraisals of their mothers agreed with how she appraised herself; however, mothers and children did not agree on assessments of the children. Finally, there was no agreement with respect to fathers' and children's characteristics in the father–child relationships. Although the correlations indicated moderate agreement with respect to mothers' characteristics, it is noteworthy that both children were in some agreement with their mothers. Perhaps children were particularly attentive towards their mothers, or perhaps mothers were particularly insightful with respect to their own qualities with each of the children.

The social relations analysis adds to the above findings by demonstrating the interplay of actor, partner, and relationship effects. When family members appraised their own qualities as husbands, wives, parents, offspring, or siblings, they regarded themselves as acting similarly across their different relationships: They indicated that they were consistently nice, helpful, mean, or hurtful. This consistency is evidenced by the strong actor effects obtained for self-ratings. A lack of partner effects in the same analyses of self-ratings provided little indication that family members elicited consistent self-appraisals from others in the family. Also, when family members directly rated their relationship partners, actor effects were less evident. Only the mothers rated other family members with significant consistency. It makes sense that family members would perceive consistency across relationships with others in the family when asked to focus on their own qualities, as they are rating a single target (self). When asked to appraise their partners in each relationship, family members should show less consistency, however, because the target of evaluation changes.

Ratings of others did provide evidence of partner effects, but only for appraisals of the children. Thus there was more general agreement on the children's qualities than on those of the parents; perhaps this indicates that the children's roles in the family (sibling, son, or daughter) are less differentiated than are the roles of adults (parents, spouse). In dynamic systems theory, Minuchin (1988) stresses the importance for family wellbeing of separating the spouse and parent roles. The lack of partner effects might indicate that the adults in these generally well-functioning community families successfully differentiate these roles. Partner effects for the children indicate that family members tended to report that children's qualities were consistent across relationships. For example, some families identified a child who was considered a problem within all three relationships: mothers, fathers and siblings reported that these children were seldom nice, often fought, and didn't share or help. Since there was little agreement within relationships on the ratings of the same target (parents didn't rate children in the same ways as children rated themselves within parent–child relationships), it is only through appraisals of relationship partners that these effects emerge.

Other recent social relations analyses tend to find more pervasive actor and partner effects (e.g., Branje et al., 2002; Cook, 2000, 2001); however, other research does not separate ratings of self from ratings of others within relationships. Additionally, all of these studies focus on adolescent children and their families, and on constructs that are quite different from the simple ratings that 4- and 5-year-olds were capable of providing in the current study; additionally, the numbers of families in each of these studies is more than double the size of the current study. Indeed, the limited sample size and the limitations of the current scale are the two major weaknesses of the current study. Nonetheless, there is some suggestive evidence across studies that constructs that lead raters to focus on the characteristics of relationship partners, such as Cook's (2001) assessment of degree of influence over others, produce stronger partner effects, than assessments of more self-oriented constructs such as anxiety (Cook, 2000) and support (Branje et al., 2002).

There are also several important methodological implications of these findings. First, actor effects could result from consistencies in family members' appraisals of themselves across relationships, or from their use of the same measuring instrument to assess their relationships (shared method variance). The finding of stronger actor effects in appraisals of self than in appraisals of others indicates that family members were largely consistent in their views of themselves, rather than in their use of the rating scale. Partner effects also indicate consistent ratings that are not a result of individual consistencies in the use of our measuring instrument because they depend on ratings provided by different family members. Additionally, somewhat different patterns for appraisals of self and others emerged from the social relations analysis of the data, despite the substantial correlations that existed in individual family members' ratings of self and other. Thus, despite the correlational evidence of reciprocity in self and other ratings ("I do unto others as they do unto me"), family members were appropriately focused on the qualities of self and of other as they completed their appraisals of their relationships with others in the family.

As predicted, the least powerful relationship effects were found in parents' self-ratings of their own characteristics in the parent–child relationships. Only the mothers' relationship to older children was significant, and it was not especially strong. This prediction was based on the premise that the role of parent is powerfully constrained by culture and community, especially as regards the affective qualities assessed in the current data. Despite the support that this hypothesis received, a far stronger assessment of the role of culture would result if cultures in which relational constraints differ were compared. For example, wherever sibling care-giving is common, siblings might offer appraisals that more closely resemble the results we found for parents. Relationship effects were also generally absent in parents' appraisals of their children, again with one exception, namely the fathers' assessments of their older children's relationships with them. For assessments of children, however, child partner effects captured variance in the children's relationship qualities; this variance was simply agreed upon by others in the families rather than being unique to particular relationships.

Ratings of self and of relationship partners were highly correlated for all family members in all relationships, indicating reciprocity in all individual family members' appraisals of their relationships. Within the Social Relationships Model, rela-

tional reciprocity is assessed as the correlation between relationship effects for two partners within each relationship. In this study, relational reciprocity was not found in any of the parent–child relationships. On the other hand, within-generation relationships did display clear reciprocity; both marital partners and siblings displayed relational reciprocity, which was especially clear in their appraisals of their relationship partners. Interestingly, Cook (2000) also found that attachment patterns in families with adolescent children were reciprocal within, but not between, generations and Branje et al. (2002) reported similar effects for perceptions of support. Thus three studies provide consistent evidence that relationships between equals demonstrate reciprocity, and those that are more hierarchical in nature do not. As the earlier two studies were of families with adolescent children, the current study extends the finding of within-generation reciprocity to families with younger children. Several explanations for this pattern of results suggest themselves. First, parents do not play the same role in their children's lives as children do in their parents' lives; the relationship is essentially complementary. Being a good parent does not depend upon having a good child; a parent might be inclined to more positive self-ratings when faced with a child they regard as a particular challenge. The problem with this interpretation, however, is that parents who rated themselves relatively positively (or negatively) rated their children in the same way. Interestingly, parents' ratings suggested slightly greater reciprocity with their spouses than with their children. It may be that relational reciprocity is more often present in relationships that are less strongly constrained by cultural expectations. Within the same generation, family members are dealing with their equals; consequently, their affection might be determined, in large part, by the affection of others toward them. With greater discretion, there is also greater agreement with regard to each other's relationship qualities; within generations family members appraised others as others appraised themselves (e.g., he says "I am often nice to my wife" and she says "My husband is often nice to me"). This suggests that within generations, family members are better attuned to one another's appraisals of their relationship and that greater awareness of how others feel sets the conditions for reciprocating those same feelings within relationships.

Family effects were quite weak in these data. Family effects were negligible in self-ratings, although significant for ratings of others. Our findings indicate that appraisals were not consistent across relationships within families, but depended on who was doing the assessments and which relationships were assessed. These findings are consistent with findings of either nonsignificant or limited family effects in other studies (e.g., Branje, et al., 2002; Cook, 2000, 2001). These findings provide an interesting contrast with views that the marital relationship, and especially marital conflict, has a pervasive effect on relationships throughout the family (e.g., Erel, Margolin, & John, 1998). Such pervasive influences would reveal themselves in strong family effects. Importantly, however, the SRM studies have not investigated conflict processes per se, but focused more often on more positive constructs within family relationships. Studies of family conflict processes using social relations analysis would provide important additions to the family conflict literature because the analysis simultaneously reveals individual, relationship, and family influences, assessed for each person and dyad within the family, as well as family effects that pervade all relationships. In this way, a social relations analysis could provide a balanced perspective that could aid in the assessment of causal processes in the area of family conflict.

In addition to illustrating the utility of the social relations analysis, our findings indicate that even the youngest children were able to provide opinions on family relationships from both their own perspectives and from the perspectives of their relationship partners. Information obtained from the youngest family members did not produce findings that were in any way discrepant from or less reliable than that obtained from older siblings or parents. Family researchers can potentially learn a great deal of new information by permitting young children to speak for themselves.

Manuscript received December 2003
Revised manuscript received June 2004

References

Arbuckle, J. L. (1996). Full information estimation in the presence of incomplete data. In G. A. Marcoulides & R. E. Schumacker (Eds.), *Advanced structural equation modeling: Issues and techniques* (pp. 243–277). Mahwah, NJ: Lawrence Erlbaum Associates Inc.

Arbuckle, J. L., & Wothke, W. (1999). *Amos 4.0 user's guide.* Chicago: SmallWaters.

Branje, S. J. T., Van Aken, M. A. G., & Van Lieshout, C. F. M. (2002). Relational support in families with adolescents. *Journal of Family Psychology, 16,* 351–362.

Brody, G. H., Stoneman, Z., & McCoy, J. K. (1992). Associations of maternal and paternal direct and differential behavior with sibling relationships: Contemporaneous and longitudinal analyses. *Child Development, 63,* 82–92.

Buhrmester, D., & Furman, W. (1987). The development of companionship and intimacy. *Child Development, 58,* 1101–1113.

Burks, V. S., & Parke, R. D. (1996). Parent and child representations of social relationships: Linkages between families and peers. *Merrill Palmer Quarterly, 42,* 368–378.

Cook, W. L. (1993). Interdependence and the interpersonal sense of control: An analysis of family relationships. *Journal of Personality and Social Psychology, 64,* 587–601.

Cook, W. L. (1994). A structural equation model of dyadic relationship within the family system. *Journal of Consulting and Clinical Psychology, 62,* 500–509.

Cook, W. L. (2000). Understanding attachment security in family context. *Journal of Personality and Social Psychology, 78,* 285–294.

Cook, W. L. (2001). Interpersonal influence in family systems: A social relations analysis. *Child Development, 72,* 1179–1197.

Cook, W. L., & Dreyer, A. (1984). A social relations model: A new approach to analysis of family-dyadic interaction. *Journal of Marriage and the Family, 46,* 679–687.

Cook, W. L., Kenny, D. A., & Goldstein, M. J. (1991). Parental affective style risk and the family system: A social relations model analysis. *Journal of Abnormal Psychology, 100,* 492–501.

Cox, M. J., & Paley, B. (2003). Understanding families as systems. *Current Directions in Psychological Science, 12,* 193–196.

Cummings, E. M., & Davies, P. T. (1995). The impact of parents on their children: An emotion security hypothesis. *Annals of Child Development, 10,* 167–208.

Cummings, E. M., Davies, P. T., & Campbell, S. B. (2000). *Developmental psychopathology and family process: Theory, research, and clinical implications.* New York: Guilford Press.

Devereux, E. C., Shouval, R., Bronfenbrenner, U., Rodgers, R. R., Kav-Venaki, S., Kiely, E., & Karson, E. (1974). Socialization practices of parents, teachers, and peers in Israel: The kibbutz versus the city. *Child Development, 45,* 269–281.

Dunn, J., & Kendrick, C. (1982). *Siblings: Lover envy and understanding.* London: Grant McIntyre.

Erel, O., Margolin, G., & John, R. S. (1998). Observed sibling interaction: Links with the marital and the mother–child relationship. *Developmental Psychology, 34,* 288–298.

Fisher, C. B., & Johnson, B. L. (1990). Getting mad at Mom and Dad: Children's changing views of family conflict. *International Journal of Behavioral Development, 13,* 31–48.

Furman, W., & Buhrmester, D. (1985). Children's perceptions of the personal relationships in their social networks. *Developmental Psychology, 21,* 1016–1024.

Gleason, T. R. (2002). Social provisions of real and imaginary relationships in early childhood. *Developmental Psychology, 38,* 979–992.

Gottman, J. M. (1994). *What predicts divorce?* Hillsdale, NJ: Lawrence Erlbaum Associates Inc.

Hinde, R. A. (1988). Introduction. In R. A. Hinde & J. Stevenson-Hinde (Eds.), *Relationships within families: Mutual influences* (pp. 1–6). Oxford: Oxford University Press.

Kashy, D. A., & Kenny, D. A. (1990). Analysis of family research designs: A model of interdependence. *Communication Research, 17,* 462–482.

Kenny, D. A., & LaVoie, L. (1984). The social relations model. In L. Berkowitz (Ed.), *Advances in experimental social psychology,* Vol. 18 (pp. 141–182). New York: Academic.

Laursen, B., Wilder, D., Noack, P., & Williams, V. (2002). Adolescent perceptions of reciprocity, authority, and closeness in relationship with mothers, fathers, and friends. *International Journal of Behavioral Development, 24,* 461–471.

MacKinnon-Lewis, C., Volling, B. L., Lamb, M. E., Dechman, K., Rabiner, D., & Curtner, M. E. (1994). A cross-contextual analysis of boys' social competence: From family to school. *Developmental Psychology, 30,* 325–333.

McHale, J. P., & Rasmussen, J. L. (1998). Coparental and family group-level dynamics during infancy: Early family precursors of child and family functioning during preschool. *Development and Psychopathology, 10,* 39–59.

Mendelson, M. J., Aboud, F. E., & Lanthier, R. P. (1994). Kindergartners' relationships with siblings, peers and friends. *Merrill-Palmer Quarterly, 40,* 416–435.

Minuchin, P. (1988). Relationships within the family: A systems perspective on development. In R. A. Hinde & J. Stevenson-Hinde (Eds.), *Relationships within families: Mutual influences* (pp. 7–26). Oxford: Oxford University Press.

Mostkoff, D. L., & Lazarus, P. J. (1983). The kinetic family drawing: The reliability of an objective scoring system. *Psychology in the Schools, 20,* 16–20.

Parker, J., & Stimpson, J. (2002). *Sibling rivalry, sibling love: What every brother and sister needs their parents to know.* London: Hodder & Stoughton.

Ross, H. S., Woody, E., Smith, M., & Lollis, S. (2000). Young children's appraisals of sibling relationships. *Merrill-Palmer Quarterly, 46,* 441–464.

Sroufe, L. A., & Fleeson, J. (1988). The coherence of family relationships. In R. A. Hinde & J. Stevenson-Hinde (Eds.), *Relationships within families: Mutual influences* (pp. 27–47). Oxford: Oxford University Press.

Stein, N. L., Trabasso, T., & Liwag, M. (1994). The rashomon phenomenon: Personal frames and future-oriented appraisals in memory for emotional events. In M. M. Haith, J. B. Benson, R. J. Roberts, & R. F. Pennington (Eds.), *The development of further-oriented processes* (pp. 409–435). Chicago: The University of Chicago Press.

Stemmler, M., & Peterson, A. C. (2000). Reciprocity and change within the affective environment in early adolescence. *International Journal of Behavioral Development, 23,* 185–198.

Stevenson, M. B., Leavitt, L. A., Thompson, R. H., & Roach, M. A. (1988). A social relations model analysis of parent-child play. *Developmental Psychology, 24,* 101–108.

Stevenson-Hinde, J., & Verchueren, K. (2002). Attachment in childhood. In P. K. Smith & C. H. Hart (Eds.), *Blackwell handbook of child social development.* Oxford: Blackwell.

Stromshak, E. A., Ballanti, C. J., Bierman, K. L., & CPPRG. (1996). The quality of sibling relationships and the development of social competence and behavior control in aggressive children. *Developmental Psychology, 32,* 79–89.

Vuchinich, S., Vuchinich, R., & Wood, B. (1993). The interparental relationship and family problem solving with preadolescent males. *Child Development, 64,* 1389–1400.

International Journal of Behavioral Development
2005, 29 (2), 120–128
http://www.tandf.co.uk/journals/pp/01650244.html

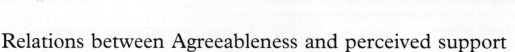

Ψ Psychology Press
Taylor & Francis Group

Relations between Agreeableness and perceived support in family relationships: Why nice people are not always supportive

Susan J. T. Branje
Utrecht University,
The Netherlands

Cornelis F. M. van Lieshout
Radboud University Nijmegen,
The Netherlands

Marcel A. G. van Aken
Utrecht University,
The Netherlands

Do more agreeable individuals perceive more support, and are they perceived as more supportive, across all family relationships or only within specific relationships? In a study of 256 Dutch two-parent families with two adolescents, we examine whether links between Agreeableness and support are generalised across relationships or occur within specific relationships. Social Relations Model analyses showed that individuals who perceive their family members as more agreeable perceive more support from family members across relationships. Also, individuals who are perceived as more agreeable are perceived as more supportive across relationships, except for mothers. In addition, individuals who perceive specific family members as more agreeable perceive these specific members as more supportive. However, individuals who are perceived as more agreeable perceive more support only within specific relationships. Thus, agreeable family members are supportive across relationships, but agreeable family members perceive support only within specific relationships.

Introduction

Individual differences in perceived support can be explained intrapersonally by characteristics of the perceiver, but also interpersonally by characteristics of the person providing the support (e.g., Lakey & Cassady, 1990; I. G. Sarason, Pierce, & Sarason, 1990). Such a characteristic is the Big Five factor Agreeableness: Individuals who are highly agreeable are motivated to maintain positive relationships with others (Jensen-Campbell & Graziano, 2001), and they tend to perceive more support from family members and are perceived as more supportive by family members (Branje, Van Lieshout, & Van Aken, 2004). However, agreeable individuals do not have to be supportive toward everyone, and not everyone will support them. These links between support and Agreeableness may occur across relationships and within relationships. The link occurs *across* relationships when an individual perceives *all* family members as agreeable and supportive or when an individual is perceived as agreeable and supportive by *all* family members. Similarly, when an individual perceives *all* family members as agreeable and is perceived as supportive by *all* family members, or when an individual perceives *all* family members as supportive and is perceived as agreeable by *all* family members, the relation is also across relationships. In contrast, the link occurs *within specific* relationships when an individual perceives a *specific* family member as agreeable and supportive, or when an individual perceives a *specific* family member as agreeable and this *specific* family member perceives the individual as supportive. Using a Social Relations Model, the present study investigated the extent to which the links between Agreeableness and support in families with two

parents and two adolescent children occur across relationships and the extent to which they occur within specific relationships.

The Social Relations Model and Agreeableness and support in the family context

The Social Relations Model (SRM; e.g., Cook, 1994; Kenny, 1994; Kenny & La Voie, 1984) is a statistical model that enables to distinguish interdependent or shared dyadic perspectives and behaviours from those that are independent and unique to each participant. The SRM enables involving the perceptions of all members of the family in the study while controlling for the statistical interdependence of the collected data of different members of the same family. Specifically, it allows to identify that part of variance in social behaviour (such as perceived support) that is due (1) to a family member's disposition to perceive support from all other family members, the *actor effect*, (2) to a particular family member's tendency of being perceived as supportive by all other family members, the *partner effect*, (3) to the *relationship effect*, or the unique relationship between two family members that makes a family member perceive support from one specific partner, but not from others, and (4) to the *family effect*, or the mean level of support perceived by all of the family members. Thus, the SRM makes a sharp distinction between the effects of dispositional characteristics of individuals, the dyadic relationships between individuals, and the family to which those individuals belong. SRM analyses have revealed that both perceived support and Agreeableness in family relationships are a function of characteristics of each partner in a relationship

Correspondence should be sent to Susan Branje, Department of Child and Adolescent Studies, Utrecht University, PO Box 80140, 3508 TC Utrecht, The Netherlands; e-mail: s.j.t.branje@fss.uu.nl.

as well as the unique relationship between the partners (Branje, Van Aken, & Van Lieshout, 2002; Branje, Van Aken, Van Lieshout, & Mathijssen, 2003). High actor variance showed that differences in perceived support and Agreeableness of individual family members are to a large extent due to actor effects, or individual family members' disposition to generally perceive support and Agreeableness from other family members. Perceivers tend to differ in the extent to which they elicit support from others, and in their stable beliefs about the supportiveness of others in general (Baldwin, 1992; Lakey & Cohen, 2000; Pierce, Baldwin, & Lydon, 1997; B. R. Sarason, Pierce, & Sarason, 1990; I. G. Sarason, Sarason, & Shearin, 1986). The extent to which two family members perceive support from each other or are agreeable to each other was also found to be partly relationship-specific, depending on the unique relationship between them. Perceptions of support are thought to be affected by the specific supportive actions of the partner: Some individuals are more likely to help and support someone than others (Lakey, McCabe, Fisicaro, & Drew, 1996a; Lakey, Adams, Neely, Rhodes, Lutz, & Sielky, 2002). Differences in perceived support or Agreeableness did not seem to depend much on individual family member's partner effects, or dispositions to be perceived as supportive or agreeable by others. More likely, the effects of perceiver and partner are likely to interact, resulting in support perceptions that are in part relationship-specific (Branje et al., 2002). In the present paper we will extend these studies by examining the *links* between the SRM components of perceived support and Agreeableness in families with adolescent children.

Links between perceived support and Agreeableness in the family context

Agreeableness is related to perceived support in close relationships (Asendorpf & Van Aken, 2003; Lakey et al., 2002). In families with adolescents, Agreeableness appeared as the Big Five personality factor most strongly related to perceived relational support (Branje et al., 2004). In fact, perceived support was linked to the Agreeableness of the perceiver as well as to the Agreeableness of the provider of support: Individuals who are more agreeable *perceive* more support from their family members and *are perceived* as more supportive by their family members. These findings may not be surprising because Agreeableness is related to motives for maintaining positive relationships with important others (Jensen-Campbell & Graziano, 2001). More agreeable individuals are likely to interpret and react more positively upon behaviours of others, and thereby facilitate social behaviours such as intimacy (Finch & Graziano, 2001). Thus, the Agreeableness of individuals may help them to maintain supportive relationships with family members.

Given this evidence, understanding how exactly perceived support and Agreeableness in the family context are related to each other becomes important. The relation between Agreeableness and perceived support may be due to individual characteristics of family members that *generalise across relationships*, but may also involve processes *within specific relationships*. That is, individuals may in part be agreeable in general, toward all their relationship partners, and therefore perceive all these relationship partners as agreeable or be perceived as agreeable by all these partners. Additionally, individuals may be differentially agreeable towards specific relationship partners,

and this relationship-specific Agreeableness may be related to the support uniquely perceived from or by this specific partner. In a sample of college students, relationship processes were found to play a role in the link between personal characteristics and support perceptions: Depending on their own traits, perceivers differ in how they combine information about target traits to judge the supportiveness of the target (Lutz & Lakey, 2001). This finding is consistent with theories on social relationships emphasising bidirectional, reciprocal processes in which dyadic partners mutually influence each other (Lollis & Kuczynski, 1997). Hence, the specific match between relationship partners seems important for support judgments and the link between Agreeableness and perceived support may also be in part relationship-specific. In dyadic relationships of families with adolescent children, we will examine to what extent links between Agreeableness and perceived support are generalised across relationship partners and to what extent they are relationship-specific.

The SRM allows us to assess links between family members' Agreeableness and perceived support across relationships and within relationships (see also Finkenauer, Engels, Branje, & Meeus, 2004). Additionally, the SRM allows us to consider these relations intrapersonally (i.e., are more agreeable family members more supportive themselves?) and interpersonally (i.e., do more agreeable family members get more support from others?). Correlated actor and partner effects of support and Agreeableness would indicate links across relationships. Intrapersonal relations across relationships would exist when individuals who perceive support from all family members perceive all family members as agreeable (correlated actor effects within a person), and also when a particular family member who is perceived as supportive by all others is perceived as agreeable by all others (correlated partner effects within a person). Interpersonal relations across relationships would be demonstrated if an individual who perceives all family members as supportive is perceived as agreeable by all others, or when an individual who perceives all family members as agreeable is perceived as supportive by all family members (actor effect–partner effect correlations of two persons).

Links *within* specific relationships would emerge when the relationship effects of perceived support and Agreeableness are correlated. Evidence for intrapersonal links within relationships would occur when a family member who perceives a specific relationship partner as supportive also perceives that specific relationship partner as agreeable (correlated relationship effects within a person). Interpersonal links within relationships would be evident when a family member who perceives a specific relationship partner as supportive is perceived as agreeable by that specific relationship partner (correlated relationship effects between two persons).

Hence, we will examine whether Agreeableness and perceived support in adolescents' families are related across relationships or within relationships. Based on the findings of high actor effects on both perceived support and Agreeableness, we hypothesise that intrapersonal links occur mainly across relationships, due to the characteristics of the perceiver. That is, family members who perceive more support across relationships are expected to perceive others as more agreeable across relationships. Interpersonally, relationship-specific links between Agreeableness and support are expected to be stronger than links across relationships. Family members will influence each other reciprocally mainly by their unique perceptions of each other, or their specific dyadic match, and not so much by their general perceptions.

Method

Participants

Participants were recruited for the Family & Personality study, a longitudinal study of 285 Dutch two-parent families with two adolescents (Haselager & Van Aken, 1999). A representative selection of 23 municipalities in the Netherlands provided lists of families with two adolescents between the ages of 11 and 15 years. After a mailing to the families announcing the study, interviewers contacted the families by phone and invited them to participate. A total of 50% of the families contacted agreed to take part in the study. Only those families were included in the study in which all four members were willing to participate. Frequently given reasons for not wanting to participate were that the family had no interest in the topic of the project, or that a specific family member did not want to collaborate. Thus for all participating families, two parents and two adolescents participated in the study. Because we employed a four-person family design in the SRM analyses (Kashy & Kenny, 1990), the two adolescents participating in the study will be distinguished as the "older" and the "younger" adolescent throughout the manuscript.

The average age was 43.9 years ($SD = 3.27$) for the fathers and 41.7 years ($SD = 3.71$) for the mothers. The older adolescents (142 boys, 143 girls) were on average 14.5 years ($SD = 0.83$), and the younger adolescents (135 boys, 150 girls) were on average 12.3 years ($SD = 0.76$). Almost all respondents were of Dutch origin. Only in 4% of the families did parents report that they were not born in the Netherlands. A small proportion of the parents, 17% of the mothers and 19% of the fathers, had finished only primary or low secondary education. Forty-six per cent of the fathers and 28% of the mothers had finished college or university education. All adolescents lived with their natural mother and father at their parental home. Concerning birth order, in 224 families (79%) the older adolescent who participated in the study was actually the oldest child in the nuclear family. Furthermore, in 219 families (77%) the younger adolescent had only one older sibling.

Procedure

Families were followed over a period of 3 years, with yearly measurement waves. In each measurement wave, trained interviewers visited the families at home and asked the mother, the father, and each of the two target adolescents to fill out a battery of questionnaires. All four family members completed questionnaires assessing the extent to which they perceive support from the three other family members and the extent to which they perceive themselves and their family members to be agreeable. The presence of the interviewer encouraged complete responding and prevented discussions regarding individual items or the topics in the questionnaires among the family members during completion of the questionnaires. Both adolescents in the family were given a CD gift certificate after completion of the questionnaires. Furthermore, 10 families who filled out all questionnaires could gain a travel voucher (value of about €900) as a reward.

Measures

Family members received a large battery of questionnaires. Only those questionnaires relevant to the questions addressed in the present study will be discussed here. All measures were adapted so as to generalise to and be appropriate in all types of relationships in the family. Relationship specificity was achieved by formulating items as statements and instructing participants to imagine each specific family member (i.e., father, mother, sibling) before rating each statement for the specific partner.

Perceived support. Perceived relational support was measured with the Relational Support Inventory (RSI; Scholte, Van Lieshout, & Van Aken, 2001). The inventory involves 24 items measured along a 5-point Likert scale ranging from *very untrue of this person* (1) to *sometimes untrue, sometimes true of this person* (3) to *very true of this person* (5).

The questionnaire includes questions on the quality of information provided (e.g., "This person explains or shows how I can make or do something"), the respect for autonomy of the relationship partner (e.g., "This person lets me solve problems as much as possible on my own but also provides help when I ask for it"), the emotional support provided (e.g., "In this person's view, I can't do anything right: he/she is always criticising me"), and the convergence of goals (e.g., "This person and I have many conflicts with regard to school achievement, the future, or career opportunities"). An overall support score for each of the 12 family relationships was computed by averaging the scores on the 24 items within each measurement wave (i.e., considering that support perceptions are directional, father→mother and mother→father are two relational perceptions). Reliabilities of these support scores were on average $\alpha = .82$ with a range of $\alpha = .80$ to $\alpha = .87$.

Agreeableness. A Dutch adaptation (Gerris, Houtmans, Kwaaitaal-Roosen, Schipper, Vermulst, & Janssens, 1998) of adjective Big Five personality markers selected from Goldberg (1992) was used to have family members judge their own Agreeableness and the Agreeableness of the other three participating family members. The Big Five factor Agreeableness was measured using six items: pleasant, helpful, friendly, obliging, agreeable, and sympathetic/nice. The participants rated the adjectives along a 7-point Likert scale ranging from (1) *very untrue of this person* to (4) *sometimes untrue, sometimes true of this person* to (7) *very true of this person*. The internal consistencies (Cronbach's alpha) ranged from .84 to .86 for judgments by fathers, from .82 to .88 for judgments by mothers, from .80 to .90 for judgments by older adolescents, and from .76 to .87 for judgments by younger adolescents.

Analyses

We used a SRM analysis to estimate the links across relationships and within relationships between Agreeableness and perceived support. A minimum sample size of 50 families is required to have enough power for an SRM analysis (Kashy & Kenny, 1990), so our sample size is large enough. A SRM analysis was performed on the covariance matrix of each family member's perceived support from the three other family members (i.e., $4 \times 3 = 12$ family relationships) and each family member's Agreeableness as judged by all family members (i.e., 4 × 4 = 16 judgments of Agreeableness). We did not estimate separate models for perceived support and Agreeableness but instead estimated both concepts in a single model. The SRM analysis explores the extent to which variance in perceived support and Agreeableness in each of the 12 family relationships is due to actor, partner, relationship, and family effects. All these effects are estimated independently, controlling for all remaining effects. That is, a relationship effect is estimated after controlling for actor, partner, and family effects.

For the four-person family design, there are 12 relationship variances, 1 for each dyadic perception. There are 12 unidirectional indicators of perceived support and 16 indicators of Agreeableness. However, to reliably estimate the 12 relationship effects (that is, without random error variances), at least 24 indicators are needed for each construct. In order to obtain enough indicators, replications of each of the observed variables can be used. Therefore, we used judgments of perceived support and Agreeableness from the first and second measurement wave as separate indicators of perceived support and Agreeableness, which produced (12 relationships × 2 scales =) 24 observed scores of perceived support and (16 judgments × 2 scales =) 32 scores of Agreeableness (see Cook, 1993, 1994, 2000).

Thus, a SRM analysis was conducted with each of the two perceived support and Agreeableness scales (the indicators) included to partition the variance in perceived support and

Agreeableness into actor, partner, relationship, and family effects for perceived support and Agreeableness, respectively. The actor, partner, relationship, and family effects technically constitute separate factors or latent variables within a confirmatory factor analysis (see Figure 1; Cook, 1994). The factor loadings (i.e., paths from the latent variables to the indicators) were all fixed at 1.0 to be able to identify the SRM factor variances (Kashy & Kenny, 1990). We allowed for correlations among measurement errors for each indicator per rating family member (e.g., for each indicator of father's perceived support, we allowed father's measurement errors for their perceived support from mother, older adolescent, and younger adolescent to correlate). The different variances for perceived support and Agreeableness were simultaneously estimated using structural equation modelling with maximum likelihood estimation procedures (LISREL 8.30; Jöreskog & Sörbom, 1996). Missing cases were deleted listwise, which reduced the sample to 256 families.

In the same SRM analysis, we also estimated the hypothesised relations between the SRM components of perceived support and Agreeableness as specified in Figure 2. The model showed an acceptable fit with our data set given the complexity of the model and the number of variables involved. The χ^2 of this model was 2041.54, $p < .01$, $df = 1381$, the Non-Normed Fit Index (NNFI) was .94, and the Root Mean Square Error of Approximation (RMSEA) was .04, indicating an acceptable fit of the overall model (Browne & Cudeck, 1989).

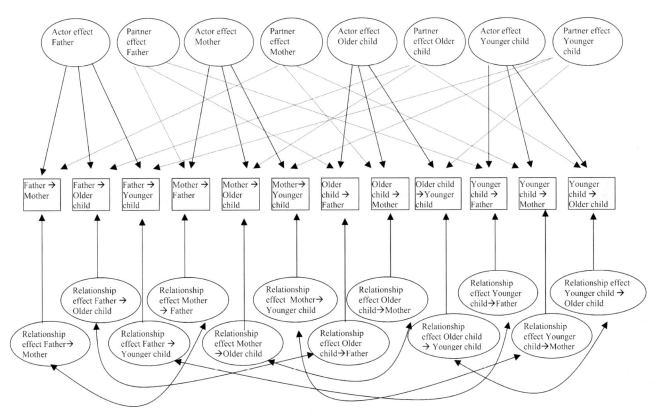

Figure 1. Parameters of the LISREL model. Rectangles represent the observed measures; ellipses represent the latent SRM components of support or Agreeableness. One-headed arrows indicate factor loadings. All loadings are fixed at 1. Double-headed arrows represent dyadic reciprocity correlations. All of the observed variables loaded on the latent SRM component "family effect", which is not included in the figure. For Agreeableness, self-reports were also included that were allowed to load on the actor effect and partner effect of the reporting person. Figure 1 displays the parameters for one indicator of perceived support or Agreeableness only; the other indicator loads on the same latent factors in a similar manner.

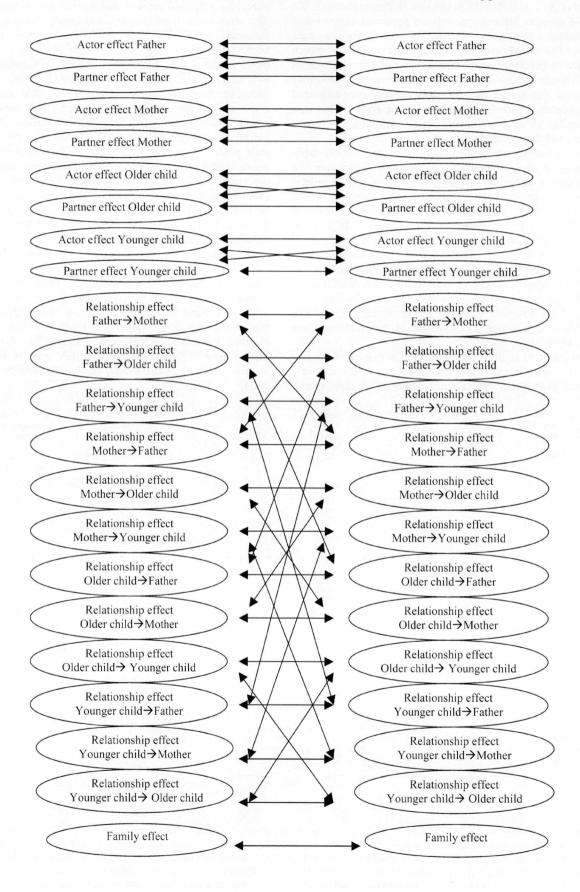

Figure 2. SRM correlations between Agreeableness and support.

Results

The simple main SRM effects (actor, partner, relationship, and family effects) for perceived support and for Agreeableness separately will not be described in the present study because they have been addressed in earlier studies (Branje et al., 2002, 2003). We will focus on the relations between different SRM effects of Agreeableness and perceived support, to address our hypotheses regarding the links between perceived support and Agreeableness across and within family relationships.

Links between perceived support and Agreeableness across family relationships

We first examined our hypotheses regarding links between Agreeableness and perceived support across family relationships. To examine whether more agreeable family members are more supportive, the correlations between a family member's actor effect for perceived support and that family member's actor effect for Agreeableness were computed, as well as the family member's partner effect for perceived support and that family member's partner effect for Agreeableness (Table 1). The significant correlations of actor effects indicate that individuals who perceive more support from all their family members perceive all their family members as more agreeable. In addition, the correlations of partner effects reveal that individuals who are perceived as more agreeable by all their family members are perceived as more supportive by all their family members as well, except for mothers. This suggests that mothers are supportive regardless of their Agreeableness. Mothers' partner effect of support was the only SRM effect that was not significant, which may be related to this finding.

To examine whether family members who are more agreeable perceive more support, the correlations between a family member's actor effect for perceived support and that family member's partner effect for Agreeableness were computed, as well as the family member's partner effect for perceived support and that family member's actor effect for Agreeableness (Table 1). The nonsignificant correlations indicate that individuals who perceive more support from all family members are not perceived as more agreeable by all family members. Also, family members who are perceived as more supportive by all family members do not perceive more Agreeableness from all family members.

Links between perceived support and Agreeableness within family relationships

Next, we examined the links between Agreeableness and perceived support within family relationships. To examine whether family members who are more agreeable within specific relationships are also more supportive in these relationships, the correlations between a family member's relationship effect for perceived support and that family member's relationship effect for Agreeableness were computed (Table 2). All correlations were significant except for the relationship of the younger child towards the mother, which indicates that individuals who perceive a specific family member as more agreeable perceive more support from this specific partner than individuals who perceive that family member as less agreeable. The strength of the correlation coefficients differed across relationships, however. z-score comparisons of correlations per family member showed that in the horizontal marital and sibling relationships, the correlations were significantly stronger than in the vertical parent–child relationships, except for the relationship of the younger children with their father and sibling.

To examine whether family members who are more agreeable within specific relationships perceive more support in these relationships, the correlations between a family member's relationship effect for perceived support and his or her dyadic partner's relationship effect for Agreeableness were computed. Most correlations were significant (Table 2), indicating that individuals who perceive a specific family member as more agreeable are perceived as more supportive by this partner than individuals who perceive a specific family member as less agreeable. Only two correlations were nonsignificant: the correlation between mothers' perceived Agreeableness from younger children and younger children's perceived support from mothers and the correlation between older adolescents' perceived Agreeableness from mothers and mothers' perceived support from older adolescents. Again, z-score comparisons showed that correlations were higher for horizontal marital and sibling relationships than for vertical parent–child relationships, except for the difference in correlations between the Agreeableness that mothers perceive from father and children and the support that fathers and children perceive from mother.

In addition, the family effect for perceived support significantly correlated with the family effect for Agreeableness ($r = .86$, $p < .01$), suggesting that in families where

Table 1

Correlations between family members' Agreeableness and perceived support across relationships

	Intrapersonal correlations		Interpersonal correlations	
	Actor effect Agreeableness– support	*Partner effect Agreeableness– support*	*Actor effect Agreeableness– partner effect support*	*Actor effect support– partner effect Agreeableness*
Father	.65**	.61**	−.07	.05
Mother	.73**	.09	.11	.06
Older adolescent	.63**	.62*	−.02	−.14
Younger adolescent	.51**	.88**	−.16	.06

*$p < .05$; **$p < .01$.

Table 2

Correlations between Agreeableness and perceived support within relationships

Relationship effect Agreeableness – support			
Intrapersonal		*Interpersonal*	
Father→mother – father→mother	.67**	Father→mother – mother→father	.46**
Father→older child – father→older child	.26**	Father→older child – older child→father	.27**
Father→younger child – father→younger child	.22**	Father→younger child – younger child→father	.23**
Mother→father – mother→father	.57**	Mother→father – father→mother	.19*
Mother→older child – mother→older child	.30**	Mother→older child – older child→mother	.24**
Mother→younger child – mother→younger child	.20**	Mother→younger child – younger child→mother	.16
Older child→younger child – older child→younger child	.76**	Older child→younger child – younger child→older child	.55**
Older child→father – older child→father	.54**	Older child→father – father→older child	.25**
Older child→mother – older child→mother	.42**	Older child→mother – mother→older child	.09
Younger child→older child – younger child→older child	.70**	Younger child→older child – older child→younger child	.38**
Younger child→father – younger child→father	.89**	Younger child→father – father→younger child	.24**
Younger child→mother – younger child→mother	.15	Younger child→mother – mother→younger child	.12*

Horizontal correlations are printed in italics.
*p < .05; **p < .01.

individuals perceive more support the individuals are also more agreeable. This relation generalises to the family as a group.

Discussion

Taken together, the results of the current study confirmed the hypothesis that family members who are more agreeable are also more supportive, both across relationships and within relationships. Individuals who perceive all family members as supportive perceive all family members as agreeable, individuals who are perceived by all family members as supportive are perceived by all family members as agreeable, and individuals who perceive specific family members as supportive perceive these specific family members as agreeable. In contrast, family members who are more agreeable perceive more support only within specific relationships. Individuals who perceive all family members as more agreeable are not perceived as more supportive by all family members, but individuals who perceive specific family members as more agreeable are perceived as more supportive by these specific family members. Thus intrapersonal links occur across and within relationships but interpersonal links occur only within specific relationships.

The results for intrapersonal links between support and Agreeableness support the idea of different levels of relational schemas. Whereas the links between perceptions of a family member's Agreeableness and supportiveness across relationships may reflect general relational schemas, the relationship-specific links may reflect relationship-specific schemas (Fletcher, 1993; Koerner & Fitzpatrick, 2002). The finding that individuals who perceive their family members as more agreeable perceive more support from these family members *across* relationships points to the influence of individuals' cognitive representations of others in interpreting their behaviour (Baldwin, 1992). It seems that a person's generalised view of others has a strong relation to that person's "sense of support" (I. G. Sarason et al., 1990). However, the link between perceived Agreeableness and perceived support across relationships is not totally due to the effect of an individual's

working model of others. The strong significant correlations between the partner effects of Agreeableness and support revealed that someone's Agreeableness as perceived and agreed upon by all family members was also related to the support all family members agree to perceive from that person. In addition, intrapersonal links occurred partly within relationships: Individuals who perceive specific family members as more agreeable also perceive these specific members as more supportive. This shows that personal characteristics are to some extent context- or relationship-specific. Individuals are differentially agreeable in specific dyadic family relationships, which affects support perceptions in these relationships. Thus, relations between Agreeableness and support are partly affected by generalised relational schemes and partly by relationship-specific schemes.

A salient result of the study was that, for interpersonal relations between Agreeableness and support, being generally agreeable to all family members does not elicit more support from all family members. Individuals who are perceived as more agreeable across relationships do not perceive more support across relationships. Instead, only when a specific family member perceives an individual as uniquely agreeable within that specific relationship, will the individual perceive more support from this member. Conversely, only when someone is perceived as uniquely unfriendly by a family member, will less support be perceived from that member. Again, this points to the significance of the specific match between two family members and reciprocity processes in dyadic relationships. The interpersonal behaviour of the dyadic partners in family members is characterised by mutuality of exchanges. Although personality characteristics are often assumed to affect individuals across contexts, our results suggest that dyadic partners have to perceive the friendly behaviour as uniquely directed towards them. Only then will they reciprocate with support.

Mothers seem to have an exceptional position in the family with regard to links between Agreeableness and support. In contrast to all other family members, mothers who are generally perceived as more agreeable are not generally perceived as more supportive by their family members. In addition, in the relationship with their husbands, a mother's perception of her husband's Agreeableness did not appear to be related to the support that he perceived from her. Being generally and unconditionally supportive seems to be inherent to the role of mother and wife, and does not depend on the personal characteristics of mothers. It may be that mothers indeed try to provide support to the members of their nuclear family independent of the personal characteristics of these members. Alternatively, family members may perceive mothers as supportive to some extent, independent of the support mothers actually provide, because the cultural stereotype of mothers is one of a supportive caregiving person. This result may be related to the low partner variance in mothers' support in these four-person families: There are no differences across families in the support that all family members perceive from the mother (Branje et al., 2002).

An additional finding was that relationship-specific processes between Agreeableness and support were more consistent and stronger in horizontal marital and sibling relationships than in vertical parent–child relationships. There were only a few exceptions to this finding: in the horizontal relationship between mothers' perceived Agreeableness from fathers and fathers perceived support from mothers, interpersonal correlation were low (as discussed above), and in the vertical adolescent–father relationship intrapersonal relationship-specific correlations for adolescents' perceptions of fathers were relatively high. These results implicate the idea that parents' specific perception of their children as agreeable is only weakly related to their level of specific perceived support from these children. Put differently, parents who perceive their children as more agreeable do not tend to perceive more support from them than parents who perceive their children as less agreeable, and the reverse may hold as well, namely that independent of the support parents perceive from their children, they may perceive their children as more or less agreeable. The finding that the relationship-specific Agreeableness and support are more strongly related in horizontal relationships, except for the Agreeableness that mothers perceive from fathers and the support that fathers perceive from mothers, suggests that reciprocity between Agreeableness and support is especially important in the sibling relationship and in fathers' relationships towards mothers. Adolescents acting in a specifically nice way towards their sibling will get more support from that sibling, and mothers acting in a specifically nice way towards their spouse will get more support from him. However, mothers are supportive toward their spouse and children regardless of how agreeable their spouse and children are.

These differences between horizontal and vertical relationships suggest that family members make relational attributions regarding the support and Agreeableness they perceive in horizontal dyads and mutually affect each other mainly in these horizontal relationships. Consistent with these findings, earlier studies revealed that relationship-specific effects and dyadic reciprocity are stronger in horizontal family relationships than in vertical ones for perceived support (Branje et al., 2000). An explanation may be that in horizontal relationships, dyad members match each other's level of exchanges to preserve equity in the relationship (Rusbult & Van Lange, 2003). In some marital or sibling relationships, the partners are nice to each other and support each other; in other such relationships, hostility is common and the partners are less likely to support each other. Compatible with this explanation is the finding that perceived mutuality in marital relationships is related to higher adjustment (Genero, Miller, Surrey, & Baldwin, 1992; Noller & White, 1990), and that perceiving support in marital partners is only related to more positive and less negative mood if support is part of an exchange in which both partners perceive and give support to each other (Gleason, Iida, Bolger, & Shrout, 2003). Relationship-specific processes are clearly a crucial aspect of horizontal relationships. Less relationship-specific processes were found for vertical parent–child interactions. In these relationships, family members' roles may affect their behaviour more strongly. For example, the parents' role is to provide care, security, and support for their children regardless of the characteristics of these children. In sum, our results suggest that a sense of mutual obligation and equal exchanges are more necessary to maintain horizontal relationships than vertical relationships. These findings emphasise the importance of distinguishing between different types of relationships.

One may argue that the concepts of Agreeableness and support are comparable and might both have been an assessment of being helpful. There are, though, several arguments against this suggestion. For instance, perceived support is assessed in terms of concrete behaviour whereas personality is assessed in terms of general traits. Also, the relational support instrument not only assesses emotional support and helpful behaviour, but also openness of communication and agreement on motives and goals. These aspects of relational support may have relations to personality factors other than Agreeableness. Furthermore, of the Big Five factors, an individual's Conscientiousness is found to be most strongly related to supportive behaviour when people are in a hurry (Reynolds & Karraker, 2003), and the partner's Conscientiousness is found to be the strongest predictor of support perceived from an unacquainted partner (Lakey, Ross, Butler, & Bentley, 1996b).

A limitation of the current study is that it addressed family relationships during adolescence only. Future research needs to examine whether support–Agreeableness links not only differ for horizontal versus vertical relationships, but also for different sex constellations, different roles within the family, or different provisions of support. Additionally, further research will need to address whether these findings can be generalised to other types of relationships in other contexts.

To conclude, our study showed that it is important to examine relations between personal characteristics such as Agreeableness and relationship qualities such as perceived support across different dyadic relationships and from the perspective of different individuals. Only then can links that are generalised across relationships be distinguished from links within specific relationships. Whereas intrapersonal relations between support and Agreeableness are partly generalised across relationships and partly relationship-specific, interpersonal relations between support and Agreeableness are only relationship-specific. Furthermore, links between Agreeableness and support within specific relationships were stronger in horizontal relationships.

References

Asendorpf, J. B., & Van Aken, M. A. G. (2003). Personality-relationship transaction in adolescence: Core versus surface personality characteristics. *Journal of Personality*, 71, 629–666.

Baldwin, M. W. (1992). Relational schemas and the processing of social information. *Psychological Bulletin*, 112, 461–484.

Branje, S. J. T., Van Aken, M. A. G., & Van Lieshout, C. F. M. (2002). Relational support in families with adolescents. *Journal of Family Psychology*, *16*, 351–362.

Branje, S. J. T., Van Aken, M. A. G., Van Lieshout, C. F. M., & Mathijssen, J. J. J. P. (2003). Personality judgments in adolescents' families: The perceiver, the target, their relationship, and the family. *Journal of Personality*, *71*, 49–81.

Branje, S. J. T., Van Lieshout, C. F. M., & Van Aken, M. A. G (2004). Relations between Big Five personality characteristics and perceived support in adolescents' families. *Journal of Personality and Social Psychology*, *86*, 615–628.

Browne, M. W., & Cudeck, R. (1989). Single sample cross-validation indices for covariance structures. *Multivariate Behavioral Research*, *24*, 445–455.

Bugental, D. B., & Goodnow, J. J. (1998). Socialization processes. In W. Damon (Series Ed.) & N. Eisenberg (Volume Ed.), *Handbook of child psychology. Vol. 3: Social, emotional, and personality development* (5th ed., pp. 389–465). New York: Wiley.

Cook, W. L. (1993). Interdependence and the interpersonal sense of control: An analysis of family relationships. *Journal of Personality and Social Psychology*, *64*, 587–601.

Cook, W. L. (1994). A structural equation model of dyadic relationships within the family system. *Journal of Consulting and Clinical Psychology*, *62*, 500–509.

Cook, W. L. (2000). Understanding attachment security in family context. *Journal of Personality and Social Psychology*, *78*, 285–294.

Finch, J. F., & Graziano, W. G. (2001). Predicting depression from temperament, personality, and patterns of social relations. *Journal of Personality*, *69*, 27–55.

Finkenauer, C., Engels, R. C. M. E., Branje, S. J. T., & Meeus, W. (2004). Not all relationships are created equal: Disclosure and relationship satisfaction in the family context. *Journal of Marriage and Family*, *66*, 195–209.

Fletcher, G. J. O. (1993). Cognition in close relationships. *New Zealand Journal of Psychology*, *22*, 69–81.

Genero, N. P., Miller, J. B., Surrey, J., & Baldwin, L. M. (1992). Measuring perceived mutuality in close relationships: Validation of the Mutual Psychological Development Questionnaire. *Journal of Family Psychology*, *6*, 36–48.

Gerris, J. R. M., Houtmans, M. J. M., Kwaaitaal-Roosen, E. M. G., Schipper, J. C., Vermulst, A. A., & Janssens, J. M. A. M. (1998). *Parents, adolescents, and young adults in Dutch families: A longitudinal study*. Nijmegen, The Netherlands: Institute of Family Studies, University of Nijmegen.

Gleason, M. E. J., Iida, M., Bolger, N., & Shrout, P. E. (2003). Daily supportive equity in close relationships. *Personality and Social Psychology Bulletin*, *29*, 1036–1045.

Goldberg, L. R. (1992). The development of markers of the Big-Five factor structure. *Psychological Assessment*, *4*, 26–42.

Hartup, W. W. (1989). Social relationships and their developmental significance. *American Psychologist*, *44*, 120–126.

Haselager, G. J. T., & Van Aken, M. A. G. (1999). *Codebook of the research project Family and Personality: Vol. 1. First measurement wave*. Nijmegen, The Netherlands: University of Nijmegen, Faculty of Social Science.

Jensen-Campbell, L. A., & Graziano, W. G. (2001). Agreeableness as a moderator of interpersonal conflict. *Journal of Personality*, *69*, 323–362.

Jöreskog, K. G., & Sörbom, D. (1996). *LISREL 8: User's reference guide*. Chicago, IL: Scientific Software International.

Kashy, D. A., & Kenny, D. A. (1990). Analysis of family research designs: A model of interdependence. *Communication Research*, *17*, 462–482.

Kenny, D. A. (1994). *Interpersonal perception: A social relations analysis*. New York: Guilford Press.

Kenny, D. A., & La Voie, L. (1984). The Social Relations Model. In L. Berkowitz (Ed.), *Advances in experimental social psychology, Vol. 18* (pp. 141–182). San Diego, CA: Academic Press.

Koerner, A. F., & Fitzpatrick, M. A. (2002). Toward a theory of family communication. *Communication Theory*, *12*, 70–91.

Lakey, B., Adams, K., Neely, L., Rhodes, G., Lutz, C. J., & Sielky, K. (2002). Perceived support and low emotional distress: The role of enacted support, dyad similarity and provider personality. *Personality and Social Psychology Bulletin*, *28*, 1546–1555.

Lakey, B., & Cassady, P. B. (1990). Cognitive processes in perceived social support. *Journal of Personality and Social Psychology*, *59*, 337–343.

Lakey, B., & Cohen, S. (2000). Social support theory and measurement. In S. Cohen, L. G. Underwood, & B. H. Gottlieb (Eds.), *Social support measurement and intervention: A guide for health and social scientists* (pp. 29–52). London: Oxford University Press.

Lakey, B., McCabe, K. M., Fisicaro, S. A., & Drew, J. B. (1996a). Environmental and personal determinants of support perceptions: Three generalizability studies. *Journal of Personality and Social Psychology*, *70*, 1270–1280.

Lakey, B., Ross, L. T., Butler, C., & Bentley, K. (1996b). Making social support judgments: The role of similarity and conscientiousness. *Journal of Social and Clinical Psychology*, *15*, 283–304.

Laursen, B., & Bukowski, W. M. (1997). A developmental guide to the organisation of close relationships. *International Journal of Behavioral Development*, *21*, 747–770.

Lollis, S., & Kuczynski, L. (1997). Beyond one hand clapping: Seeing bidirectionality in parent–child relations. *Journal of Social and Personal Relationships*, *14*, 441–461.

Lutz, C. J., & Lakey, B. (2001). How people make support judgments: Individual differences in the traits used to infer supportiveness in others. *Journal of Personality and Social Psychology*, *81*, 1070–1079.

Maccoby, E. E. (1992). The role of parents in the socialization of children: An historical overview. *Developmental Psychology*, *28*, 1006–1017.

Noller, P., & White, A. (1990). The validity of the Communication Patterns Questionnaire. *Psychological Assessment*, *2*, 478–482.

Pierce, T., Baldwin, M. W., & Lydon, J. E. (1997). A relational scheme approach to social support. In G. R. Pierce, B. Lakey, I. W. Sarason, & B. R. Sarason (Eds.), *Sourcebook of social support and personality. The Plenum series in social/clinical psychology* (pp. 107–140). New York: Plenum Press.

Reynolds, B., & Karraker, K. (2003). A Big Five model of disposition and situation interaction: Why a "helpful" person may not always behave helpfully. *New Ideas in Psychology*, *21*, 1–13.

Rusbult, C. E., & Van Lange, P. A. M. (2003). Interdependence, interaction and relationships. *Annual Review of Psychology*, *54*, 351–375.

Russell, A., Pettit, G. S., & Mize, J. (1998). Horizontal qualities in parent–child relationships: Parallels with and possible consequences for children's peer relationships. *Developmental Review*, *18*, 313–352.

Sarason, B. R., Pierce, G. R., & Sarason, I. G. (1990). Social support: The sense of acceptance and the role of relationships. In B. R. Sarason, I. G. Sarason, & G. R. Pierce (Eds.), *Social support: An interactional view* (pp. 97–128). New York: John Wiley.

Sarason, I. G., Pierce, G. R., & Sarason, B. R. (1990). Social support and interactional processes: A triadic hypothesis. *Journal of Social and Personal Relationships*, *7*, 495–506.

Sarason, I. G., Sarason, B. R., & Shearin, E. N. (1986). Social support as an individual difference variable: Its stability, origins, and relational aspects. *Journal of Personality and Social Psychology*, *50*, 845–855.

Scholte, R. H. J., Van Lieshout, C. F. M., & Van Aken, M. A. G. (2001). Perceived relational support in adolescence: Dimensions, configurations, and adolescent adjustment. *Journal of Research in Adolescence*, *11*, 71–94.

International Journal of Behavioral Development
2005, 29 (2), 129–138
http://www.tandf.co.uk/journals/pp/01650244.html

Ψ Psychology Press
Taylor & Francis Group

DOI: 10.1080/01650250444000469

Sibling aggression: Sex differences and parents' reactions

Jacqueline L. Martin
University of Waterloo, Canada

Hildy S. Ross
University of Waterloo, Canada

Thirty-nine families were observed extensively at home when children were 2½ and 4½ years of age and again 2 years later. The Social Relations Model is used to investigate children's sex differences in aggression and parents' prohibiting aggression during sibling conflict. In the first observation period, boys engaged in more severe and mild physical aggression, grabbing, insulting, and property damage than girls. At Time 2, boys engaged in more mild physical aggression and insulting, than girls, but there were no sex differences in other forms of aggression. At Time 1, parents' responses were relatively uninfluenced by the sex of the children. However, parents were more likely to prohibit mild physical aggression, grabbing, and property damage by and towards girls at the second time period. Conversely, parents showed more tolerance for boys' mild physical aggression at Time 2, suggesting that this socialisation message may play a role in boys' greater use of physical aggression both at home and with peers.

Introduction

Children show sex differences in aggression (e.g., Coie & Dodge, 1997; Loeber & Hay, 1997), and parents react differently to the aggression of their boys and their girls (e.g., Mills & Rubin, 1990; Parke & Slaby, 1983). Consistent evidence of sex differences in early childhood comes from the peer domain. Important differences may emerge when sibling aggression is studied because of the greater long-term interdependence, stability, and intimacy of sibling relationships. This study fills a gap in the literature by examining sibling aggression and parents' reactions to their male and female children in the same sample, thereby allowing investigation of parents' possible role in sex differences in children's aggression. There is an advantage to studying these processes in siblings instead of peers because parents are close at hand and have the option of reacting immediately to their own children's aggression. In the present study we investigate these questions using Kenny's (1994) Social Relations Model (SRM) because this design makes it possible to analyse the dual role that siblings play as both perpetrators and targets of the aggression and allows for an unconfounded analysis of sex differences in both of these roles. Despite the suitability of the SRM model for studying sex differences in sibling aggression, prior studies have not utilised this methodology. Varied forms of physical aggression (severe, mild, property damage, grabbing objects) and verbal aggression (insults, threats) were studied because sex differences are not uniformly found for all forms of aggression, and because parents' reactions to different kinds of aggression have not been studied separately.

Sex differences in children's aggression

There are different developmental patterns of sex differences in aggression between siblings and peers. Male and female siblings show minor sex differences that seem to peak in the preschool-age period whereas sex differences in peer aggression are substantial, begin at 2 to 3 years of age, and continue to strengthen over time. When sex differences are found, however, boys are reported to be more aggressive than girls.

Within sibling relationships, no sex differences were found for physical aggression of 2- and 4-year-old siblings observed in the laboratory (Vespo, Pedersen, & Hay, 1995), or between 1- and 3-year-olds and their older siblings observed at home (Abramovitch, Corter, & Lando, 1979; Kendrick & Dunn, 1983). Amongst slightly older siblings (2½ to 5 years old), boys engaged in more physical aggression than girls (Abramovitch et al., 1979); however, approximately 1½ and 3½ years later, when only a broad category of agonistic behaviour was examined, no sex differences were found (Abramovitch, Corter, Pepler, & Stanhope, 1986; Pepler, Abramovitch, & Corter, 1981). Additionally, in closely spaced toddler to preschool-aged sibling pairs, boys engaged in more verbal aggression than girls, whereas with larger age differences, girls engaged in more verbal aggression than boys (Abramovitch et al., 1979). Once again, when the siblings were observed later, male and female siblings engaged in similar levels of verbal aggression. Finally, Brody, Stoneman, MacKinnon, and MacKinnon (1985) found that preschool-aged male siblings engaged in more agonistic behaviour than female pairs, but no sex differences were found among school-aged pairs.

Correspondence should be sent to Jacqueline L. Martin, Judge Baker Children's Center, Harvard Medical School, 53 Parker Hill Avenue, Room 408, Boston, MA 02120-3225, USA; e-mail: jmartin@jbcc.harvard.edu.

Although there are contrary findings, sex differences in sibling aggression tend to be found in preschool-aged children, and are less likely to be found in either very young or school-aged children. In contrast, sex differences in peer aggression are more apparent.

Toddler peers of both sexes appear to be quite similar in their use of aggression (Hay, Vespo, Zahn-Waxler & Radke-Yarrow, 1993; Vespo et al., 1995), but by 3 to 6 years of age, it is well documented that boys engage in higher rates of overt physical aggression with peers than girls, and this sex difference continues into middle childhood and adolescence (Cairns & Cairns, 1994; Coie & Dodge, 1997; Crick, 1997; Loeber & Hay, 1997; Maccoby & Jacklin, 1974; Parke & Slaby, 1983; Zahn-Waxler, 1993). For example, Maccoby and Jacklin (1987) observed three cohorts of 4½-year-old children in a nursery school setting while the children engaged in free play in a mobile lab with two other familiar, same-sex playmates. Boy trios engaged in significantly more rough-and-tumble play than girl trios, and boys engaged in low levels of physical aggression whereas girls did not engage in this behaviour at all during the observations (Maccoby, 1988). It has been argued that aggressive behaviour peaks at 2 years of age, when it is of equal magnitude for both girls and boys, but declines steeply and abruptly for girls, and more slowly for boys (Goodenough, 1931; Smetana, 1989). Several investigators have argued that girls are more inclined to use verbal aggression than physical aggression (Bjorkqvist, Lagerspetz, & Kaukiainen, 1992; Ledingham, 1991; Loeber & Hay, 1997); however, studies of sex differences in young children's verbal aggression generally find that boys threaten, harass, tease, command, and taunt more often than girls (Galen & Underwood, 1997; Koyama & Smith, 1991; Maccoby & Jacklin, 1987; Miller, Danaher, & Forbes, 1986). One exception is an observational study of elementary-school children, which indicated that girls used more verbal aggression than boys in the classroom (Archer, Pearson, & Westeman, 1988).

There are diverse and important differences between the contexts of sibling and peer aggression that might account for the different patterns found in the sex difference literature. The long-term interdependence, stability, intimacy, and nurturance of sibling relationships (Abramovitch et al., 1979; Dunn, 2002), the greater vulnerability of peer relationships to dissolution (Collins & Laursen, 1992; Laursen & Collins, 1994), and the tendency of boys and girls to associate in same-gender peer groups (Maccoby & Jacklin, 1987) are among the important factors that may contribute to differences in findings. However, the current study focuses on the potential role of parents' reactions to the aggression of their boys and girls as a potential contributor to the pattern of sex differences found amongst siblings.

Differential socialisation of girls' and boys' anger and aggression

After children reach 2 years of age, it is argued that parents begin to consistently hold them responsible for their actions (Zahn-Waxler, Cole, & Barrett, 1991), and also at this time overt expression of anger and aggression decline abruptly and sex differences in aggression begin to emerge (Goodenough, 1931; Smetana, 1989). Differences in girls' and boys' aggression may be related to parental feedback concerning the appropriateness of such displays (Zahn-Waxler, 1993), or

parents may be reacting in correspondence with their observations that their daughters are better able than their sons to regulate their negative emotions and behaviour (Weinberg & Tronick, 1997). Parents report that they would be more accepting of anger and aggression in boys than in girls (Birnbaum & Croll, 1984; Brody, 1985; Fivush, 1991; Mills & Rubin, 1990). However, a meta-analysis by Lytton and Romney (1991) that summarised studies based on parent interview, child report, and responses to vignettes, found only a trend for parents to prohibit girls' physical aggression more than boys' aggression. When looking at parents' observed responses to aggression in their children, Power and Parke (1986) found that parents were more likely to discourage physical aggression and encourage prosocial behaviour in their 11-, 14-, and 17-month-old daughters than their same-aged sons. Additionally, mothers show more tolerance for their infant sons' displays of anger than for those of their daughters (Malatesta & Haviland, 1982).

Parents also actively encourage intense physical play, competitiveness, and play with action toys—activities that may promote physical aggression—more often with boys than girls (Block, 1983; Maccoby & Jacklin, 1974; Parke & Slaby, 1983). Parents use physical punishment more with boys than girls, thereby modelling physical aggression (Lytton & Romney, 1991). Parents' use of induction (noting the consequences of misbehaviour for others), and explanations following their daughters' transgressions may reduce future aggression because they emphasise children's sensitivity to others, whereas power assertive methods (e.g., commands, punishment) are more frequently implemented following boys' transgressions (Fivush, 1991; Lytton & Romney, 1991; Smetana, 1989). Thus, particularly in observational studies, there is evidence that parents are more likely to discourage physical aggression and related behaviours shown by their daughters than their sons.

Hypotheses

Overall, we hypothesise that boys would engage in more physical aggression, and particularly in severe forms of physical aggression (e.g., kicking, hitting, property damage), than girls. In peer aggression and in some reports of sibling aggression, sex differences become more prevalent after 2 to 3 years of age due to a more dramatic decline for girls' than boys' physical aggression (e.g., Abramovitch et al., 1979; Brody et al., 1985; Loeber & Hay, 1997). However, sex differences in sibling aggression appear to decline after the preschool-age period, whereas the opposite is true for peers. Thus, the question of whether boys and girls will become more similar or increasingly divergent in the frequency of their physical aggression over time was examined. Because of the reciprocity effect, which suggests that there are strong relations found between behaviours given and received among children (e.g., Ross, Cheyne, & Lollis, 1988), boys were also expected to be more frequent targets of physical aggression than girls, irrespective of the perpetrator's sex. Results from studies of children's verbal aggression also generally indicate that young boys engage in higher rates of aggression than girls (e.g., Koyama & Smith, 1991). Thus, we predicted that brothers would also be more verbally aggressive than sisters.

We expected that patterns of parents' responses to children's aggression would mirror patterns found in the children's aggressive behaviour, such that parents would generally show greater tolerance for the aggression of boys than girls. Following from results of previous observational studies of parents' responses to toddlers' aggression (e.g., Power & Parke, 1986), and emerging patterns of children's sex differences slightly thereafter (Abramovitch et al., 1979; 1986), parents were expected to be more likely to prohibit their daughters' than their sons' physical and verbal aggression at Time 1, and particularly severe forms of physical aggression. Consistent with this hypothesis, parents were also expected to discourage physical aggression more often when the victim was a girl than when a boy was the target. Given the inconsistencies in the literature concerning sex differences in children's aggression in the early school period, and in parents' responses as their children enter school, predictions cannot be precise for Time 2; however, parallels between sex differences in children's aggression and parents' reactions to their children's aggression are expected.

Method

Participants

Forty Caucasian families each consisting of a mother, father, and two children participated in this study. Families were recruited based on birth announcements in the local newspaper of a medium-sized Canadian city. In an initial interview, the overall goals of the study were described: Parents were told that we were interested in the relationship between their two children, as well as in how children learn family rules and parents' expectations for interpersonal behaviour. Specific mention of interest in children's aggression, of parents' reactions to these behaviours, or of sex differences was not made, although it was clear that parent behaviour was also recorded. The children were told that observers were coming into their home and would watch how they played together.

Families were observed at two different time periods, separated by approximately 2 years. The older children were between 3.6 and 4.9 years of age ($M = 4.4$ years) at Time 1 and 5.4 and 7.0 years of age ($M = 6.3$ years) at Time 2; the younger children were between 1.9 and 2.6 years of age ($M = 2.4$ years) at Time 1, and 3.8 and 4.8 years of age ($M = 4.4$ years) at Time 2. There were 10 of each possible sister/brother combination at Time 1. One family was not observed at Time 2 because they had moved away, resulting in a sample of 39 families. Parents' ages at the beginning of the study ranged from 23 to 48 years ($M = 30.8$ years for mothers; $M = 32.6$ years for fathers). Twenty-nine per cent of the parents had completed a university degree, 15% had completed a college programme, 41% had completed high school, and 15% had not graduated from high school.

Procedure

Behavioural observations. The data came from six 90-minute sessions in the families' homes at each time period. Sessions occurred at a time that was convenient for the family. During three of the sessions the whole family was present and in the remaining three, the mother and children were observed without the father. These two situations were chosen because

it was felt that they represented the most common constellations in these families. For the purpose of the present study, both session types were collapsed and analysed as a unit. Occasionally it was necessary to shorten an observation session and in these situations the observations were completed at a later time. In two families the parents had divorced by Time 2, and six sessions of interaction with the mother were recorded; two families were undergoing separation at Time 2, and in those cases either one or two sessions were recorded with the father. Additionally, there were up to three sessions missing in three other families and their data was pro-rated to be equivalent to 9 hours. Ten families had a third child by the time of the second set of observations, and these children were generally present during the home observation sessions; however, the behaviour of and behaviour directed to the third child was not included in the present analyses. Analyses comparing the families who experienced divorce or separation and those who experienced the birth of a third child with the remaining families indicated that these changes in family structure did not appear to systematically affect the results reported below.

During the observational periods, families were asked to go about their natural everyday interactions. Parents were asked not to interact with the observer, and additionally, children were told to pretend that the observer was not there. Across the two time periods there were 11 different female observers. To maintain stability and rapport, only two observers were assigned to each family at each time period. To minimise the intrusiveness of the situation, only one observer was present during each session. Observers were aware that the study investigated sibling conflict but were unaware of the focus on sex differences. Observers used hand-held, unidirectional microphones to record the families' talk onto one track of a stereo tape-recorder while at the same time filling in the details of their actions on the other track by means of lapel microphones. Observers did not initiate conversations with family members or direct their activities, but did briefly respond to comments that were addressed to them and moved their position when appropriate in order to create as natural a situation as possible. For observations to proceed, only the family members were present in the house, children were in the same room, and parents were either in the same room as their children or in an adjacent room. Allowances were made for brief absences of family members. Televisions, video games, and other major distractions were not allowed. Whenever these conditions were not met, observers stopped recording and waited until the family members were able to meet the above requirements or arranged to observe at a more convenient time.

The participating families and the data from these observation sessions have been the focus of previous publications. For example, the data have been used to answer questions about family rules for sibling behaviour (Ross, Filyer, Lollis, Perlman, & Martin, 1994), how mitigating circumstances influence sibling aggression (Martin & Ross, 1996), and the role of parent intervention in the quality and extent of sibling conflict (Perlman & Ross, 1997). No previous studies have examined sex differences in sibling aggression or parents' reactions.

Coding of children's physical and verbal aggression

First, the audiotaped records of the observation sessions were transcribed. Before being coded, all evidence of the sex of the children was removed from the transcripts (e.g., children's names, sex-specific pronouns). Each act of aggression by the siblings that occurred during conflict was coded into a mutually exclusive category. The coding categories of physical aggression included severe physical aggression (e.g., biting, hitting, kicking, throwing or hitting with hard objects, hitting with any object above the neck), mild physical aggression (e.g., pushing a sibling away, physically blocking a sibling, restraining a sibling, hitting with soft objects below the neck), property damage (e.g., breaking a sibling's toy, writing on a sibling's drawing), and grabbing (e.g., forcefully pulling objects from a sibling's grasp). The verbal aggression categories were insulting (e.g., calling names, making derogatory statements) and threatening (e.g., stating an intention to hurt sibling, with or without conditions). Conflicts could involve a variety of different categories of aggression by one or both siblings.

Coding of parents' responses to children's aggression

Each instance of children's aggressive behaviour was given a corresponding parent response code indicating whether either parent prohibited their child's aggression. Prohibit responses gave children the message that their behaviour was inappropriate or that the parents disapproved of the action in some way. Prohibitions took the form of simple commands (e.g., "stop that"), reasoning (e.g., "that's your sister's toy"), rule statements (e.g., "you are not allowed to hit"), and, rarely, physical interventions (e.g., grabbing a toy from a child, spanking). All forms of parental prohibition were considered together in the current study because they all conveyed the message that their children should not behave aggressively. Despite extensive behavioural observations, it was not possible to consider differences in the form of children's aggression and to simultaneously distinguish among the ways in which parents attempted to control that aggression. The data also would not reliably support differentiation between mothers' and fathers' responses. Parents' responses prohibiting aggression were reported as a proportion of the frequency of each category of aggression used by each child at each time period. For example, the number of incidents of property damage by a younger sibling at Time 1 that were prohibited by parents was divided by the total number of times that the child damaged the sibling's property at Time 1.

Reliability

Reliability was calculated in two phases: First, the reliability of *observing* was estimated, based on analysis of 27 additional 20-minute pre-sessions that took place prior to the beginning of the data recording in all families (17 sessions at Time 1 and 10 sessions at Time 2). The two observers assigned to that family each independently recorded and transcribed the behaviour of family members during these sessions and their records were compared. Child actions and parent responses were observed in both pre-session records 92% of the time at the first time period, and 86% of the time at the second time period. Second, the *coding* of children's aggressive behaviour and parents' responses to these behaviours was examined in the transcripts of the regular observation sessions. The first author and one other coder independently categorised these actions in 32 of

the same transcripts. One transcript was taken from 32 of the 40 families, 16 transcripts from each time period, and an equal number of transcripts for each possible gender combination of sibling pairs. Children's actions were categorised both in terms of whether they were or were not some form of aggression, and what type of aggression was shown. Kappa for children's aggression categories was .94, and Kappa for the parents' prohibit response was .77.

Rationale for the analysis

The Social Relations Model (SRM) provides a statistical design for studying interdependence and reciprocity between interaction partners or groups of individuals (Kenny, 1994). In this study, the SRM makes it possible to analyse both the interdependent interaction between two siblings and the dual role that siblings play as both actor and partner (Kenny, 1994). Following from Kenny (1994), the design of this study includes effects of sex of actor, sex of partner, the type of relationship between the actor and the partner (i.e., sibling status: older vs. younger sibling), and the longitudinal effect of time of measurement. Additionally, it represents an expansion of Seay and Kay's (1983) design, modelled after a method developed by Kraemer and Jacklin (1979). This method made an important statistical contribution to the study of sex differences in sibling pairs because it allowed for the consideration of sex as a single factor in analyses that included both same- and mixed-sex pairs.

A major advantage to the SRM is the ability to perform a principled analysis that examines sex of actor together for both older and younger siblings. The traditional repeated measures ANOVA is inappropriate for this purpose because the sex of the older siblings and the sex of the younger siblings would have to be separate factors, resulting in an analysis that confounds the effect of the sex of the child who is acting aggressively with the sex of the aggressor's sibling. For example, a main effect of older siblings' sex would include both the contrast between the aggression of older boys versus older girls and the aggression of younger siblings who have older brothers versus older sisters, regardless of the younger child's own sex. The SRM eliminates this problem because it allows for comparison of all girls and boys in the form of a main effect of sex of actor (the child who aggresses) that allows a determination of whether similar sex effects extend to both children. To date, this procedure has not been used in the sibling literature, which typically looks separately at sex of older and younger siblings, or examines four combinations of sex of dyad (e.g., older girl with younger boy, older girl with younger girl, etc.). Neither of these methods allow for examination of one overall effect of sex of actor, sex of partner, or their interaction.

The data were analysed following Seay and Kay's (1983) methodology. Similar to a matched *t*-test, the correlation between the paired scores from a dyad is important in this analysis, and the mathematical model used to derive the statistical tests can be conceptualised as a variant of an ANOVA with fixed effects. All main effects and interactions among the four independent variables were assessed, and separate analyses were conducted for each category of aggression (severe physical aggression, mild physical aggression, property damage, grab, insult, and threaten) and parents' responses to each type of child aggression. The steps that were

Table 1

Levels of aggression by older and younger children and at Time 1 and Time 2

	Older	Younger	Time 1	Time 2
Severe aggression[a]	8.26 (8.72)	5.59 (5.70)	7.90 (6.95)	5.96 (7.47)
Mild aggression[a]	4.62 (4.08)	2.59 (2.59)	4.09 (3.20)	3.12 (3.47)
Property Damage[a,b]	3.25 (3.32)	4.22 (4.18)	4.32 (3.63)	3.15 (3.87)
Grab[a,b]	10.26 (5.56)	5.82 (5.11)	11.15 (6.59)	4.92 (4.08)
Insult[a]	3.70 (4.47)	2.13 (3.34)	2.69 (4.21)	3.14 (3.59)
Threaten[a,b]	4.21 (5.26)	1.49 (2.94)	2.01 (3.62)	3.69 (4.59)

[a]Statistically significant main effects of sibling status.
[b]Statistically significant effects of time.

taken and equations that were used in the analysis are listed in Appendix A.

Results

Children's physical and verbal aggression

Effects of sibling status and time. The rates of different types of aggression for younger and older siblings and for the children at each time period are reported in Table 1. Averaging across both time periods, older children engaged in more severe physical aggression, $t(35) = 2.85$, $p < .05$, mild physical aggression, $t(35) = 5.05$, $p < .01$, grabbing, $t(35) = 5.07$, $p < .01$, insulting, $t(35) = 3.82$, $p < .05$, and threatening, $t(35) = 5.56$, $p < .05$, than their younger siblings, but younger children damaged property more often than older children, $t(35) = -2.08$, $p < .05$. In general, the overall level of physical aggression tended to decrease from Time 1 to Time 2, but the time main effect was only significant for property damage, $t(35) = 2.22$, $p < .05$, and grab, $t(35) = 7.91$, $p < .01$. In contrast, there was more threatening at Time 2 than at Time 1, $t(35) = -2.53$, $p < .05$.

Sex differences in children's aggression (actor effects). As hypothesised, there was a main effect of sex of actor for severe physical aggression, $t(35) = 2.51$, $p < .05$, mild physical aggression, $t(35) = 2.58$, $p < .05$, and property damage, $t(35) = 2.39$, $p < .05$, which showed that boys engaged in higher levels of aggression than girls (Table 2). However, there were also significant interactions between sex of actor and time for severe physical aggression, $t(35) = 2.55$, $p < .05$, and property

damage, $t(35) = 2.71$, $p < .05$, indicating that boys engaged in higher levels of these behaviours than girls at Time 1, but this difference was no longer present at Time 2. Similarly, there was an interaction between sex of actor and time for grab, $t(35) = 2.29$, $p < .05$, that showed that boys grabbed more than girls at Time 1, but there was little difference between boys' and girls' grabbing at Time 2. As shown in Table 2, both girls' and boys' physical aggression tended to decline over time, but boys showed the more dramatic drop.

In terms of verbal aggression, a sex of actor main effect confirmed that boys insulted more than girls, $t(35) = 2.38$, $p < .05$, but there was no significant difference between the frequency of boys' and girls' threats (Table 2).

Sex of partner effects. Contrary to the hypothesis, boys were not more often the recipients of either physical or verbal aggression than girls. However, there was a sex of partner by sibling status interaction effect for mild physical aggression, $t(35) = -2.21$, $p < .05$, showing that older siblings, regardless of sex, aggressed more against girls than boys whereas younger siblings aggressed more against boys than girls (Table 3). The same interaction effect was found for property damage, $t(35) = -2.24$, $p < .05$ (Table 3). A three-way interaction for grab, between sex of partner, sex of actor, and time showed that at Time 1, boys were much more likely to grab from girls than from boys ($M = 16.88$, $SD = 9.22$ vs. $M = 9.20$, $SD = 3.04$), $t(35) = -2.15$, $p < .05$. There was also a three-way interaction between sex of partner, sibling status and time, for grab, that showed younger siblings grabbed more often from girls than boys at Time 1 ($M = 10.43$, $SD = 6.68$ vs. $M = 5.85$, $SD = 3.00$), $t(35) = 2.18$, $p < .05$.

Table 2

Sex of actor effects at Time 1 and Time 2

	Time 1		Time 2	
	Boys	Girls	Boys	Girls
Severe aggression[a,b]	10.69 (7.58)	5.08 (4.83)	6.60 (7.96)	5.07 (6.56)
Mild aggression[a]	5.14 (3.67)	3.03 (2.22)	3.74 (4.21)	2.48 (2.37)
Property damage[a,b]	5.55 (3.97)	3.12 (2.79)	3.32 (3.86)	2.93 (3.54)
Grab[b]	12.90 (7.80)	9.42 (4.58)	5.06 (3.45)	4.76 (4.63)
Insult[a]	3.46 (5.37)	1.91 (2.49)	4.15 (3.67)	2.10 (3.25)
Threaten	1.94 (3.80)	2.09 (3.50)	4.35 (4.18)	2.98 (4.22)

[a]Statistically significant main effects of sex of actor.
[b]Statistically significant interactions of sex of actor by time.

Table 3

Sex of partner effects for older versus younger children

	Older siblings		Younger siblings	
	To boys	*To girls*	*To boys*	*To girls*
Mild aggression[a]	3.97 (2.75)	5.25 (4.87)	3.16 (3.04)	1.98 (1.91)
Property damage[a]	2.36 (2.54)	4.09 (3.72)	4.89 (4.46)	3.52 (3.39)
Grab	9.31 (4.30)	11.16 (6.47)	4.93 (3.65)	6.76 (5.60)

[a]Statistically significant interactions of sex of partner by sibling status.

Parents' responses

Effects of sibling status and time. The rates of parents' prohibit responses to all categories of children's aggression are reported as mean proportions. The average proportion of prohibition across both time periods of children's severe physical aggression was .31, mild physical aggression was .26, property damage was .25, grab was .18, insult was .19, and threat was .17. A time by sibling status interaction showed that at Time 1, parents were more likely to prohibit older children's property damage ($M = .33$, $SD = .32$) than younger children's property damage ($M = .23$, $SD = .22$), but they were equally likely to prohibit both siblings at Time 2 ($M = .21$, $SD = .30$ vs. $M = .20$, $SD = .24$), $t(13) = 2.45$, $p < .05$.

It was necessary to omit the verbal aggression categories (insult and threaten) from the following analyses because there were a number of cases in which both siblings in a family did not insult or threaten one another at both time periods (especially younger siblings at Time 1). To calculate proportions, there must be at least one instance of child behaviour, and to calculate the current within-subjects effects, there cannot be missing data in any cell.

Parents' responses to their daughters' and sons' physical aggression. The sex of the child aggressor did not significantly impact parents' behaviour, even for severe physical aggression and property damage (Table 4). For mild physical aggression there was a sex of actor by time interaction, indicating that at Time 1 parents were more likely to prohibit boys' mild physical aggression ($M = .37$, $SD = .24$) than girls' mild physical aggression ($M = .24$, $SD = .27$), but the opposite was true at Time 2 ($M = .28$, $SD = .38$ for girls, $M = .17$, $SD = .23$ for boys), $t(19) = 2.55$, $p < .05$. Similarly, for mild physical aggression, there was a sex of partner by time interaction, showing that at Time 1 parents prohibited children who were aggressive to boys more often than children who were aggressive to girls ($M = .36$, $SD = .33$ vs. M= .26, $SD =$

.18). At Time 2, however, parents more frequently prohibited children who were aggressive to girls ($M = .25$, $SD = .32$) than children who were aggressive to boys ($M = .20$, $SD = .30$), $t(19) = 2.45$, $p < .05$. In addition, for grab, there was a complex three-way interaction involving sex of actor by sex of partner by time that indicated that at Time 2, parents were much more likely to prohibit girls from grabbing from their sisters than from their brothers, $t(28) = -2.05$, $p < .05$.

Sibling status also influenced parents' responses to their sons and daughters (Table 5). A sex of partner by sibling status interaction for grab indicated that parents were more likely to prohibit older children from grabbing from their brothers than from their sisters, but for younger children, they were more likely to prohibit younger children's grabbing from their sisters than from their brothers, $t(28) = 2.60$, $p < .05$. Similarly, parents were more likely to prohibit older children's damage of their brothers' property than their sister's property, but for younger children, they were more likely to prohibit younger children's damage of their sisters' property than their brothers' property, $t(13) = 2.14$, $p < .05$.

Discussion

Do boys engage in more aggression than girls?

Boys displayed more physical and verbal aggression than girls, but for severe physical aggression, property damage, and grabbing, this effect was only found at the first time period when the younger children were approximately 2½ years of age and the older children approximately 4½ years of age. Mild physical aggression and insults continued to be used more by boys than girls at the second time period. The higher level of aggression of 2½- and 4½-year-old boys is consistent with sex differences in the peer aggression literature and in the preschool period for sibling aggression (e.g., Abramovitch et al., 1979; Loeber & Hay, 1997).

Table 4

Parents' reactions to children's aggression: Significant actor and partner interactions with time

		Time 1		Time 2	
		Boys	*Girls*	*Boys*	*Girls*
Mild aggression[a]	To boys	.39 (.31)	.32 (.34)	.19 (.25)	.21 (.34)
	To girls	.35 (.17)	.16 (.19)	.15 (.21)	.35 (.42)
Grab[b]	To boys	.18 (.17)	.21 (.18)	.19 (.24)	.05 (.09)
	To girls	.21 (.14)	.19 (.17)	.13 (.16)	.25 (.30)

[a]Sex of actor and sex of partner each interacted with time.
[b]Sex of actor by sex of partner by time interaction was significant.

Table 5

Parents' reactions to children's aggression: Significant actor and partner interactions with sibling status

	Older		Younger	
	To boys	*To girls*	*To boys*	*To girls*
Property damage[a]	.35 (.37)	.20 (.22)	.19 (.23)	.27 (.20)
Grab[a]	.22 (.20)	.15 (.13)	.09 (.14)	.24 (.25)

[a]Sex of partner by sibling status is significant for both variables.

It is noteworthy that there are two groups of 4½-year-old children in this study: older siblings at Time 1, and younger siblings at Time 2. Different patterns of sex differences were found for the two types of 4½-year-old children. Older 4½-year-old boys at Time 1 engaged in more mild and severe forms of physical and verbal aggression than their female counterparts, whereas younger 4½-year-old male siblings at Time 2 only engaged in more mild physical aggression and insulting than their female counterparts. Also, younger 4½-year-old siblings at Time 2 tend to be the least physically aggressive overall. This result suggests that context plays an important role in understanding gender differences in sibling aggression. It is possible that the difference stems from the age of the partner, given that the older 4½-year-olds at Time 1 are aggressing against 2½-year-old siblings, whereas younger 4½-year-olds at Time 2 are aggressing against 6½-year-old siblings. Six-year-olds would be better able to control the aggression of their younger siblings and this could act to eliminate sex differences in aggression that might otherwise be found.

Loeber and Hay (1997) comment that there has been little research in the differential decline of peer aggression for boys and girls; however, they suggest that, "it seems probable that girls during the preschool period outgrow conflict more speedily than boys" (p. 388). In the present study, the frequency of girls' and boys' physical aggression tended both to decline and to become more similar over time. The interaction effect for severe physical aggression, property damage, and grabbing was attributable to a greater decline in boys' and more stability in girls' physical aggression over time. These results correspond with findings in other studies of sibling aggression that show that sex differences tend to disappear after the preschool age period (Abramovitch et al., 1986; Brody et al., 1985). However, male siblings' greater use of mild physical aggression and insulting persisted across time, replicating effects of gender differences found in the peer literature (e.g., Koyama & Smith, 1991; Loeber & Hay, 1997; Maccoby, 1988).

Why did brothers' and sisters' overall levels of severe physical aggression, property damage, and grabbing become more similar over time, whereas findings from the peer aggression literature would suggest that they should diverge within this same time period? It is possible that less stringent conduct rules surrounding the use of physical conflict may be present in sibling interaction than in peer interaction. Girls appear to be less comfortable than boys in an angry environment (Cummings, Iannotti, & Zahn-Waxler, 1985; El-Sheikh & Reiter, 1995); thus, girls may prefer to be involved with less outwardly conflictual peer groups. Indeed, strong restrictions appear to surround the use of overt aggressive behaviour in girls' peer groups, and girls risk rejection if they engage in such behaviour (Crick, 1997; Maccoby & Jacklin,

1987). Unlike with peers, in a sibling relationship girls do not have the option of excluding siblings who act aggressively, making girls less effective in controlling the aggression of their siblings. In terms of boys, their more rapid decline in aggression in sibling than peer interaction might be partially understood by the consistency of their interaction partner. Aggression serves as a method to establish social hierarchy amongst males and, given that peer groups tend to be in transition, then aggression levels would stay high. However, in the sibling relationship aggression might decrease over time because the dyadic hierarchy has been established and there are no newcomers to challenge it. Indeed, at Time 1, younger 2½-year-old children were just entering into relationships in which their behaviour presents a challenge to their older siblings. Thus, it would be a time for dominance to be established, especially for brothers, and it is also at this time period that aggression levels are particularly high. Parents' supervision might also have led to less aggression over time for boys at home. Boys engaged in more frequent aggression than girls, leading to more frequent parent reprimands, even though the proportion of parents' responses remained the same for boys and girls. Additionally, sex differences in siblings' mild physical aggression and insulting persisted over time. Perhaps, within boys' peer groups, and without the close supervision of adults, mild physical aggression and verbal aggression increase and potentially escalate into severe forms of aggression, accounting for the sex differences favouring males' greater use of aggression among peers.

The influence of the sex of the recipient of aggression

The sex of the recipient of aggression on its own did not consistently influence levels of aggression displayed by the perpetrator. However, there were interaction effects that showed that older siblings, regardless of sex, engaged in more mild physical aggression and property damage when the victim was a girl, whereas younger siblings aggressed more against older brothers. Older siblings may aggress more when their victims are most vulnerable and least likely to retaliate, whereas younger siblings may aggress more if they imitate the higher levels of aggression shown by their older brothers. Previous studies have shown that younger, second-born children are more likely to imitate their brothers or sisters than their older siblings are (Abramovitch et al., 1979, 1986; Pepler et al., 1981). In addition, Martin and Ross (1995) found that older siblings' aggression was stable over time but younger children's aggression was predicted by the earlier aggression of their older siblings. Specifically, more aggressive younger siblings at Time 2 had older siblings who were aggressive towards them at Time 1.

Grabbing, which is a relatively frequent but less intense form of aggression, showed the same pattern of findings but only at the first time period. At Time 1 only, girls were more likely to be the target of this behaviour; boys were more likely to grab from their little sisters than brothers, and younger siblings, irrespective of sex, were more likely to grab from older sisters than brothers. Thus all but older sisters were more likely to grab things from children who were less likely to grab themselves, or to otherwise retaliate.

Parents' responses to their daughters' and sons' physical aggression

Previous research shows support for parents' greater tolerance of physical aggression and anger expression in boys than in girls (e.g., Brody, 1985; Malatesta & Haviland, 1982; Power & Parke, 1986; Zahn-Waxler et al., 1991). In this study, parents did not differentially prohibit boys' and girls' severe physical aggression and property damage at either time period. However, for mild physical aggression and grabbing at Time 2, parents were more likely to prohibit girls' aggression than boys' aggression. They also were more likely to prohibit both mild aggression and grabbing behaviour targeted at girls than at boys at Time 2. Thus, there is some evidence that as girls get older, parents are more vigilant about preventing aggression used by or directed towards girls in sibling conflict.

There are important parallels between parents' responses and children's aggression, suggesting that parents' socialisation might relate to levels of girls' and boys' aggression. Specifically, at Time 2, boys engaged in significantly more mild physical aggression than girls and parents were more likely to prohibit girls' use of this behaviour. Parents' tolerance of boys' use of mild physical aggression at the second time period could communicate to boys that use of this behaviour with peers is also acceptable, helping to explain the prevalence of physical aggression in boys' peer groups. At Time 2, parents were more likely to prohibit grabbing done by girls, and directed towards girls. At Time 1 girls were more likely to be the target of this behaviour than were boys. Given that girls were no longer more likely to be the victim of grabbing at Time 2, it suggests that the parents' socialisation message might have acted to diminish this behaviour.

Sibling status also influenced how parents responded to aggression directed towards their male and female children. Specifically, for grabbing and property damage, parents were more likely to prohibit their older children from aggressing against a younger brother, whereas they were more likely to prohibit younger children from aggressing against an older sister. For property damage, this result fits with the finding discussed above, that older children were more likely to damage the property of girls, and younger children were more likely to damage the property of boys. The more consistent the prohibition, the less frequent the aggression.

Limitations and strengths

It is important to consider limitations and strengths of this study. There were 39 families, each with 2 children, resulting in 78 children to compare for sex of actor effects and 78 to compare for sex of partner effects, and these effects were compared at two time periods. Thus the study had sufficient power to examine the hypotheses related to sex differences in children's aggression and parents' responses. The study was based on extensive observational data, which is the least biased of data collection methods. There were two time periods in this longitudinal study. Although time-consuming and costly, a better understanding of sex differences would have come from collecting data at three or four time points. Such data would allow for examination of whether sex differences in aggression move in a consistent direction across time and whether the patterns of sex differences change as siblings become older. The data for the current analyses come from 18 hours of observation in each family, approximately 700 hours in total. This amount of data enabled us to consider a variety of different forms of aggression, but we were only able to examine parent responses to those that occurred often enough to give instances in most children at both time periods. Furthermore, it was impossible to also provide reliable data breaking down the parents' responses either according to type of prohibition or to compare mothers versus fathers. Due to the young age of the younger siblings at Time 1, their verbal skills were weak, making the incidence of verbal aggression quite low. Thus despite the substantial amount of data collected, we did not have the opportunity to explore all of the potentially interesting questions concerning children's aggression and parents' responses to it.

The current study makes an important contribution to the understanding of sex differences in sibling aggression. Other studies have assessed this question, but previous studies have not broken down aggression into different types, nor have parents' responses been considered in the same sample. Additionally, the SRM allowed for analysis of the dual role that siblings play as both perpetrator and target of the aggression and allowed for an unconfounded analysis of sex differences in both of these roles. The results clearly demonstrated that boys engaged in higher levels of physical aggression than girls at the first time period. In addition, boys' physical aggression tended to decline more than girls' physical aggression over time. Although sex differences in severe physical aggression, property damage, and grabbing in sibling conflict were only present at Time 1, boys continued to engage in more mild aggression and insulting at Time 2 than girls. These results support the idea that analysing different types of aggression is a significant strength of the current study. A variable not emphasised in previous studies, the sex of the recipient of the aggression, had a minimal impact on the level of children's aggression. At Time 1, parents' responses to boys' and girls' aggression was similar, but at Time 2, parents were less tolerant of mild physical aggression by and directed towards girls, and grabbing and property damage that was directed towards girls. It is noteworthy that at the second time period girls' use of these behaviours diminishes. Likewise, parents show greater tolerance for 4½- and 6½-year-old boys' use of mild physical aggression, a behaviour that could contribute to boys' continued greater use of this behaviour at home, as well as play a role in the sex difference favouring boys' greater use of physical aggression with peers. Thus, there is some evidence that parents recognise children's sex in their response to aggression and that these socialisation messages may impact levels of children's aggressive behaviour.

References

Abramovitch, R., Corter, C., & Lando, B. (1979). Sibling interaction in the home. *Child Development*, 50, 997–1003.

Abramovitch, R., Corter, C., Pepler, D., & Stanhope, L. (1986). Sibling and peer interaction: A final follow-up and a comparison. *Child Development*, 57, 217–229.

Archer, J., Pearson, N., & Westeman, K. (1988). Aggressive behavior of children aged 6–11: Gender differences and their magnitude. *British Journal of Social Psychology*, *27*, 371–384.

Birnbaum, D. W., & Croll, W. L. (1984). The etiology of children's stereotypes about sex differences in emotionality. *Sex Roles*, *10* (9–10), 677–691.

Bjorkqvist, K., Lagerspetz, K., & Kaukiainen, A. (1992). Do girls manipulate and boys fight? Development trends in regard to direct and indirect conflict. *Aggressive Behavior*, *18*, 117–127.

Block, J. (1983). Differential premises arising from differential socialization of the sexes: Some conjectures. *Child Development*, *54*, 1335–1354.

Brody, L. (1985). Gender differences in emotional development: A review of theories and research. *Journal of Personality*, *53*, 102–149.

Brody, L., Stoneman, Z., MacKinnon, C., & MacKinnon, R. (1985). Role relationships and behavior between preschool-aged and school-aged sibling pairs. *Developmental Psychology*, *21*, 124–129.

Cairns, R., & Cairns, B. (1994). *Lifelines and risks: Pathways of youth in our time.* Cambridge: Cambridge University Press.

Coie, J., & Dodge, K. (1997). Aggression and antisocial behavior. In W. Damon & N. Eisenberg (Eds.), *Handbook of child psychology: Vol. 3*, (5th ed.). New York: John Wiley.

Collins, W. A., & Laursen, B. (1992). Conflict and the transition to adolescence. In C. U. Shantz & W. W. Hartup (Eds.), *Conflict in child and adolescent development* (pp. 216–241). Cambridge: Cambridge University Press.

Crick, N. (1997). Engagement in gender normative versus non-normative forms of conflict: Links to social-psychological adjustment. *Developmental Psychology*, *33*, 610–617.

Cummings, E., Iannotti, R., & Zahn-Waxler, C. (1985). Influence of conflict between adults on the emotions and conflict of young children. *Developmental Psychology*, *21*, 495–507.

Dunn, J. (1993). *From preschool to adolescence: A ten-year follow-up of siblings in Cambridge.* Presented to Centre for Family Research, Cambridge, UK.

Dunn, J. (2002). Sibling relationships. In P. K. Smith & C. H. Hart (Eds.), *Blackwell handbook of childhood social development* (pp. 223–237). Oxford: Blackwell.

Dunn, J., & Kendrick, C. (1982). *Siblings: Love, envy, and understanding.* Cambridge, MA: Harvard University Press.

El-Sheikh, M., & Reiter, S. (1995). *Children's responding to live angry interactions: The role of form of anger expression.* Poster presented at the biennial meeting of the Society for Research in Child Development, Indianapolis, Indiana, March 30–April 2, 1995.

Fivush, R. (1991). Gender and emotion in mother–child conversations about the past. *Journal of Narrative and Life History*, *1*, 325–341.

Galen, B., & Underwood, M. (1997). A developmental investigation of social aggression among children. *Developmental Psychology*, *33*, 589–600.

Goodenough, F. (1931). *Anger in young children.* Minneapolis, MN: University of Minnesota Press.

Hay, D., Vespo, J., Zahn-Waxler, C., & Radke-Yarrow, R. (1993). *Patterns of family conflict when the mother is depressed.* Presented at the 6th European Conference of Developmental Psychology, Bonn, Germany.

Kendrick, C., & Dunn, J. (1983). Sibling quarrels and maternal responses. *Developmental Psychology*, *19*, 62–70.

Kenny, D. A. (1988). The analysis of data from two-person relationships. In S. Duck (Ed.), *Handbook of personal relationships* (pp. 57–77). New York: John Wiley.

Kenny, D. A. (1994). *Interpersonal perception: A social relations analysis.* New York: Guilford Press.

Koyama, T., & Smith, P. (1991). Showing-off behaviour of nursery children. *Aggressive Behavior*, *17*, 1–10.

Kraemer, H., & Jacklin, C. (1979). Statistical analysis of dyadic social behavior. *Psychological Bulletin*, *86*, 217–224.

Laursen, B., & Collins, W. A. (1994). Interpersonal conflict during adolescence. *Psychological Bulletin*, *115*, 197–209.

Ledingham, J. (1991). Social cognition and aggression. In D. Pepler & K. Rubin (Eds.), *The development and treatment of childhood aggression* (pp. 279–285). Hillsdale, NJ: Lawrence Erlbaum Associates Inc.

Loeber, R., & Hay, D. (1997). Key issues in the development of conflict and violence from childhood to early adulthood. *Annual Review of Psychology*, *48*, 371–410.

Lytton, H., & Romney, D. (1991). Parents' differential socialization of boys and girls: A meta-analysis. *Psychological Bulletin*, *109*, 267–296.

Maccoby, E. (1988). Gender as a social category. *Developmental Psychology*, *24*, 755–765.

Maccoby, E., & Jacklin, C. (1974). *The psychology of sex differences.* Stanford, CA: Stanford University Press.

Maccoby, E., & Jacklin, C. (1987). Gender segregation in childhood. In H. Reese (Ed.), *Advances in child development and behavior: Vol. 20* (pp. 239–288). Orlando, FL: Academic Press.

Malatesta, C., & Haviland, J. (1982). Learning display rules: The socialization of emotion expression in infancy. *Child Development*, *53*, 991–1003.

Martin, J., & Ross, H. (1995). The development of aggression within sibling conflict. *Early Education and Development*, *6*, 335–358.

Martin, J., & Ross, H. (1996). Do mitigating circumstances influence family reactions to sibling physical aggression? *Child Development*, *67*, 1455–1466.

Miller, P., Danaher, D., & Forbes, D. (1986). Sex-related strategies for coping with interpersonal conflict in children aged five and seven. *Developmental Psychology*, *22*, 543–548.

Mills, R., & Rubin, K. (1990). Parents' beliefs about problematic social behaviors in early childhood. *Child Development*, *61*, 138–151.

Parke, R., & Slaby, R. (1983). The development of conflict. In P. Mussen (Series Ed.) & E. Hetherington (Vol. Ed.), *Handbook of child psychology: Vol. 4. Socialization, personality and social development.* New York: Wiley.

Pepler, C., Abramovitch, R., & Corter, C. (1981). Sibling interaction in the home: A longitudinal study. *Child Development*, *52*, 1344–1347.

Perlman, M., & Ross, H. S. (1997). The benefits of parent intervention in children's disputes: An examination of concurrent changes in children's fighting styles. *Child Development*, *64*, 690–700.

Power, T., & Parke, R. (1986). Patterns of early socialization: Mother and father infant interaction in the home. *International Journal of Behavioral Development*, *9*, 331–341.

Ross, H., Cheyne, A., & Lollis, S. (1988). In S. Duck (Ed.), Defining and studying reciprocity in young children. *Handbook of personal relationships* (pp. 143–176). New York: John Wiley.

Ross, H., Filyer, R., Lollis, S., Perlman, M., & Martin, J. (1994). The administration of justice in the family. *Journal of Family Psychology*, *8*, 254–273.

Seay, M., & Kay, E. (1983). Three-way analysis of dyadic social interactions. *Developmental Psychology*, *19*, 868–872.

Smetana, J. (1989). Toddlers' social interactions in the context of moral and conventional transgressions in the home. *Developmental Psychology*, *25*, 499–508.

Vespo, J., Pederson, J., & Hay, D. (1995). Young children's conflicts with peers and siblings: Gender effects. *Child Study Journal*, *25*, 189–212.

Weinberg, K., & Tronick, E. (1997). Maternal depression and infant maladjustment: A failure of mutual regulation. In J. Noshpitz (Series Ed.), & S. Greenspan, S. Wieder, & J. Osofsky (Vol. Eds.), *The handbook of child and adolescent psychiatry: Vol. 1. Infants and preschoolers: Development and syndromes* (pp. 177–191). New York: John Wiley.

Zahn-Waxler, C. (1993). Warriors and worriers: Gender and psychopathology. *Development and Psychopathology*, *5*, 79–89.

Zahn-Waxler, C., Cole, P., & Barrett, K. (1991). Guilt and empathy: Sex differences and implications for the development of depression. In J. Garber & K. Dodge (Eds.), *The development of emotion regulation and dysregulation* (pp. 243–272). Cambridge: Cambridge University Press.

Appendix 1

For each category of child aggression and parents' responses to each type of child aggression, the following 5 steps were taken:

1. Mean (M) and difference scores (D) were created within each family.

a. Mean (M) represents the overall level of each variable, regardless of sibling status (older vs. younger) or time (time 1, time 2): $MAG = (oAG\_1 + oAG\_2 + yAG\_1 + yAG\_2)/4$, where older's (o) aggression (AG) at Time 1 and Time 2 = oAG_1 and oAG_2 respectively, and younger's (y) aggression (AG) at Time 1 and Time 2 = yAG_1 and yAG_2.

b. Difference (D) provides the contrasts for the within-subjects effect of sibling status (older vs. younger): $DAG = (oAG\_1 + oAG\_2 - yAG\_1 - yAG\_2)/4$.

c. Mean and difference scores were also calculated for the within-subject effect of time ($MtAG$) and for the interaction of time and sibling status ($DtAG$): $MtAG = (oAG\_1 - oAG\_2 + yAG\_1 - yAG\_2)/4$ and $DtAG = (oAG\_1 - oAG\_2 - yAG\_1 + yAG\_2)/4$.

2. Means and estimated variances for all M and D values from step 1 were calculated for each possible sex pairing: i.e., two brothers (oByB); older brother, younger sister (oByG); older sister, younger brother (oGyB); and two sisters (oGyG).

3. Unbiased estimators for all main and interaction effects were calculated as follows:

Sex of actor effect (α) = $(MAG\_oByB - MAG\_oGyG + DAG\_oByG - DAG\_oGyB)/4$

Sex of partner effect (β) = $(MAG\_oByB - MAG\_oGyG - DAG\_oByG + DAG\_oGyB)/4$

Sibling status effect (γ) = $(DAG\_oByB + DAG\_oByG + DAG\_oGyB + DAG\_oGyG)/4$

Time effect (Υ) = $(MtAG\_oByB + MtAG\_oByG + MtAG\_oGyB + MtAG\_oGyG)/4$

$\alpha\beta$ = $(MAG\_oByB - MAG\_oByG - MAG\_oGyB + MAG\_oGyG)/4$

$\alpha\gamma$ = $(DAG\_oByB - DAG\_oGyG + MAG\_oByG - MAG\_oGyB)/4$

$\beta\gamma$ = $(DAG\_oByB - DAG\_oGyG - MAG\_oByG + MAG\_oGyB)/4$

$\alpha\beta\gamma$ = $(DAG\_oByB - DAG\_oByG - DAG\_oGyB + DAG\_oGyG)/4$

$\alpha\Upsilon$ = $(MtAG\_oByB - MtAG\_oGyG + DtAG\_oByG - DtAG\_oGyB)/4$

$\beta\Upsilon$ = $(MtAG\_oByB - MtAG\_oGyG - DtAG\_oByG + DtAG\_oGyB)/4$

$\alpha\beta\Upsilon$ = $(MtAG\_oByB - MtAG\_oByG - MtAG\_oGyB + MtAG\_oGyG)/4$

$\gamma\Upsilon$ = $(DtAG\_oByB + DtAG\_oByG + DtAG\_oGyB + DtAG\_oGyG)/4$

$\alpha\gamma\Upsilon$ = $(DtAG\_oByB - DtAG\_oGyG + MtAG\_oByG - MtAG\_oGyB)/4$

$\beta\gamma\Upsilon$ = $(DtAG\_oByB - DtAG\_oGyG - MtAG\_oByG + MtAG\_oGyB)/4$

$\alpha\beta\gamma\Upsilon$ = $(DtAG\_oByB - DtAG\_oByG - DtAG\_oGyB + DtAG\_oGyG)/4$

4. Estimated variances (EV) were calculated using the following equations:

EV (α or β) = $(evMAG\_oByB + evMAG\_oGyG + evDAG\_oByG + evDAG\_oGyB)/16N$

EV ($\alpha\beta$) = $(evMAG\_oByG + evMAG\_oByG + evMAG\_oGyB + evMAG\_oGyG)/16N$

EV ($\alpha\gamma$ or $\beta\gamma$) = $(evMAG\_oByG + evMAG\_oGyB + evDAG\_oByB + evDAG\_oGyG)/16N$

EV (γ or $\alpha\beta\gamma$) = $(evDAG\_oByB + evDAG\_oByG + evDAG\_oGyB + evDAG\_oGyG)/16N$

EV (Υ or $\alpha\beta\Upsilon$) = $(evMtAG\_oByB + evMtAG\_oByG + evMtAG\_oGyB + evMtAG\_oGyG)/16N$

EV ($\alpha\Upsilon$ or $\beta\Upsilon$) = $(evMtAG\_oByB + evMtAG\_oGyG + evDtAG\_oByG + evDtAG\_oGyB)/16N$

EV ($\alpha\gamma\Upsilon$ or $\beta\gamma\Upsilon$) = $(evMtAG\_oByG + evMtAG\_oGyB + evDtAG\_oByB + evDtAG\_oGyG)/16N$

EV ($\gamma\Upsilon$ or $\alpha\beta\gamma\Upsilon$) = $(evDtAG\_oByB + evDtAG\_oByG + evDtAG\_oGyB + evDtAG\_oGyG)/16N$

where ev = estimated variance found in step 2 above, 16 = the square of the number of groups and N = the number of subjects per group

5. The test statistic for all effects divided by its respective standard error (the square root of EV) is distributed as a t with $n_{oByB} + n_{oByG} + n_{oGyB} + n_{oGyG} - 4$ degrees of freedom.

International Journal of Behavioral Development
2005, 29 (2), 139–145
http://www.tandf.co.uk/journals/pp/01650244.html

Ψ Psychology Press
Taylor & Francis Group

© 2005 The International Society for the
Study of Behavioural Development
DOI: 10.1080/01650250444000397

Stability of aggression during early adolescence as moderated by reciprocated friendship status and friend's aggression

Ryan E. Adams and William M. Bukowski
Concordia University, Montreal, Canada

Catherine Bagwell
University of Richmond, Richmond, VA, USA

The effect of friendship reciprocation and friend aggression on the stability of aggression across a 6-month period following the transition to secondary school was studied in a sample of 298 Grade 6 children from a predominately white, middle-class, Midwestern American community. The stability of aggression was generally high but it varied as a function of (1) the level of aggression of both individuals in the friendship and (2) whether the friendship was reciprocated. For children with high initial levels of aggression, those with unreciprocated aggressive friends were the most stable in their aggression. For children with low initial levels of aggression, most children remained stably low in aggression, with type of friendship and friend aggression having little effect on stability. Adolescents who were high in aggression at time 1 (T1) and had an aggressive friend (reciprocated or not) remained aggressive at time 2 (T2), but those who were aggressive at T1 and had nonaggressive friends actually displayed much lower levels of aggression at T2. The opposite did not occur for those adolescents low in aggression at T1. Those low in aggression with aggressive friends at T1 did not increase in aggression. These findings were discussed in light of current thinking about the effect of friendship on development.

Introduction

Characteristics of the individual, characteristics of their friends, and characteristics of the friendships have separately been shown to play a role in understanding aggression in individuals. But each of these three different sources of information are not independent of one another. Friends influence the characteristics of one another and each member of the dyad influences the characteristics of the friendship. Because each of these sources of information are interdependent, the importance of simultaneously examining all three sources is clear, but accounting for the interdependence of the data in any analysis has been difficult until recently. The current study deals with the issue of interdependence through the Actor-Partner Interdependence Model (APIM: Kashy & Kenny, 2000; Campbell & Kashy, 2002) by utilising Hierarchical Linear Modeling (HLM) to separately estimate the effects of the child (i.e., the actor), their friend (i.e., the partner), and the friendship (i.e., the dyad) on the stability of aggression during early adolescence.

The question regarding the stability of aggression in individuals seems not to be whether aggression is stable or not stable but rather how stable. Regardless of whether aggression is examined in short-term or long-term studies, in studies utilising peer ratings or those utilising observations, in studies with child participants or with adult participants, research typically reveals that the stability of aggression varies from a moderate to a high level. Stability has been found to range from a correlation of .25 from age 8 peer report to age 30 self-reports (Huesmann, Eron, Lefkowitz, & Walder, 1984) to a stability coefficient of .75 resulting from a meta-analysis (Olweus, 1979). Stability of aggression typically increases from childhood to early adolescence and then tapers off until increasing again in adulthood (Loeber & Hay, 1997). While it is fair to say that, on average, aggression is a stable characteristic, there is variation across individuals in the level of stability in aggression (Loeber, 1982). In other words, some people are quite stable in their aggressive behaviour while others are less so. Identifying which factors promote stability is important in understanding aggressive behaviour and also in creating programmes that aim to reduce aggressive behaviour.

As a critical developmental context (Newcomb, Bukowski, & Bagwell, 1999), friendships are likely to be an important source of the stability or instability of aggression. Although aggression is, at least in part, a dyadic experience, it is typically studied at the level of the individual. The basic premise of the current study is that characteristics of each person in the friendship (separately and in combination) and the type of dyad (i.e., reciprocated or unreciprocated friendships) play unique roles in the maintenance of aggression. Three questions have been posed by W. W. Hartup (1996) as key to understanding the effects of friendship: Does a child have a friend? What are the characteristics of the friend? What are the characteristics of the relationship? The current study focuses

---

Correspondence should be sent to Ryan Adams, Center for Research in Human Development, Concordia University, 7141 Sherbrooke St West, Montreal, Quebec, H4B 1R6, Canada; e-mail: radams@vax2.concordia.ca.

on how the first two questions, separately and in combination, might contribute to understanding the stability of aggression during early adolescence.

Friend's aggression as the predictor of aggression and its stability

Having a close friend might be ideal for successful development, but what if that friend possesses a less than ideal characteristic such as aggression? It is our hypothesis that having an aggressive friend will not only predict absolute levels of a child's aggression but having a friendship with an aggressive peer would promote the stability of aggression. Alternatively, having a friendship with a nonaggressive peer should be associated with instability in aggression. These predictions derive from the idea that friends seek common ground and experiences in the effort to maintain the relationship. To find common ground and experiences, certain behaviours, such as aggression, are deemed acceptable and thus are reinforced within the relationship (Gottman, 1983).

As a developmental context, friendships can be viewed as a product of the characteristics that each child brings to the relationship. It is known, however, that the qualities of each child in the relationship are not independent of one another, especially since friends are often similar to each other. Indeed, friends look for common ground and experiences as they try to create shared environments based on common experiences to both create a friendship and to maintain it (Cairns, Cairns, Neckerman, Gest, & Gariepy, 1988; Gottman, 1983; Hartup, 1992). As a result, friends are similar and can become more similar to one another. It is known already, for example, that children like and are liked by others with similar levels of aggression (Nangle, Erdley, & Gold, 1996), that friends are similar in their level of aggression even before a friendship is formed (Newcomb et al., 1999), that friends become more similar in aggression over the course of the friendship (Newcomb et al., 1999), and finally that similarity in aggression between friends predicts stability of the friendship (Newcomb et al., 1999; Poulin & Boivin, 2000).

In their efforts to maintain this common ground, friends may also sanction certain standards of behaviour that could be either positive or negative depending on the individuals in the friendship. In this way friendships can be seen as moral events in which individuals become accountable to one another (Bukowski & Sippola, 1996). Friendships define and constrain which behaviours are acceptable and provide the context where morality can be learned and achieved. Children with friends who hold less than ideal values should be more accepting of these less socially acceptable values. For example, children with aggressive friends have been found to become more tolerant of aggression over time (Newcomb et al., 1999).

Friends do not just sanction certain standards of behaviour; they also mutually regulate these behaviours (Newcomb & Brady, 1982). Friendships are ideal for maintaining certain behaviours because friends provide a higher frequency of reinforcement and more positive reinforcement than nonfriends (Hartup, Glazer, & Charlesworth, 1967). A good example of friends reinforcing aggressive behaviour comes from deviancy training research (Dishion, McCord, & Poulin, 1999). Here positive affect, such as laughing, during a discussion of a rule-breaking topic can be operationalised as the reinforcement of delinquency. The rate of this reinforcement, or deviancy training, has been shown to be predictive of increases in self-reported delinquency and increases in self- and police-reported violent behaviour. In fact, the effects of early involvement with deviant peers in predicting growth from 4th to 12th grade in new forms of antisocial behaviour in the same boys is completely mediated by deviancy training during the 8th grade (Patterson, Dishion, & Yoerger, 2000). In other words, the effects of childhood deviant friends on increases in antisocial behaviour from childhood to late adolescence are through the mechanism of deviancy training.

In sum, the desire to achieve common ground leads to similarity between friends in aggression. Maintaining this common ground leads to sanctioning and reinforcing certain standards of behaviour, such as aggression, resulting in those with aggressive friends being more tolerant of aggression and more reinforcing of aggressive behaviours. Thus similarity in aggression, tolerance of aggression, and reinforcement of aggression, are all mechanisms with which aggressive friends help maintain the stability of aggression.

Friendship status as a predictor of aggression and its stability

While friends influence one another's aggressive behaviours, not having a close friend is also expected to be associated with the stability of aggression. Typically, aggression is thought to lead to friendship difficulty, but it is our contention that difficulty in forming and maintaining friendships can also lead to aggression and is a context that can support the stability of aggression. This contention is based on the assumption that the need to be in close relationships is a fundamental human motivation and the absence of a reciprocated friendship will lead to aggression.

Baumeister and Leary (1995) propose that all humans are instilled with a fundamental human motivation to form lasting, positive, and significant interpersonal relationships. The need to belong is met through frequent, affectively pleasant interactions that take place in the context of a stable and enduring framework of emotional concern for each other's welfare. When this need is not met, negative affect, such as loneliness, anxiety, and jealousy, results and these negative emotions, in turn, lead to aggression. Similarly, and also more specific to the developmental period under study in the current investigation, Sullivan (1953) proposed that early adolescence is a period in which a specific type of relationship, "chumships", are the most critical for development. Close, intimate, mutual relationships with same-sex "co-equals" during this developmental period provide critical experiences for development. It is our contention that the absence of these experiences as a result of being chumless leads to aggression.

It should be mentioned that both Baumeister and Leary's and Sullivan's theories require relationships that are stable and marked by positive and frequent interaction. While unreciprocated best friendships might partially meet some of these requirements, it is only reciprocated friendships that are able to truly fulfil all of the requirements. In comparison to unreciprocated friendships, reciprocated friendships last longer (Bukowski & Newcomb, 1984; Gershman & Hayes, 1983) and have higher levels of contact, positive affect, equity, closeness, liking, and loyalty (Newcomb & Bagwell, 1995). Thus the current investigation focuses on comparisons of reciprocated and unreciprocated friendships.

The few studies that have examined the effects of not having a mutual friend on aggression have produced inconsistent findings. For instance, a study of friendships during summer camp found that those with no reciprocal friendships had higher peer reputations of getting mad easily and that those who readily dissolved and formed friendships had a peer reputation for hitting and starting fights (Parker & Seal, 1996). Interestingly, suggesting that one might be alone in the future can also lead to aggression (Twenge, Baumeister, Tice, & Stucke, 2001). In a series of experiments, individuals who were told that their responses to a personality survey indicated that they would end up alone later in life behaved more aggressively in response to negative interactions and even neutral interactions when compared to control groups. On the other hand, it has also been shown that that the link between aggression and friendship status might not be so clear. A study of social networks found that highly aggressive children had approximately the same probability of having a reciprocated friend as a matched control group (Cairns et al., 1988). Because this study allowed for an unlimited number of best friend nominations, one explanation for this finding is that the friends might not be the close, intimate friends, that are the focus of the current study.

Hypotheses

To examine the stability of aggression, friendship patterns and levels of aggression were assessed twice, once at the beginning of 6th grade, just after the participants had made the transition to a secondary school environment and then again 6 months later. While a child's time 1 (T1) level of aggression and their friend's T1 level of aggression were expected to individually predict the child's time 2 (T2) aggression, it was predicted that the stability of the child's aggression would be the product of whether a child was in a reciprocated friendship, the friend's aggression score, and the child's initial level of aggression. Specifically, it was predicted that aggression would be the most stable for children who are aggressive at T1 with unreciprocated friends who were also high in aggression. This was expected because these children are subject to the processes of seeking common ground with this aggressive friend (i.e., acceptance of aggressive behaviour and reinforcement of aggressive behaviour) and at the same time have unfulfilled intimacy needs (Baumeister & Leary, 1995; Sullivan, 1953). Alternatively, children low in aggression at T1 with reciprocated friends who were low in aggression should have the most stably low aggression because they too are subject to the processes of seeking common ground with their nonaggressive friends and, in addition, will have their intimacy needs fulfilled. The least stable groups of children should be (1) children initially low in aggression with unreciprocated friends high in aggression and (2) children initially high in aggression with reciprocated friends low in aggression. Here it is thought that the discrepancy between friends on aggression, along with the discrepancy between what the need for intimacy model would expect for the friendship types, will create instability in aggression. Specifically, the first group should become more aggressive because their friends are aggressive and their need for intimacy is not fulfilled, and the second group should become less aggressive for the opposite reason; their friends are not aggressive and their intimacy needs are fulfilled.

Method

Participants

Participants were predominantly white, middle-class, Caucasian students from public schools in a suburban, Midwestern American community (see Bukowksi & Newcomb, 1984; Newcomb & Bukowski, 1983). Within this community, students were recruited from 16 classrooms from five schools in one school district. At each time more than 90% of the potential pool of students participated. Participants were assessed on two different occasions: time 1 (T1) occurred at the beginning of the 6th-grade school year after the students had made the transition to a single middle-school ($N = 334$; 175 boys and 159 girls) and time 2 (T2) was 6 months later ($N = 321$; 165 boys and 156 girls). The average age of the participants was approximately 11.5 years old at T1. They were nearly all within 1 year of each other in age and were in the same school grade. Only those students who were present at both time periods with complete data were included in the reported analyses. This resulted in a sample size of 298, representing 89% and 93% of the participants in the sample at T1 and T2, respectively. Participants who were in the sample at just one time did not differ on aggression from the 298 who were part of the final sample.

Instruments

Friendship type. At each meeting, participants were provided with a list of class names presented in alphabetical order. Students were asked to name three same-sex participants who were their best friends. Each participant was coded as having either a reciprocated friendship (coded as -1) or an unreciprocated friendship (coded as 1). For the purpose of the current study, reciprocated friendships were friendships where first or second same-sex best friend nomination also nominated them as their first or second same-sex best friend. Unreciprocated friendships were those friendships where nominations were not reciprocated. While other studies often utilise all the nominations, the current study is limited to the first and second nominations because this was a more conservative estimate of close best friend status. It should be mentioned that none of the children in the unreciprocated category would have been in the reciprocated group if their third nomination was utilised.

Aggression. Students also completed a peer assessment procedure typically known as the class play. Each participant was given a list of 14 descriptions and were asked to nominate up to three individuals in the classroom who fit each description. The descriptions were factor analysed and four factors emerged (see Newcomb & Bukowski, 1983). For the purpose of the current study only the factor containing the aggression items was examined. In a previous study (Newcomb & Bukowski, 1983) this factor was comprised of five items: *someone who is a mean cruel boss, someone who picks on smaller kids, someone who causes a lot of trouble, someone who is selfish,* and *someone who is stuck up.* The final two items concerning self-centredness were dropped from the current aggression measure because they did not seem valid for current conceptualisations of aggression. Each child was given a score on each of the remaining three items according to how often the child was chosen for that item. Composite scores aggregated across these three items were reliable at both T1 and T2 (Cronbach's alpha = .83 and .85, respectively). All scores were standardised within sex to account for differences in the number of boys and girls in the sample.

Procedure

Prior to starting the study, each participant had explicit parental permission to take part in the study and provided informed consent. At both time points, participants completed questionnaires at their classroom desks during a regularly scheduled class period.

Creating friendship dyads

Because the proposed analyses examined the effects of both the child and their friend, the friend's aggression score and the child's aggression score were needed for each participant. When more than one reciprocal nomination occurred for a participant, their first choice was retained for analysis. This was to ensure that no participant was represented more than once in the analyses. For those with only unreciprocated friendships, the unreciprocated participant was designated as the chooser and a student was designated as the friend (i.e., the chosen) who both (1) was nominated as a friend but did not reciprocate the nomination and (2) was not part of a reciprocated friendship. This procedure resulted in 149 dyads (66 reciprocated dyads and 83 unreciprocated dyads) and thus 298 participants for analysis.

Plan of analysis

Following the procedures described by Campbell and Kashy (2002), multilevel modelling was used to assess the effects of the actor, the partner, and the dyad (i.e., actor × partner effect) on the stability of aggression across the 6-month interval. The level 1 HLM model consisted of two entries per dyad, one for each of the children in the pair. For each child, the T2 aggression score was used as the dependent variable and the child's T1 aggression score (i.e., the actor

effect) and the peer's T1 aggression score (i.e., the partner effect) were used as predictors. These predictors were entered as fixed effects. The intercept calculated in the level 1 model was designated as a random effect. In the level 2 model, three variables were used as predictors of variability in the level 1 intercept. They were type of friendship (i.e., reciprocated or non-reciprocated), the two-way interaction between the child's aggression and their friend's aggression (i.e., dyad effects), and the three-way interaction between type of friendship and child aggression and friend aggression. Specifically the models that we assessed were as follows: the level 1 model

$$Y = \beta_0 + \beta_1 \text{ (Child Aggression)} + \beta_2 \text{ (Friend Aggression)} + r$$

and the level 2 model

$$\beta_0 = \gamma_{00} + \gamma_{01} \text{ (Type of Friend)} + \gamma_{02}$$
$$\text{(Child} \times \text{Friend Aggression)} + \gamma_{03}$$
$$\text{(Type} \times \text{Child} \times \text{Friend)} + u_0$$
$$\beta_1 = \gamma_{10}$$
$$\beta_2 = \gamma_{20}$$

Results

Preliminary analyses examined friends' similarity in aggression. Correlations between T1 child aggression and T1 friend aggression found that reciprocated friends were more similar to each other ($r = .55$, $p < .001$) than unreciprocated friends ($r = .21$, $p < .01$), z-score difference = 3.39, $p < .001$.

The coefficients for the two fixed effects estimated in the level 1 model were .44 ($t = 11.07$, $p < .01$) for T1 child aggression and .10 ($t = 2.49$, $p < .05$) for T1 friend aggression (see Table 1). The strong coefficient for the effect of the T1 child aggression score on the T2 child aggression score (i.e., the outcome variable) indicated that aggression was, as expected, generally stable. In the same model, the significant main effect for T1 friend aggression suggests that T1 friend aggression adds to the stability of the child aggression score from T1 to T2.

As shown above, three variables were used in the level 2 model to explain the variability in the intercept across dyads.

Table 1

Effects of T1 child aggression, T1 friend aggression, the dyad, and type of friend on T2 aggression

Model	T2 child aggression		
	Coefficient	SE	t
Intercept β_0			
Intercept γ_{00}	−0.09	0.03	2.93**
Type of Friend γ_{01}	0.05	0.03	1.73
Child × Friend Aggression γ_{02}	0.11	0.02	5.22***
Type × Child × Friend γ_{03}	0.03	0.02	2.10*
Child aggression β_1			
Intercept γ_{10}	0.44	0.04	11.07***
Friend aggression β_2			
Intercept γ_{20}	0.10	0.04	2.49*

Child × Friend aggression = two-way interaction between TI child aggression and T1 friend aggression and Type × Child × Friend = three-way interaction between type of friendship, T1 child aggression, and T1 friend aggression. Level 1 coefficients df = 292 and Level 2 coefficients df = 145.
* $p < .05$; ** $p < .01$; *** $p < .001$.

The analysis revealed a significant effect for the two-way interaction between child and friend aggression (coefficient = .11, $t = 5.22$, $p < .001$) and a significant effect for the three-way interaction between type of friendship, child aggression, and friend aggression (coefficient = .03, $t = 2.10$, $p < .05$). Because the effects of the first two level 2 predictors were qualified by the three-way interaction between the type of friend and the dyad effect, the three-way interactions are explained.

The interaction is examined using Figure 1. It should be mentioned that instead of using the typical values of -1 SD for low values and $+1$ SD for high values to plot the interaction, -0.66 and $+1.33$ were used for values of high and low T1 child aggression because the lowest score for any individual was -0.66. Because smaller difference between T1 and T2 child aggression indicates higher stability in aggression over the period, the easiest way to examine stability using this figure is to see how close the T2 child aggression score is to the value of the T1 child aggression score. For instance, at high levels of T1 child aggression (i.e., child aggression score of 1.33 at T1), those with aggressive unreciprocated friends were the most stable in aggression because their T2 aggression score of 0.93 was closest to 1.33. While the next most stable were those with aggressive reciprocated friends, the least stable were those with reciprocated and unreciprocated friends low in aggression, with most decreasing by 1 SD in aggression between the time periods (because their T2 aggression score was near 0.3). While the type of friend and the friend's aggression had a large effect on stability when children were initially high in aggression, the type of friendship and the friend's aggression had little effect on T2 child aggression when children were low in aggression at T1. Even though children with reciprocated low aggressive friends had the most stably low levels of aggression, there was little difference in stability based on

friendship type and friend aggression with most children remaining low in aggression (because their T2 scores remain near -0.66).

Discussion

The goal of this paper was to assess the effect of friendship type and friend characteristics on the stability of aggression. The findings show that although aggression was generally stable this stability varied as a function of (1) the level of aggression of both individuals in the friendship and (2) whether that friendship was reciprocated. As predicted, those children initially high in aggression with unreciprocated friends who were also high in aggression were the most stably high in aggression, but the predictions for those children initially low in aggression were not clearly supported. For children initially low in aggression, those with reciprocated friends low in aggression were the most stably low in aggression, as predicted, but the type of friendship and the initial level of the friend's aggression had little effect on the stability of aggression, as indicated by the fact that all four of the friendship type by friend level of aggression combinations remained stably low in aggression. Because most long-term studies of aggression tend to focus on the highly aggressive children and not children low in aggression, it is difficult to interpret this finding in context of previous research. Needless to say the results do suggest that aggression seems to depend on stable individual characteristics, such as temperament, rather than contextual influences (i.e., friendships) for the children initially low in aggression. Interestingly the opposite seems to be true for those children initially high in aggression.

For children initially high in aggression, there is large variability in the stability of aggression depending on both the

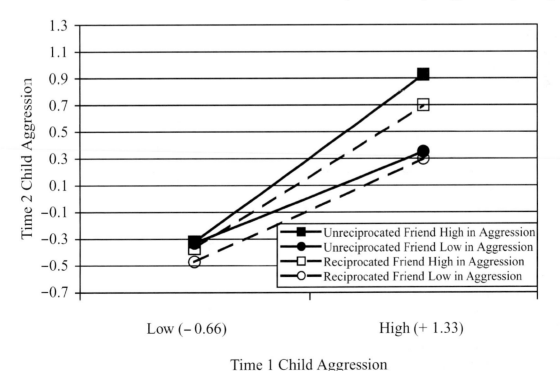

Figure 1. Estimation of time 2 child aggression based on time 1 child aggression, time 1 friend aggression, and type of friendship. (Stability increases as the child T2 aggression score gets closer to the values of the child T1 aggression score. -0.66 and $+1.33$ were used for values of low and high child T1 aggression because the lowest score for any individual was -0.66. All values are z-scores.)

type of friendship and the aggressiveness of their friend, suggesting that aggression thrives in very specific types of friendships. Just having one person in the friendship with high levels of aggression did not sustain aggression, as was the case with those who were aggressive at T1 with nonaggressive friends, nor did it promote aggression, as was the case with those who were not aggressive at T1 with reciprocated aggressive friends. Aggression thrived in contexts where both the child and their friend were aggressive. Stable aggressive behaviour in the context of a reciprocated friendship between two aggressive adolescents replicates the deviancy training research (Dishion et al., 1999), but the absence of a reciprocated friendship being linked directly to stability of aggression could not be found in previous studies (most likely due to the fact that most studies of friendship tend to only examine reciprocated friendships) even though it was predicted by the need for intimacy model. It seems clear that it would be fruitful for future research to examine the mechanisms that promote the stability of aggression in children with unreciprocated friendships and how these children are at more risk for aggressive behaviour than those with reciprocated aggressive friends. We promote the need for intimacy model as an explanation but more information is needed to know if it is heightened negative emotions, as predicted by Baumeister and Leary (1995), or if it is a lack of critical experiences, as predicted by Sullivan (1953), that sustain the aggression in these children.

The finding that had the most practical importance for interventions for aggression was not initially predicted. Adolescents who were high in aggression at T1 and had an aggressive friend (reciprocated or not) remained aggressive at T2, but those who were aggressive at T1 and had nonaggressive friends actually displayed much lower levels of aggression at T2. Unexpectedly, the opposite did not occur for those adolescents low in aggression at T1. Those low in aggression with aggressive friends at T1 did not increase in aggression. Together these findings have important implications. They suggest that while intervention programmes should be careful about fostering friendships among two aggressive children, as has been shown in the deviancy training research (Dishion et al., 1999), pairing aggressive children with nonaggressive children might be beneficial for the aggressive child without detrimental effects for the nonaggressive child. Previous work with younger children supports this idea. Having a nonaggressive friend was associated with decreases in aggression over the course of the year for children who were initially high in aggression (Warman & Cohen, 2000), but it also been shown that pairing aggressive children with nonaggressive children does not necessarily cause the nonaggressive child to become more aggressive (Hektner, August, & Realmuto, 2003).

When interpreting the current results one should keep in mind that a rather global index of aggression was utilised rather than a more specific index such as reactive or proactive aggression. While the broader index provided a reliable global measure of aggression, it is difficult to make conclusions about an adolescent's functioning in the peer group due to measuring aggression with such a broad index. For instance, interpreting low aggression scores as a good thing in those adolescents in unreciprocated friendships might be misleading. Recent work on the positive effects of aggression suggests that the link between proactive aggression and competency is not linear. Those with high and those with low proactive aggression scores have been shown to be less competent than those with average levels of proactive aggression (Little, Brauner, Jones, Nock, & Hawley, 2003). On the other hand, the link between reactive aggression and competence is linearly negative. Thus, our broad measure of aggression makes it difficult to interpret low aggression as a general indication of positive adjustment. In addition to providing better interpretive value, more differentiated aggression indices could also lead to alternative results. For instance, friends seem to be more similar in proactive but not reactive aggression (Poulin & Boivin, 2000), which indicates that the current findings involving reciprocated friendships might apply only to proactive aggression. This would fit with our thinking because proactive aggression has a value for the aggressor that reactive aggression does not, and it is this value that aggressive friends are most likely to share. In addition, it is likely that friends would be more likely to reinforce proactive aggression rather than reactive aggression because reactive aggression is just as likely to be targeted at the friend as at others.

In sum, the results reveal the importance of examining aggression in the context of friendships. Consideration of this context revealed two important findings. First, the association of aggressive adolescents with a friend who was low in aggression was predictive of a large decrease in aggressive behaviour over the course of the 6 months, but for those initially low in aggression having a friend who was high in aggression did not lead to a large increase in aggression. Second, the often-overlooked group of children in unreciprocated friendships exhibited the most stable levels of aggression: Those initially high in aggression with unreciprocated aggressive friends had the most stably high aggression. Both findings suggest friendship is an important context for understanding aggression and how it might be reduced.

References

Baumeister, R. F., & Leary, M. R. (1995). The need to belong: Desire for interpersonal attachments as a fundamental human motivation. *Psychological Bulletin, 117*, 497–529.

Bukowski, W. M., & Newcomb, A. F. (1984). Stability and determinants of sociometric status and friendship choice: A longitudinal perspective. *Developmental Psychology, 20*, 941–952.

Bukowski, W. M., & Sippola, L. K. (1996). Friendship and morality: (How) are they related? In W. M. Bukowski (Ed.), *The company they keep: Friendship in childhood and adolescence* (pp. 238–261). New York: Cambridge University Press.

Cairns, R. B., Cairns, B. D., Neckerman, H. J., Gest, S. D., & Gariepy, J. L. (1988). Social networks and aggressive behavior: Peer support or peer rejection? *Developmental Psychology, 24*, 815–823.

Campbell, L., & Kashy, D. A. (2002). Estimating actor, partner, and interaction effects for dyadic data using PROC MIXED and HLM: A user-friendly guide. *Personal Relationships, 9*, 327–342.

Dishion, T. J., McCord, J., & Poulin, F. (1999). When interventions harm: Peer groups and problem behavior. *American Psychologist, 54*, 755–764.

Gershman, E. S., & Hayes, D. S. (1983). Differential stability of reciprocal friendships and unilateral relationships among preschool children. *Merrill Palmer Quarterly, 29*, 169–177.

Gottman, J. M. (1983). How children become friends. *Monographs of the Society for Research in Child Development, 48* [No 201], 86.

Hartup, W. W. (1992). Friendships and their developmental significance. In H. McGurk (Ed.), *Childhood social development: Contemporary perspectives* (pp. 175–205). Hillsdale, NJ: Lawrence Erlbaum Associates Inc.

Hartup, W. W. (1996). The company they keep: Friendships and their developmental significance. *Child Development, 67*, 1–13.

Hartup, W. W., Glazer, J. A., & Charlesworth, R. (1967). Peer reinforcement and sociometric status. *Child Development, 38*, 1017–1024.

Hektner, J. M., August, G. J., & Realmuto, G. M. (2003). Effects of pairing aggressive and nonaggressive children in strategic peer affiliation. *Journal of Abnormal Child Psychology, 31*, 399–412.

The functions of aggression refer to the motive of the aggressor and have generally been distinguished along the lines of instrumental versus reactive aggression (e.g., Dodge & Coie, 1987). Instrumental aggression (also called proactive or "cold-blooded" aggression) refers to that which is deliberate and directed toward obtaining desired goals. Reactive aggression (also called defensive or hot-blooded aggression) refers to that which is an angry, often emotionally dysregulated, response to perceived offences or frustrations. These functions of aggression derive from different theoretical perspectives, which posit that differing social-cognitive processes are responsible for enacting each function of aggression (see Crick & Dodge, 1994, 1996; Dodge & Coie, 1987). Substantial evidence suggests that reactive aggression is more strongly related to several aspects of maladjustment than is instrumental aggression (Little, Brauner, Jones, Nock, & Hawley, 2003; Little, Jones, Henrich, & Hawley, 2003; Prinstein & Cillessen, 2003; Schwartz et al., 1998; Vitaro, Brendgen, & Tremblay, 2002). In fact, emerging evidence exists that some aggression (likely instrumental in nature) is not related to maladjustment and could be related to positive adjustment (see Hawley & Vaughn, 2003).

Social status is now also recognised as a multi-faceted construct. In this study, we consider four aspects of social status: victimisation, peer influence, perceived popularity, and social preference. Victimisation refers to the degree to which children are the victims of their peers' aggression or intentional exclusion from the group. It is conceptually distinct from other measures of social status (e.g., peer rejection) because it describes specific events that happen to the child (rather than attitudes that may be held by peers but not expressed); however, victimisation is highly related to other measures of social status (see Card, 2003; Hodges & Perry, 1999) and can serve as an indicator of children's adaptation with their peers. Peer influence is an aspect of social status that is central to resource control and evolutionary theories (see Hawley, Little, & Pasupathi, 2002), and refers to an individual's ability to affect their peers' behaviour. Perceived popularity refers to children's perceptions that certain individuals are popular within the peer group; a construct that exhibits high but not perfect overlap with social preference (LaFontana & Cillessen, 1999, 2002; Parkhurst & Hopmeyer, 1998). Finally, social preference, which is the most commonly used measure of social status (and, until recently, was often used synonymously with the term social status), refers to tendencies to be highly liked and not disliked by peers (see Bierman, 2004; Newcomb, Bukowski, & Pattee, 1993; Parker & Asher, 1987).

Social relations modelling of children's peer world

The Social Relations Model (SRM) is a conceptual, methodological, and analytic approach that captures the interpersonal nature of perception. This approach has been thoroughly described in previous writings (e.g., Kenny, 1994) and in the other works in this issue, so we will describe it only briefly here, focusing on three aspects of the model that will be examined in the current study: group means, variance partitioning, and reciprocity. First, the SRM provides unbiased estimates of mean levels of perception within groups. It also partitions the variance in interpersonal perceptions into two components. The first variance component is that due to individual differences among perceivers' tendencies to view others in a particular manner (actor variance). The second variance

component is that due to individual differences in targets' tendencies to be viewed in certain ways by others (partner variance), and is the component typically examined among peer nomination. If multiple items or multiple time points are available, it is also possible to distinguish unique perceptions into that due to stable relationship effects and that due to random error. Finally, the SRM allows the computation of two indexes of reciprocity. Generalised reciprocity refers to tendencies of individuals who perceive others in a certain way to also be perceived by others as high or low on that characteristic (e.g., if a child views others as aggressive, is this child also viewed as aggressive by others?). Dyadic reciprocity refers to the tendency for one child's view of a peer to be related to that particular peer's view of the child (e.g., if child A views child B as aggressive, does child B also view child A as aggressive?).

Although children spend much of their lives with peers, relatively little is known about the interpersonal perceptions that occur within these contexts from a social relations perspective. Malloy and colleagues (Malloy, Sugarman, Montvilo, & Ben-Zeev, 1995) examined the actor and partner variances among first- through sixth-graders' ratings of random subsamples of peers on cognitive ability, positive affect, attractiveness, popularity, physical strength, and positive behaviour. Their results generally indicated greater partner than actor variance, especially among older children. In artificial play groups of third-grade boys, social relations analyses of aggressive behaviours (Coie et al., 1999) and aggression-encouraging social cognitions (Hubbard, Dodge, Cillessen, Cole, & Schwartz, 2001) revealed generally significant actor and partner variances (more so for instrumental aggression and supporting outcome expectancies than for reactive aggression and supporting hostile attribution biases). However, these findings do not directly speak to perceptions of aggression. In a study of 20- and 30-month-old children's play behaviour, modest actor and partner variances were found for play and conflict behaviours (Ross & Lollis, 1989), though, again, these findings speak to behaviours rather than perceptions. Finally, a few studies have examined children's interpersonal behaviours using designs suggested by the SRM, but did not analyse data in a manner that provided variance partitioning or reciprocity estimates of interest in the current design (e.g., Hawley, 2002; Hawley & Little, 1999).

In summary, we are aware of only one prior study in which social relations analyses of children's interpersonal perceptions (rather than behaviours) were performed (i.e., Malloy et al., 1995). In our view, a more thorough examination of young people's interpersonal perceptions in general, and of perceptions within and across gender in particular, will contribute to our understanding of children's peer relations, specifically of peer reputations for aggression and social status.

Hypotheses of the current study

In predicting patterns of mean rates of nominations among boys and girls, two alternate views can be taken. First, given the existence of intergroup biases (i.e., more favourable views of in-group than of out-group members) among children (Bigler, Jones, & Lobliner, 1997; Egan & Perry, 2001; Martin & Halverson, 1981; Powlishta, 1995), nominations may be distributed such that children nominate same-sex peers more for positive features and cross-sex peers more for negative features. On the other hand, given the gender-segregated nature of children's peer worlds (see Maccoby, 1998), children may more often observe the behaviours and be more aware of the social status of their same-sex peers relative to their opposite-sex peers. This view would suggest that children are more likely to nominate same-sex peers for both positive and negative qualities.

We are aware of no previous studies examining sex differences in actor and partner variances on interpersonal perception among children. This state of affairs is unfortunate because such work has the potential to elucidate the role of gender in processes of children's interpersonal perception. Studies of adult men and women generally have not focused on sex differences, and those that we reviewed generally reported an absence of sex differences (e.g., Malloy & Albright, 1990, found no differences between groups of male and female college students in actor and partner variances of ratings on several cognitive, emotional, and social characteristics). However, we can still offer several hypotheses based on extensions from prior theory and research.

One interpretation of actor variance is as an index of assimilation, a tendency to see others in a similar way (Boldry & Kashy, 1999; Kenny, 1994). As described above, gender is a salient factor in children's group categorisation. Given well-known tendencies for individuals to see out-group members as more homogeneous than in-groups members (e.g., Linvile, Fischer, & Salovey, 1989; Park & Rothbart, 1982), we hypothesised that actor variance would be greater for cross-sex nominations than for same-sex nominations.

Partner variance can be considered an index of consensus, the extent to which peers agree that particular targets are high or low in a characteristic (Kenny, 1994; Kenny, Albright, Malloy, & Kashy, 1994). It has been suggested that the degree of acquaintance among individuals should be positively related to the degree of consensus (though a review of the literature on ratings of personality traits failed to support this; Kenny et al., 1994). Given the higher amount of interaction among same-sex than among opposite-sex children (Maccoby, 1998), we hypothesised that partner variance would be stronger for same-sex than for cross-sex nominations.

In terms of the two indexes of reciprocity (i.e., generalised and dyadic), there exists no prior research of which we are aware to guide hypothesis generation. An exception is made for liking: A review of the literature on adults (see Kenny, 1994) suggested almost no generalised reciprocity in liking (i.e., that those who like others tend to be liked), but quite substantial evidence of positive dyadic reciprocity in liking (i.e., if person A likes person B, person B tends to like person A). There is also evidence of dyadic reciprocity in children's liking and disliking (see Hartup & Abecassis, 2002). Given the absence of prior literature examining either type of reciprocity in either adults or children for perceptions of other aspects of social status or for aggression, examination of these correlations in the current study will be exploratory.

Method

Participants

Participants were 351 sixth-grade (M age = 10.5 years) boys (n = 178) and girls (n = 173) from 17 classes within 9 elementary schools located in a mid-sized city in northeastern United States. Representative of the population of these schools,

participants were 68% Caucasian, 22% African American, 5% Hispanic, and 5% of other or mixed ethnicity. The communities in which these schools were located are generally lower- to upper-middle class.

Procedure and measures

In the fall of the school year, participants were asked to complete a variety of paper-and-pencil questionnaires during three 45-minute testing sessions. Questionnaires were administered by two trained research assistants; one research assistant read the questionnaires aloud while a second assisted participants with any questions. In addition to demographic information about sex, ethnicity, and age, the primary instrument utilised for the current report was a peer nomination inventory.

The peer nomination inventory consisted of 18 items in which participants were asked to nominate which of their grademates fit the description provided in each item. Both same- and cross-sex nominations were allowed, as were cross-class nominations within the same school. These cross-class nominations represented a small percent of total nominations, and were not analysed in the current report (see next section).

Twelve items of the peer nomination inventory were combined to form eight constructs: (1) overt aggression (nominations on "Who pushes, kicks, or punches others because they've been angered by them?" plus nominations on "Who hurts others to get what they want?"; possible values of 0, 1, or 2); (2) relational aggression ("Who keeps people from being in their group of friends if they've been hurt by them?" plus "Who ignores or stop talking to others in order to get what they want?"; 0, 1, or 2); (3) instrumental aggression ("Who hurts others to get what they want?" plus "Who ignores or stop talking to others in order to get what they want?"; 0, 1, or 2); (4) reactive aggression ("Who pushes, kicks, or punches others because they've been angered by them?" plus "Who keeps people from being in their group of friends if they've been hurt by them?"; 0, 1, or 2); (5) victimisation ("Who gets pushed around by others?" plus "Who is not played with or hung out with by others?"; 0, 1, or 2); (6) peer influence ("Who gets others to go along with what they say?" plus "Who has good ideas or suggestions that the others like to follow?"; 0, 1, 2); (7) perceived popularity ("Who is the most popular?" minus "Who is most unpopular?"; −1, 0, or 1); and (8) social preference ("Who do you like to hang out with?" minus "Who do you not like to hang out with?"; −1, 0, or 1). It should be noted that the above scores were multiplied by 100 (e.g., instrumental aggression scores could be 0, 100, or 200; social preference could be −100, 0, 100) in order to both facilitate presentation and avoid potential small-number rounding errors, with no effect on analyses of interest in this study.

It should be noted that participants were limited to 10 nominations. Although it might be expected that this would limit the variability in individual differences to nominate more or fewer peers for the items (thus reducing actor variance), only a small percentage of participants nominated the maximum number of peers on any item (ranging from 0.3% to 4.6% for all items used to form constructs, with the exception of "Who do you like to hang out with?", for which 15.4% of participants nominated 10 peers). Thus, it was expected that this limitation would minimally attenuate actor variance, with the possible exception of that for social preference.

Data analytic strategy

All data were analysed using the SRM; specifically using *SOREBIG*, a version of the *SOREMO* program modified to accommodate group sizes of up to 45 individuals (compared to 25 individuals accommodated by *SOREMO*; see Kenny, 1998). In order to test hypotheses that variances (actor and partner) and reciprocity correlations (generalised and dyadic) were different from zero, between-group *t*-tests were performed in which estimates of each parameter (weighted by number in group minus 1) were obtained within each of the 17 classes, then we tested whether the dispersion of this parameter estimate across classes (distributed as a *t*-distribution with 16 degrees of freedom) warrants rejection of the null hypothesis (that the parameter equals 0; Kenny, 1994; Kenny & La Voie, 1984; cf. Lashley & Bond, 1997).

In order to test for potential sex effects of the nominator or targets, the overall (irrespective of sex) round-robin design of nominations within the classroom was decomposed into two round-robin designs (for boys' and girls' same-sex nominations) and two half-block designs (for boys' nominations of girls and girls' nominations of boys). This decomposition is represented in Figure 1. After social relations parameter estimates within each design were computed, a series of 2 (sex of nominators) × 2 (sex of targets) within-class ANOVAs were performed to test for significant sex-of-nominator, sex-of-target, and interaction effects (with variance/covariance estimates from each class weighted by the geometric mean of the number of boys and the number of girls in the class; see Boldry & Kashy, 1999). Significant interactions were further examined through simple effects within genders. It should be noted that nominator and target sex differences can be considered actor and partner effects, respectively. However, to avoid confusion we use the terms nominator and target effects to refer to the fixed effects of sex, and the terms actor and partner to refer to the random effects of individuals within each group (overall class or sex subgroup).

Results

Mean levels of nominations

In order to compare nominations made by boys and girls of other boys and girls, the mean percentages of peers nominated for each of the eight constructs under investigation (overt

aggression, relational aggression, instrumental aggression, reactive aggression, victimisation, peer influence, perceived popularity, and social preference) were computed for the four combinations of male and female nominators and targets: boys' nominations of boys, boys' nominations of girls, girls' nominations of boys, and girls' nominations of girls. Tests of nominator sex, target sex, and nominator × target sex interaction effects were examined through within-group comparisons of these means within the 17 classes studied. Although this is a conservative test in terms of the ability to detect these effects, it was chosen because it parallels hypothesis testing procedures in subsequent sections.

As shown in Table 1, there were no significant nominator, target, or interaction sex effects for nominations of overt aggression. In other words, boys and girls did not reliably differ in their tendencies to nominate others or to be nominated, and the frequency of nominations was not predicted by the interaction of the sexes of nominators and targets. However, nominations for relational aggression did exhibit a significant actor difference: Girls nominated more peers as relationally aggressive than did boys. This effect was moderated by a significant nominator sex by target sex interaction. Follow-up analyses revealed that girls nominated others as relationally aggressive more so than boys when the targets were other girls: paired $t(16) = 3.88$, $p < .001$ when targets were girls and $t(16) = 1.32$, *ns* when targets were boys. Girls were more frequently nominated than boys when nominators were girls, $t(16) = 2.59$, $p < .05$, but boys and girls did not differ in their frequency of being nominated as relationally aggressive by boys, $t(16) = 1.23$, *ns*.

Nominations for instrumental aggression also did not reveal significant nominator, target, or interaction sex effects. Nominations for reactive aggression did not indicate significant nominator or target sex main effects, but a significant nominator by target interaction was evident. Follow-up analyses indicated that boys more often nominated other boys than they nominated girls as reactively aggressive, paired $t(16) = 2.57$, $p < .05$, whereas girls did not differ in their tendencies to nominate boys or girls, $t(16) = 1.05$, *ns*. Girls were less often nominated as reactively aggressive by boys than by girls, $t(16) = 3.77$, $p < .01$, whereas boys did not differ in the nominations received by boys and girls, $t(16) = 0.99$, *ns*.

Girls were found to nominate others as victimised more often than did boys, but this nominator main effect was qualified by a significant sex of nominator by sex of target

Table 1

Mean percentage of peers nominated by sex

	Boys' nominations of		Girls' nominations of				
	Boys	Girls	Boys	Girls	Nominator	Target	N × T
Overt agg	6.82	3.17	6.04	4.63	0.12	2.00	1.80
Relational agg	6.00	3.47	4.22	10.07	8.65**	0.92	10.41**
Instrumental agg	5.67	3.81	4.58	6.29	0.66	0.00	2.50
Reactive agg	7.15	2.83	5.68	8.42	2.93	0.16	16.29***
Victimisation	8.96	2.26	8.05	8.01	5.68*	2.84	10.82**
Influence	13.27	4.85	5.38	16.77	4.43	1.12	32.55***
Popularity	3.64	0.66	−3.45	6.10	0.52	2.99	13.56**
Social pref	20.75	0.64	−1.08	20.64	0.17	0.17	84.13***

Nominator, target, and interaction effects of sex based on within-group comparisons across the 17 groups, within-group $F(1, 16)$ for each effect.

*$p < .05$; **$p < .01$; ***$p < .001$.

interaction. Follow-up analyses revealed that girls nominated others more than boys only when potential targets were other girls, paired $t(16) = 3.25, p < .01$; girls and boys did not differ in their tendencies to nominate boys as victimised, $t(16) = 0.92$, *ns*. Boys nominated girls as victimised less frequently than they nominated boys, $t(16) = 3.83, p < .001$, whereas girls did not differ in their nominations of boys and girls, $t(16) = 0.02$, *ns*.

Peer nominations of influence did not reveal significant nominator or target sex differences (though there was a marginal trend for girls to nominate more peers than did boys, $p = .052$, which is similar to previous research with college students; Lord, Phillips, & Rush, 1980). However, a significant nominator by target interaction emerged in which youths nominated same-sex peers as influential more often than they nominated opposite-sex peers. Specifically, all four paired comparisons were significant: boys more often nominated boys than they nominated girls, paired $t(16) = 3.38, p < .01$, girls more often nominated girls than they nominated boys, $t(16) = 5.88, p < .001$, boys were more often nominated by boys than by girls, $t(16) = 4.77, p < .001$, and girls were more often nominated by girls than by boys $t(16) = 5.26, p < .001$.

Nominations of perceived popularity and of social preference followed similar trends in which no nominator or target main effects were evident, but youths viewed same-sex peers more favourably (i.e., more popular and liking more) than cross-sex peers. In terms of perceived popularity, girls viewed other girls as more popular than they viewed boys, paired $t(16) = 3.44, p < .01$, whereas boys did not view boys or girls as different in popularity, $t(16) = 1.30$, *ns*; and girls were perceived as more popular by girls than by boys, $t(16) = 3.26, p < .01$, whereas boys were perceived as more popular by boys than by girls, $t(16) = 2.99, p < .01$. Nominations of social preference differed in all four follow-up comparisons of the nominator by target interaction: boys liked other boys more than they liked girls, $t(16) = 6.93, p < .001$, whereas girls liked other girls more than they liked boys, $t(16) = 7.03, p < .001$, and boys were more liked by other boys than by girls, $t(16) = 6.16, p < .001$, whereas girls were more liked by other girls than by boys, $t(16) = 7.27, p < .001$. In summary, nominations of perceived popularity and social preference

suggested more positive views of same-sex than of cross-sex peers.

Variance partitioning

As outlined earlier, the variance in nominations of these constructs were first partitioned into actor and partner (and relationship/error) variances without reference to sex by performing a round-robin social relations analysis with each class as a distinct group (see left portion of Figure 1). As shown in the first columns of Tables 2 and 3, statistically reliable actor and partner variances were found for each of the eight constructs investigated.

In order to examine whether the magnitude of these actor and partner variances differed by the sexes of the nominators and targets, these variances were estimated separately for four patterns of nominations: boys nominating boys, boys nominating girls, girls nominating boys, and girls nominating girls. The first and last patterns were analysed as two round-robin designs, while the second and third were analysed as two half-block designs. Tests of differences in actor or partner variances by the sexes of nominators or targets (or the interaction) were examined through within-class comparisons in the 17 classrooms.

As shown in Table 2, actor variances for these constructs were generally reliably different from zero across the four combinations of nominator and target sexes, though actor variances of boys' nominations of boys were less consistent. Only one significant sex difference was evident: Actor variance for popularity was stronger when girls served as nominators (i.e., actors) than when boys served as nominators ($M = .019$ versus .052); $t(16) = 2.39, p < .05$.

Partner variances for these constructs were also generally significant across the four combinations of nominator and target sexes (see Table 3). However, the sizes of these partner variances in several instances differed depending on the sexes of the nominators and targets. Partner variances for relational aggression and for popularity were more pronounced when girls served as nominators than when boys served as nominators ($M = .063$ versus .017); $t(16) = 2.19, p < .05$.

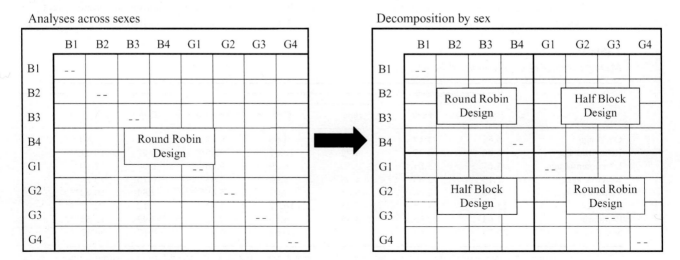

Figure 1.   Decomposition to examine sex-of-nominator and sex-of-target effects. (B1, B2, etc. represent boy1, boy2, etc. in the class, and G1, G2, etc. represent girl1, girl2, etc. in class.)

Table 2

Relative actor variances of peer nominations by sex

	Overall	Boys' nominations of		Girls' nominations of		Nominator	Target	N × T
		Boys	Girls	Boys	Girls			
Overt agg	.029**	.020	.025*	.041*	.019**	0.07	1.22	0.72
Relational agg	.024**	.034	.028*	.027*	.044***	0.06	0.07	0.26
Instrumental agg	.033**	.019	.052**	.034*	.026**	0.67	0.28	1.35
Reactive agg	.025***	.033	.045**	.039**	.033**	0.20	0.25	0.42
Victimisation	.031***	.038**	.048**	.034*	.048***	0.01	0.00	0.14
Influence	.023***	.053**	.042*	.038*	.023**	0.50	1.36	0.47
Popularity	.033**	.026**	.011	.035*	.070*	5.72*	0.02	1.88
Social pref	.034***	.037	.072	.037*	.049**	0.06	0.68	0.05

Nominator, target, and interaction effects of sex based on within-group comparisons across the 17 groups, within-group $F(1, 16)$ for each effect. $*p < .05; **p < .01; ***p < .001$.

The partner variance for perceived popularity also differed depending on the sex of those nominated; partner variance was greater, on average, when boys were being nominated than when girls served as targets. These main effects of nominator and target sex on perceived popularity partner variance were qualified by a nominator by target sex interaction. Follow-up analyses revealed an especially large partner variance for girls' nominations of boys as popular, relative to both girls' nominations of other girls, paired $t(16) = 3.72, p < .01$, and boys' nominations of boys, $t(16) = 3.38, p < .01$.

Reciprocity of nominations

Tables 4 and 5 provide summaries of findings regarding two indexes of reciprocity, generalised (i.e., between an individual's perceptions of peers in general and peers' perceptions of the individual) and dyadic (i.e., between an individual's perception of a particular peer and that peer's perception of the individual).

Across sexes, those who viewed (i.e., nominated) others as victimised tended to be viewed by others as less victimised ($r = -.21$), those who saw others as influential were viewed by others as influential ($r = .26$), and those who liked others (more positive social preference nominations) tended to be better liked by others ($r = .33$). These and other generalised reciprocity correlations are shown in Table 4. Also shown in this table are sex effects of nominators and targets (and interactions). Although the sexes of the nominator or target did

not affect the generalized reciprocity correlations, there was a significant interaction between the sexes of nominator and target for instrumental aggression. Here, the generalised reciprocity correlation in instrumental aggression nominations was more positive for girls' nominations of other girls than for either girls' nominations of boys, paired $t(16) = 2.64, p < .05$ or boys' nominations of girls, $t(16) = 2.39, p < .05$.

As shown in Table 5, significant positive dyadic reciprocity correlations were found for nominations of liking ($r = .29$), peer influence ($r = .10$), and instrumental aggression ($r = .08$). Because dyadic reciprocities of boys' nominations of girls and girls' nominations of boys were necessarily identical, possible sex differences were explored by performing a three-level (boys, cross-sex, and girls) within-class ANOVA. No significant differences were evident across these three levels for any of the variables under study.

Discussion

Our goal was to examine sixth-grade children's peer nominations of aggression and social status using various aspects of the Social Relations Model (i.e., group means, actor and partner variance, generalised and dyadic reciprocity) in order to better understand the nature of interpersonal perception of these constructs among children. Typical usage of peer nomination instruments has implicitly considered only partner variances; however, our results using the SRM revealed a great deal of

Table 3

Relative partner variances of peer nominations by sex

	Overall	Boys' nominations of		Girls' nominations of		Nominator	Target	N × T
		Boys	Girls	Boys	Girls			
Overt agg	.097**	.089*	.030*	.057**	.054*	0.57	0.70	2.37
Relational agg	.056***	.024	.009	.047*	.079**	4.79*	0.01	1.18
Instrumental agg	.073**	.040	.036*	.065*	.070**	1.43	0.00	0.24
Reactive agg	.084***	.071*	.030*	.091**	.083**	1.90	0.48	1.10
Victimisation	.166***	.165**	.039**	.137**	.144***	1.19	2.11	4.24
Influence	.062***	.049**	.064*	.017	.092**	0.00	0.96	3.86
Popularity	.150***	.032**	.085**	.177***	.023*	4.94*	6.79*	15.74**
Social pref	.052***	.040*	.042*	.072**	.063**	1.31	0.14	0.01

Nominator, target, and interaction effects of sex based on within-group comparisons across the 17 groups, within-group $F(1, 16)$ for each effect. $*p < .05; **p < .01; ***p < .001$.

Table 4

Generalised reciprocity correlations of peer nominations by sex

| | Overall | Boys' nominations of | | Girls' nominations of | | Nominator | Target | $N \times T$ |
		Boys	Girls	Boys	Girls			
Overt agg	−.01	.22	−.02	−.09*	.03	0.89	0.00	1.23
Relational agg	.22*	−.07*	−.01	−.04	.21*	1.91	3.78	1.28
Instrumental agg	.14	.06	−.08	−.06	.19*	1.47	3.44	6.56*
Reactive agg	.08	−.02	−.07*	−.06	.29*	1.40	0.81	1.96
Victimisation	−.21*	−.07	−.01	.09	−.11	0.07	0.75	0.20
Influence	.26*	.43**	.01	.22*	.17	0.36	1.95	1.92
Popularity	−.09	.16	.02	−.03	.07	0.83	0.00	2.95
Social pref	.33***	.15	.13	.07	−.02	0.64	0.18	0.84

Nominator, target, and interaction effects of sex based on within-group comparisons across the 17 groups, within-group $F(1, 16)$ for each effect.
  * $p < .05$; ** $p < .01$; *** $p < .001$.

complexity in the qualities of interpersonal perceptions inherent in peer nomination data. Moreover, differences in these variances emerged depending on the sexes of both nominators and targets. The results of our study provide some unique insights to the gender-segregated nature of interpersonal perceptions.

Peer nominations of the various dimensions of aggression (overt, relational, instrumental, and reactive) were characterised by reliable actor and partner variances, indicating that children tend to differ in the degree to which they perceive others as enacting these aspects of aggression, and that there is consensus within the peer group about who enacts these aggressive behaviours. We found evidence of generalised reciprocity in nominations of relational aggression (but not overt aggression), and evidence of dyadic reciprocity in instrumental aggression. Although there exist several potential explanations for reciprocity in interpersonal perception (see Kenny, 1994), we believe that the positive reciprocity of relational aggression is due to individuals using this form of aggression eliciting these aggressive behaviours from their peers, which in turn influences the individuals' perceptions of their peers' relational aggressiveness. In other words, children who are relationally aggressive might elicit relational aggression

from their peers (in general and from specific peers), which in turn causes these children to have the perception that their peers (in general and specific peers) are relationally aggressive. Similar processes with individual peers might explain the dyadic reciprocity of instrumental aggression indicated by our results. These explanations assume that peers' nominations (i.e., partner effects) accurately reflect the child's behaviour; thus, it is unclear why similar findings were not evident for overt forms of aggression, which are readily observable by peers. Perhaps this lack of reciprocity may be due to more clearly defined power differentials between overt aggressors and their victims, resulting in little retaliation. This explanation may be examined further within longitudinal studies, as it might suggest that reciprocal perceptions in aggression will increase with familiarity (e.g., as the school year progresses).

We did not find gender differences in the rates of nominations for overt or instrumental aggression; however, same-sex nominations for relational and reactive aggression were more common than cross-sex nominations. Relational and reactive aggression may be relatively more visible to (and hence, more often nominated by) same-sex than cross-sex peers because these types of aggression may occur more often than other types (overt and instrumental aggression) within

Table 5

Dyadic reciprocity correlations of peer nominations by sex

	Overall	Boys' nominations of boys	Cross-sex nominations[a]	Girls' nominations of girls[b]	$F(2,32)$
Overt agg	.01	.03	−.01	.04	1.25
Relational agg	.06	.04	.01	.06	0.16
Instrumental agg	.08*	.02	.00	.09*	1.35
Reactive agg	.00	−.02	−.01	.02	0.18
Victimisation	−.01	−.02	−.01	−.01	0.36
Influence	.10**	.02	.01	.15**	3.12
Popularity	.01	−.03	.01	.00	1.18
Social pref	.29***	−.01	.07*	.10*	2.98

Nominator, target, and interaction effects of sex based on within-group comparisons across the 17 groups, within-group $F(1, 16)$ for each effect.

[a] Dyadic reciprocities of boys' nominations of girls and girls' nominations of boys were necessarily equivalent.

[b] In one class with only three girls it was not possible to estimate a dyadic reciprocity correlation. Dyadic reciprocity values of zero were substituted for girls' nominations of girls in this class, with no impact on the results.

*$p < .05$; **$p < .01$; ***$p < .001$.

same-sex friendships and cliques (see Card, Rosenfeld, Isaacs, Beasley, & Hodges, 2001; Grotpeter & Crick, 1996). The failure to find a sex of target effect for overt aggression is surprising given consistent findings that boys are more overtly aggressive than girls, including when assessed by peer nominations (e.g., Crick, 1997; Crick & Grotpeter, 1995; Lancelotta & Vaughn, 1989; Salmivalli et al., 2000; Tomada & Schneider, 1997). Although we initially suspected that this failure to detect such a difference could be due to the conservative method of detecting these mean-level sex differences (i.e., within class comparisons), post hoc analyses performed at the level of the individual rather than the class indicated only a nonsignificant trend of boys receiving more nominations for overt aggression than girls, $t(349) = 1.69$, $p = .092$.

Sex differences in nominations for relational aggression indicate a gender-segregated pattern. Namely, the previous research showing that girls have higher levels of peer-nominated relational aggression than boys appears to be accurate only among same-sex peer nominations (e.g., Crick & Grotpeter, 1995; Lancelotta & Vaughn, 1989). Our findings did not reveal sex differences in the magnitudes of actor or partner variances in nominations of overt, reactive, or instrumental aggression. However, we did find that consensus (i.e., partner variance) in relational aggression was greater when girls were nominators than when boys were nominators, suggesting that girls may be more aware, and in greater agreement, of who is relationally aggressive. Generalised reciprocity of perceptions of instrumental aggression also differed by sex. Here, only girls' nominations of other girls were marked by positive reciprocity. Thus, the previously noted failure to detect generalised reciprocity in instrumental aggression was apparently due to sex differences in which this reciprocity is evident among girls but not boys; instrumentally aggressive girls may elicit similar behaviour from their peers, thus resulting in their view that others are aggressive. That this occurred among girls but not boys may be due to the different forms typical of each: relational aggression (for which there is reciprocity) among girls and overt aggression (for which there is no evidence of reciprocity) among boys. Sex differences in the degree of dyadic reciprocity of perceptions of aggressiveness were not indicated.

We found significant actor and partner variances for all four measures of social status (victimisation, peer influence, perceived popularity, and social preference). The actor and partner variances indicate that young people tend to both differentially perceive and show consensus in their perceptions of social status. Positive generalised reciprocities were also found for peer nominations of social preference and peer influence: Young people who tend to like their peers (i.e., give positive social preference nominations) tend to also be liked by their peers, and young people who view others as influential are viewed as influential by others. In contrast, we found negative generalised reciprocity for victimisation: Young people who view others as victimised tend to be not viewed as victimised by others, whereas young people who do not view others as victimised tend to be perceived as victimised by their peers. This pattern suggests the existence of social comparison processes for victimisation: Young people who are highly victimised may tend to not notice or perceive others' treatment by peers as victimisation. In terms of dyadic reciprocity, positive reciprocity was indicated for perceptions of peer influence and social preference: Young people who view a

particular peer as high in these aspects of status also tend to be viewed as high in these characteristics by these particular peers. For example, if Child A likes Child B, Child B tends to like Child A; whereas if Child A dislikes Child B, Child B also tends to dislike Child A. This pattern is likely to be due to frequent expressions of one's feelings within relationships based on mutual liking or disliking (i.e., friendships and antipathetic relationships; see Card, Giordano, Rakamaric, Santana, Mancuso, & Hodges, 2002). Similarly, we found reciprocal perceptions for peer influence, suggesting that certain dyads within the peer group may mutually influence one another (e.g., mutually influential friendships; see Berndt, 1982; Kandel, 1978; Poulin, Dishion, & Haas, 1999), or otherwise be aware of one another's ability to influence peers.

Perceptions of social status also differed by gender. For all four measures of social status, same-sex nominations were more frequent than cross-sex nominations: Young people tend to view their same-sex peers as more victimised, more influential, and more popular than cross-sex peers, and they also tend to prefer same-sex over cross-sex peers. In-group bias in liking has been demonstrated in numerous previous studies (see Maccoby, 1998), and these findings suggest that this bias extends to perceived popularity. Our finding of greater same-sex than cross-sex nominations on influence is consistent with Maccoby's (1990, 1998) conclusion that influence more often occurs within sex than between the sexes. Maccoby also suggested that boys would be especially unresponsive to much of girls' influence; however, our post hoc comparisons did not reveal a difference in the rates of boys' and girls' cross-sex nominations of influence.

Regarding sex differences for actor and partner variances on social status nominations, only one actor variance estimate was significantly different: Actor variance for perceived popularity was more pronounced when girls served as nominators than when boys were nominators. In other words, differences in viewing others as popular or unpopular were more pronounced among girls than boys. Partner variance for perceived popularity was also related to the sex of nominators, although this was qualified by an interaction with target sex: Partner variance of perceived popularity was largest among girls' nominations of boys. In other words, we found high consensus among girls as to which boys were popular and unpopular. This may indicate that qualities that differentiate boys' popularity among girls at this age are especially observable (e.g., physical dominance; see Pellegrini & Long, 2003). Sex differences in generalised or dyadic reciprocity of nominations were not indicated for any of the social status variables.

Taken together, these results indicate higher rates of same-sex than of cross-sex nominations on both positive (e.g., social preference) and negative (e.g., victimisation) aspects of social status, whereas only relational and reactive aggression showed this pattern. Perhaps these aspects of aggression are more embedded within the gender-segregated social milieu, whereas overt forms and instrumental functions (e.g., bullying) of aggression are more readily viewable to cross-sex peers. That the sex differences found among six of the eight variables exhibited the same pattern of greater same-sex than cross-sex nominations is consistent with our hypothesis that the gender-segregated nature of children's social worlds (e.g., Maccoby, 1998) would result in more same-sex than cross-sex nominations for both desirable and undesirable characteristics. These findings run counter to the alternate hypothesis based on intergroup biases that suggested that same-sex nominations would be greater than cross-sex nominations only for positive features, but that cross-sex nominations would be greater than same-sex nominations on negative features. Thus, traditional paradigms based on in-group/out-group biases seem to be inadequate to explain the gender-segregated worlds of children at this age.

Sex differences in actor variances were generally not evident. In addition to individual differences in the tendency to view others in a particular manner, actor variance reflects assimilation, or tendencies for individuals to have homogeneous perceptions of others (Boldry & Kashy, 1999; Kenny, 1994). The absence of sex differences thus suggests that young people do not adopt a more assimilative, or stereotyped, view of their cross-sex than same-sex peers, as would be suggested by the well-established principle of out-group homogenisation (e.g., Linville et al., 1989; Park & Rothbart, 1982). Together, the higher rate of same-sex than cross-sex nominations across positive and negative characteristics and the general failure to find sex differences in actor variances suggest that young people's interpersonal perceptions are not well explained by classic in-group / out-group processes of bias and homogenisation. Instead, children's interpersonal perceptions tend to be marked by greater saliency of same-sex peers' than cross-sex peers' characteristics (i.e., aggressiveness and social status), but similar processes (i.e., degrees of assimilation and consensus) explain these perceptions. It is worth noting that evidence for such an outcome could not be found using traditional partner-effects-only approaches to peer nominations. That young people are prone to sex-segregated perceptions even in the context of sex-diverse school environments suggests lines of future research on the effects of salient demographic factors (e.g., ethnicity, socioeconomic status) and peer group aspects (e.g., cliques, social status groups) on children's interpersonal perception.

In addition to illuminating the effects of sex on children's interpersonal perception, these findings have implications for the use of peer nomination instruments to assess aggression and social status. That there were reliable partner variances across the measures of aggression and social status supports the traditional usage of peer nomination inventories to assess individual differences in tendencies to be nominated on these constructs by peers. There is a degree of consensus (see Kenny, 1994; Kenny et al., 1994) within peer groups about which young people are aggressive (overtly, relationally, instrumentally, and reactively) and about social status (who is victimised, influential, popular, and preferred). That is, meaningful individual differences in children's tendencies to be nominated by their peers can be obtained by aggregating the number of nominations they receive. The existence of reliable actor variances, however, indicates that additional information can be gleaned from peer nominations; namely, young people's tendencies to perceive others as aggressive and as having high or low social status. Further examination of actor effects may be a potentially fruitful avenue for future research. For example, tendencies to view peers as aggressive may be a product of biased social information processing (i.e., hostile attributional biases; see Crick & Dodge, 1994; Dodge & Coie, 1987). Thus, an important adjunct to the partner effects of peer nomination data is the rich information that can be obtained through consideration of the interpersonal nature of peer nominations.

Several limitations of this study warrant mention. First, this study used single variables assessed at one time point to represent each construct. Therefore, it was not possible to differentiate stable relationship variance from unstable error. Relationship effects offer a potentially important additional source of variance in children's peer nominations. Previous research has shown that relationship effects are an important explanatory factor of actual aggressive behaviour (Coie et al., 1999) and supporting social cognitions (Hubbard et al., 2001); they are also likely to account for interpersonal perceptions of aggressiveness, as well as social status. This study was also limited in terms of age. Malloy and colleagues (1995) demonstrated that the magnitudes of actor and partner variances in children's peer perceptions vary with age. Whether the actor and partner variances, as well as the indexes of reciprocity and sex differences, differ with age represents an important question for future research. It might be especially interesting to explore these sex differences in mid- to late-adolescence when the amount of cross-sex interaction increases (see Rubin, Bukowski, & Parker, 1998). Finally, this study examined children's interpersonal perceptions in the fall of the school year, when children have had only a couple of months of interaction. Although most of these sixth-graders had probably known one another for several school years—indeed, the evidence of consensus across all constructs studied suggests familiarity—it will be important to explore these effects later in the school year after the classes have had longer periods of interaction.

Despite these limitations, this study adds to the extant literature by elucidating the impact of children's gender-segregated social worlds on interpersonal perceptions of aggression and social status. Moreover, this study demonstrates how additional information can be gained from peer nomination instruments beyond individual differences in number of nominations received, namely individual differences in tendencies to perceive others as high or low social status or as aggressive (i.e., actor variances). Further examination of these individual differences and their correlates requires going beyond typical usage of peer nomination inventories and adapting sophisticated techniques of conceptualising and analysing the dyadic nature of interpersonal perception, such as that offered by the Social Relations Model.

References

Berndt, T. J. (1982). The features and effect of friendship in early adolescence. *Child Development*, 53, 1447–1460.

Bierman, K. L. (2004). *Peer rejection: Developmental processes and intervention strategies.* New York: Guilford Press.

Bigler, R. S., Jones, L. C., & Lobliner, D. B. (1997). Social categorization and the formation of intergroup attitudes in children. *Child Development*, 68, 530–543.

Boldry, J. G., & Kashy, D. A. (1999). Intergroup perception in naturally occurring groups of differential status: A social relations perspective. *Journal of Personality and Social Psychology*, 77, 1200–1212.

Cairns, R. B., Cairns, B. D., Neckerman, H. J., Ferguson, L. L., & Gariépy, J. L. (1989). Growth and aggression: I. Childhood to early adolescence. *Developmental Psychology*, 25, 320–330.

Card, N. A. (2003, April). Victims of peer aggression: A meta-analytic review. In N. A. Card & A. Nishina (Chairs), *Whipping boys and other victims of peer aggression: 25 years of research, now where do we go?* Poster symposium presented at the meeting of the Society for Research in Child Development, Tampa, FL.

Card, N. A., Giordano, N. J., Rakamaric, D., Santana, M., Mancuso, A. F., & Hodges, E. V. E. (2002, August). *Enemy relationships in adolescence: Formation, maintenance, impact, and typologies.* Poster presented at the meeting of the International Society for the Study of Behavioural Development, Ottawa City, Ottawa.

Card, N. A., Rosenfeld, L. B., Isaacs, J., Beasley, T. M., & Hodges, E. V. E. (2001, August). *Aggression within children's friendships*. Poster presented at the meeting of the American Psychological Association, San Francisco, CA.

Coie, J. D., Cillessen, A. H. N., Dodge, K. A., Hubbard, J. A., Schwartz, D., Lemerise, E. A., & Bateman, H. (1999). It takes two to fight: A test of relational factors and a method for assessing aggressive dyads. *Developmental Psychology, 35*, 1179–1188.

Crick, N. R. (1997). Engagement in gender normative versus nonnormative forms of aggression: Links to social-psychological adjustment. *Developmental Psychology, 33*, 610–617.

Crick, N. R., & Dodge, K. A. (1994). A review and reformulation of social information-processing mechanisms in children's social adjustment. *Psychological Bulletin, 115*, 74–101.

Crick, N. R., & Dodge, K. A. (1996). Social information-processing mechanisms in reactive and instrumental aggression. *Child Development, 67*, 993–1002.

Crick, N. R., & Grotpeter, J. K. (1995). Relational aggression, gender, and social-psychological adjustment. *Child Development, 66*, 710–722.

Dodge, K. A., & Coie, J. D. (1987). Social information-processing factors in reactive and instrumental aggression in children's playgroups. *Journal of Personality and Social Psychology, 53*, 1146–1158.

Egan, S. K., & Perry, D. G. (2001). Gender identity: A multidimensional analysis with implications for psychosocial adjustment. *Developmental Psychology, 37*, 451–463.

Grotpeter, J. K., & Crick, N. R. (1996). Relational aggression, overt aggression, and friendship. *Child Development, 67*, 2328–2338.

Hartup, W. W., & Abecassis, M. (2002). Friends and enemies. In P. K. Smith & C. H. Hart (Eds.), *Blackwell handbook of childhood social development* (pp. 285-306). Oxford: Blackwell.

Hawley, P. H. (2002). Social dominance and prosocial and coercive strategies of resource control in preschoolers. *International Journal of Behavioral Development, 26*, 167–176.

Hawley, P. H., & Little, T. D. (1999). On winning some and losing some: A social relations approach to social dominance in toddlers. *Merrill-Palmer Quarterly, 45*, 185–214.

Hawley, P. H., Little, T. D., & Pasupathi, M. (2002). Winning friends and influencing peers: Strategies of peer influence in late childhood. *International Journal of Behavioral Development, 26*, 466–474.

Hawley, P. H., & Vaughn, B. E. (2003). Aggression and adaptive functioning: The bright side to bad behavior. *Merrill-Palmer Quarterly, 49*, 239–242.

Hodges, E. V. E., & Perry, D. G. (1999). Personal and interpersonal consequences of victimization by peers. *Journal of Personality and Social Psychology, 76*, 677–685.

Hubbard, J. A., Dodge, K. A., Cillessen, A. H. N., Coie, J. D., & Schwartz, D. (2001). The dyadic nature of social information processing in boys' reactive and proactive aggression. *Journal of Personality and Social Psychology, 80*, 268–280.

Kandel, D. B. (1978). Homophily, selection, and socialization in adolescent friendships. *American Journal of Sociology, 84*, 427–436.

Kenny, D. A. (1994). *Interpersonal perception: A social relations analysis*. New York: Guilford.

Kenny, D. A., (1998). *SOREMO (Version 2)* [Computer software and manual]. University of Connecticut.

Kenny, D. A., Albright, L., Malloy, T. E., & Kashy, D. A. (1994). Consensus in interpersonal perception: Acquaintance and the Big Five. *Psychological Bulletin, 116*, 245–258.

Kenny, D. A., & La Voie, L. J. (1984). The social relations model. In L. Berkowitz (Ed.), *Advances in experimental social psychology*, Vol. 18 (pp. 142–182). San Diego, CA: Academic Press.

LaFontana, K. M., & Cillessen, A. H. N. (1999). Children's interpersonal perceptions as a function of sociometric and peer-perceived popularity. *Journal of Genetic Psychology, 160*, 225–242.

LaFontana, K. M., & Cillessen, A. H. N. (2002). Children's perceptions of popular and unpopular peers: A multimethod assessment. *Developmental Psychology, 38*, 635–647.

Lagerspetz, K. M. J., Björkqvist, K., & Peltonen, T. (1988). Is indirect aggression typical of females? Gender differences in aggressiveness in 11- to 12-year-old children. *Aggressive Behavior, 14*, 403–414.

Lancelotta, G. X., & Vaughn, S. (1989). Relation between types of aggression and sociometric status: Peer and teacher perceptions. *Journal of Educational Psychology, 81*, 86–90.

Lashley, B. R., & Bond, C. F., Jr (1997). Significance testing for round robin data. *Psychological Methods, 2*, 278–291.

Linville, P. W., Fischer, G. W., & Salovey, P. (1989). Perceived distributions of the characteristics of in-group and out-group members: Empirical evidence and a computer simulation. *Journal of Personality and Social Psychology, 57*, 165–188.

Little, T. D., Brauner, J., Jones, S. M., Nock, M. K., & Hawley, P. H. (2003). Rethinking aggression: A typological examination of the functions of aggression. *Merrill-Palmer Quarterly, 49*, 343–369.

Little, T. D., Jones, S. M., Henrich, C. C., & Hawley, P. H. (2003). Disentangling the "whys" from the "whats" of aggressive behaviour. *International Journal of Behavioral Development, 27*, 122–133.

Lord, R. G., Phillips, J. S., & Rush, M. C. (1980). Effects of sex and personality on perceptions of emergent leadership, influence, and social power. *Journal of Applied Psychology, 65*, 176–182.

Maccoby, E. E. (1990). Gender and relationships: A developmental account. *American Psychologist, 45*, 513–520.

Maccoby, E. E. (1998). *The two sexes: Growing up apart, coming together*. Cambridge, MA: Harvard University Press.

Malloy, T. E., & Albright, L. (1990). Interpersonal perception in a social context. *Journal of Personality and Social Psychology, 58*, 419–428.

Malloy, T. E., & Kenny, D. A. (1986). The social relations model: An integrative method for personality research. *Journal of Personality, 54*, 199–225.

Malloy, T. E., Sugarman, D. B., Montvilo, R. K., Ben-Zeev, T. (1995). Children's interpersonal perceptions: A social relations analysis of perceiver and target effects. *Journal of Personality and Social Psychology, 68*, 418–426.

Martin, C. L., & Halverson, C. F. (1981). A schematic processing model of sex typing and stereotyping in children. *Child Development, 52*, 1119–1134.

Newcomb, A. F., Bukowski, W. M., & Pattee, L. (1993). Children's peer relations: A meta-analytic review of popular, rejected, neglected, controversial, and average sociometric status. *Psychological Bulletin, 113*, 99–128.

Park, B., & Rothbart, M. (1982). Perception of outgroup homogeneity and levels of social categorization: Memory for the subordinate attributes of ingroup and outgroup members. *Journal of Personality and Social Psychology, 42*, 1050–1060.

Parke, R. D., & Slaby, R. G. (1983). The development of aggression. In P. Mussen & M. Hetherington (Eds.), *Handbook of child psychology: Vol. 3, Socialization, personality, and social development* (4th ed., pp. 547–641). New York: Wiley.

Parker, J. G., & Asher, S. R. (1987). Peer relations and later personal adjustment: Are low accepted children at risk? *Psychological Bulletin, 102*, 357–389.

Parkhurst, J. T., & Hopmeyer, A. G. (1998). Sociometric popularity and peer-perceived popularity: Two distinct dimensions of peer status. *Journal Early Adolescence, 18*, 125–144.

Pellegrini, A. D., & Long, J. D. (2003). A sexual selection theory of longitudinal analysis of sexual segregation and integration in early adolescence. *Journal of Experimental Child Psychology, 85*, 257–278.

Phillipsen, L. C., Deptula, D. P., & Cohen, R. (1999). Relating characteristics of children and their friends to relational and overt aggression. *Child Study Journal, 29*, 269–289.

Poulin, F., Dishion, T. J., & Haas, E. (1999). The peer influence paradox: Friendship quality and deviancy training within male adolescent friendships. *Merrill-Palmer Quarterly, 45*, 42–61.

Powlishta, K. K. (1995). Gender bias in children's perception of personality traits. *Sex Roles, 32*, 17–28.

Prinstein, M. J., & Cillessen, A. H. N. (2003). Forms and functions of adolescent peer aggression associated with high levels of peer status. *Merrill-Palmer Quarterly, 49*, 310–342.

Ross, H. S., & Lollis, S. P. (1989). A social relations analysis of toddler peer relations. *Child Development, 60*, 1082–1091.

Rubin, K. H., Bukowski, W. M., & Parker, J. G. (1998). Peer interactions, relationships, and groups. In W. Damon (Series Ed.) & N. Eisenberg (Ed.). *Handbook of child psychology: Vol. 3, Social, emotional, and personality development* (pp. 619–700). New York: Wiley.

Salmivalli, C., Kaukiainen, A., & Lagerspetz, K. (2000). Aggression and sociometric status among peers: Do gender and type of aggression matter? *Scandinavian Journal of Psychology, 41*, 17–24.

Schwartz, D., Dodge, K. A., Coie, J. D., Hubbard, J. A., Cillessen, A. H. N., Lemerise, E. A., & Bateman, H. (1998). Social-cognitive and behavioral correlates of aggression and victimization in boys' play groups. *Journal of Abnormal Child Psychology, 26*, 431–440.

Tomada, G., & Schneider, B. H. (1997). Relational aggression, gender, and peer acceptance: Invariance across culture, stability over time, and concordance among informants. *Developmental Psychology, 33*, 601–609.

Vitaro, F., Brendgen, M., & Tremblay, R. E. (2002). Reactively and instrumentally aggressive children: Antecedent and subsequent characteristics. *Journal of Child Psychology and Psychiatry, 43*, 495–505.

International Journal of Behavioral Development
2005, 29 (2), 156–164
http://www.tandf.co.uk/journals/pp/01650244.html

Ψ Psychology Press
Taylor & Francis Group

© 2005 The International Society for the
Study of Behavioural Development
DOI: 10.1080/01650250444000342

Adolescent perceptions of friendship and their associations with individual adjustment

William J. Burk and Brett Laursen
Florida Atlantic University, Fort Lauderdale, FL, USA

This study of 282 dyads examines early- and mid-adolescents' perceptions of friendship quality and their association with daily disagreements, self- and mother reports of behaviour problems, and school grades. Actor and partner analyses identify unique associations between perceptions of friendship quality and perceptions of daily conflict. Actor effects reveal links between friendship negativity and self-perceptions of conflict affective intensity, relationship impact, post-conflict interaction, and post-conflict separation, and between friendship positivity and self-perceptions of relationship impact. Partner effects reveal links between friendship negativity and partner perceptions of conflict outcomes. Perceptions of relationship quality were also associated with self- and mother reports of behaviour problems and with school grades, such that individual and dyadic views of friendship negativity were linked to detrimental outcomes. The worst outcomes tended to be reserved for dyads in which one or both friends reported high levels of relationship negativity.

Friendship quality is a key indicator of adolescent psychosocial adjustment. Participant perceptions are a strong predictor of individual well-being, but friends may have differing views about positive and negative features of their relationship (Rubin, Bukowski, & Parker, 1998). Most previous research concerning perceptions of friendship has exclusively focused on the individual, despite the dyadic nature of the relationship. Partner perceptions presumably contribute to the overall quality of a relationship, but ascertaining the unique contribution of each partner is difficult because friends' perceptions are not independent (Furman, 1996). As a consequence, little is known about distinctions between shared and unique perceptions of friendship quality and their links to interpersonal competence and individual adjustment. The present investigation will address some of the limitations of traditional parametric approaches by applying data analytic techniques designed for interdependent relationship reports (Griffin, Murray, & Gonzalez, 1999; Kashy & Kenny, 2000). Adolescent friends completed identical questionnaires concerning negativity and positivity in order to identify shared and unique relationship perceptions associated with conflict, behaviour problems, and school grades.

Most conceptual models that address the provisions of friendship include separate dimensions that describe negative and positive features of the relationship (Furman, 1989). Negative friendship qualities encompass rivalry, betrayal, hostility, antagonism, and competition. Positive friendship qualities encompass companionship, intimacy, assistance, loyalty, caring, warmth, closeness, and trust. There is considerable overlap in friends' perceptions of these relationship qualities. Children report the greatest congruence in

perceptions of positive friendship qualities, whereas adolescents report the most congruence in perceptions of negative friendship qualities (Furman, 1996; Parker & Asher, 1993). Dyadic-level variation in shared relationship views has received less attention. Some have suggested that incongruent perceptions of a friendship reflect poor relationship skills and, as such, may be an indicator of maladjustment (Buhrmester, 1990; Parker, Rubin, Price, & DeRosier, 1995). Thus, independent and shared perceptions of friendship should be linked to social competence and individual well-being. Indirect support for this assertion comes from a study indicating that perceptions of friendship quality differ as a function of sociometric status (Brendgen, Little, & Krappmann, 2000). Low levels of agreement about perceptions of closeness were more characteristic of low accepted children and their friends than of average and high accepted children and their friends.

The present study examines adolescent views of friendship for links with dyadic perceptions of conflict management. Conflict behaviours are a microcosm of functioning in close relationships (Laursen & Collins, 1994). Although the frequency of conflict has received the most attention, the manner in which conflicts are managed may be a better marker of friendship quality (Laursen, Hartup, & Koplas, 1996). Most conflicts between adolescent friends are settled amicably. Friends tend to avoid coercion in favour of mitigation strategies that minimise negative affect and unequal outcomes (Adams & Laursen, 2001; Laursen, Finkelstein, & Betts, 2001). Here too, dyadic differences are poorly articulated. Research on the topic has been limited to studies of hypothetical conflict management in samples of middle child-

---

Correspondence should be addressed to Brett Laursen, Department of Psychology, Florida Atlantic University, 2912 College Ave., Fort Lauderdale, Florida, 33314-7714, USA; e-mail: wjburk26@aol.com or laursen@fau.edu.

This research was supported by a grant to Brett Laursen from the US National Institute of Child Health and Human Development (HD 33006).

We would like to acknowledge the cooperation of the students, parents, faculty, and staff of the Broward and Miami/Dade county public schools.

Special thanks to Ryan Adams, Angela Friedli, Rosamond Parker, and Carly Sacher for their assistance with this project and to David Bjorklund, Steven Hecht, and Louise Perry for comments on an earlier draft of this manuscript.

hood friends and to laboratory observations of conflict between married couples. In each case, reports of conflict goals and strategies were linked to negative relationship qualities, but not to positive relationship qualities (Gottman, 1979; Rose & Asher, 1999). This suggests that perceptions of relationship negativity may be a better marker of relationship conflict than perceptions of relationship positivity.

The present study also examined views of friendship quality for links with adolescent adjustment. There is evidence that positive friendship qualities are associated with adolescent school involvement and academic achievement, and that negative friendship qualities are associated with adolescent behaviour problems (Berndt & Keefe, 1992; Loeber, Farrington, Stouthamer-Loeber, & Van Kammen, 1998). These findings have focused exclusively on self-reports of predictor and outcome variables, raising concerns that shared reporter variance may inflate the magnitude of associations between friendship quality and adolescent adjustment. Although there is general agreement that shared perceptions of friendship should promote individual adjustment (Buhrmester & Prager, 1995), outcomes associated with positive and negative views of adolescent friendship have yet to be identified.

To summarise, standard parametric statistics cannot easily accommodate interdependent assessments of friendship, so scholars have tended to rely on self-reports of relationship quality that omit shared views of the affiliation and inflate estimates of association with self-report measures of adjustment. To address these concerns, the present investigation employs two complementary statistical methods designed for interdependent data. The first method, the Actor-Partner Interdependence Model (APIM: Kashy & Kenny, 2000), uses regression-based procedures involving pooled estimates of between-dyad and within-dyad variance. APIM analyses examine whether self-perceptions of friendship negativity and positivity are linked to self-perceptions of conflict (actor effects) and to friend perceptions of conflict (partner effects). The second method, a trichotomised variable approach (Griffin et al., 1999), uses absolute difference score correlations and ANOVA-based procedures to determine whether individual and dyadic reports of friendship negativity and positivity are associated with school grades and self- and mother reports of behaviour problems.

Three questions will be addressed. (1) Do participants and friends have interdependent perceptions of friendship negativity and friendship positivity? Interdependence is a prerequisite for statistical models that address dyadic views of relationships. We anticipated a moderate degree of interdependence between the reports of adolescent friends, consistent with previous studies of adolescent perceptions of relationship qualities (Buhrmester, 1990). (2) Are perceptions of friendship negativity and friendship positivity linked to self-perceptions and partner perceptions of daily conflict? Hypothetical reports from preadolescents suggest that perceptions of friendship negativity should be more strongly linked to reports of conflict management than perceptions of friendship positivity (Rose & Asher, 1999). (3) Are perceptions of friendship positivity and friendship negativity linked to adolescent adjustment? Consistent with previous studies (Berndt & Keefe, 1992; Loeber et al., 1998), negative friendship qualities were expected to be linked to behaviour problems and positive friendship qualities were expected to be linked to school grades. Reports from preadolescents suggest that shared views of friendship are linked to social adjustment

(Brendgen et al., 2000), which gives rise to the prediction that discrepant perceptions of negativity and positivity may be associated with behaviour problems and difficulties with school.

Method

Participants

A total of 282 adolescents and their same-sex friends participated in this investigation. Adolescents were recruited from 18 public schools in the greater Miami and Fort Lauderdale metropolitan area. The final sample consisted of 171 early-adolescents (11 to 13 years of age, $M = 11.53$) and 111 mid-adolescents (14 to 16 years of age, $M = 14.71$). In each ethnic group there were 21 to 27 early-adolescent males, 30 to 37 early-adolescent females, 10 to 21 mid-adolescent males, and 18 to 34 mid-adolescent females. Mothers of 103 adolescents also participated, including mothers of 61 early-adolescents (22 male and 39 female) and mothers of 42 mid-adolescents (16 male and 26 female).

All adolescent participants were United States citizens, born in the USA, and fluent in English. Participation was restricted to adolescents in three ethnic groups: (1) non-Hispanic African Americans, (2) non-Hispanic Anglo Americans, and (3) Hispanic Americans. Hispanic American participants were of Cuban (50%), South American (17.4%), Central American (16.3%), and Caribbean (16.3%) ancestry. English was the primary language spoken in African American and Anglo American households; Spanish was the primary language spoken in Hispanic American homes. Of the 550 adolescents who returned parental consent forms, 100 were not selected because they did not meet one or more of these qualifying criteria.

Socioeconomic status (SES) was assessed with the Hollingshead (1974) four-factor index, which potentially ranges from 8 to 66. In the present study, Hollingshead scores ranged from 11 to 66 ($M = 37.77$, $SD = 10.0$). A 2 (age group) × 3 (ethnicity) × 2 (gender) ANOVA revealed ethnic group differences on SES, $F(2, 265) = 5.50$, $p < .01$. Tukey HSD comparisons indicated that Anglo Americans reported higher SES ($M = 40.52$, $SD = 9.4$) than Hispanic Americans ($M = 36.41$, $SD = 9.2$) and African Americans ($M = 35.72$, $SD = 11.1$). There were no statistically significant main effects or interactions involving age group or gender.

Instruments

Participants and friends completed two instruments. The first, the Network of Relationships Inventory (Furman & Buhrmester, 1985), describes negative and positive provisions of relationships. The second, the Interpersonal Conflict Questionnaire (Laursen 1993), assays characteristics of disagreements from the previous weekday. Participants also completed the Youth Self-Report (Achenbach, 1991a) and mothers completed the Child Behavior Checklist (Achenbach, 1991b), both of which provide an assessment of behaviour problems. School grades were obtained from academic records.

Network of Relationships Inventory. Participants and friends separately completed a 33-item instrument describing 11 characteristics of their relationship. Each subscale consisted of three items measured on a 5-point scale ranging from 1 (*little or none*) to 5 (*the most*). Three factors emerged from separate principal components factor analyses of the participant and friend subscales, replicating the results of previous studies (Furman, 1996): negativity, positivity, and relative power. The present study focuses on two of these factors. *Friendship negativity* had eigenvalues of 1.86 and 1.82, and accounted for 17% of the variance in participant and friend reports. Two subscales loaded above .88 on this factor: annoying behaviours and conflict. Internal reliabilities were high for participant ($\alpha =$ .86) and friend ($\alpha = .88$) reports. *Friendship positivity* had eigenvalues of 5.25 and 5.48, and accounted for approximately 50% of the variance in participant and friend reports. Eight subscales loaded above .72 on this factor: admiration, affection, companionship, instrumental aid, intimacy, nurturance, reliable alliance, and satisfaction. Internal reliabilities were high for participant ($\alpha = .94$) and friend ($\alpha = .95$) reports. For each factor, item scores were summed and averaged.

Interpersonal Conflict Questionnaire. Participants and friends described characteristics of daily conflict in their relationship. From a list of 33 conflict issues, adolescents were asked to identify all disagreements with this friend that arose during the previous weekday. Adolescents then described several distinct components of each disagreement. *Affective intensity* describes the emotional tenor: How did you feel after the disagreement? Participants rated each disagreement on a 5-point scale ranging from 1 (*friendly*) to 5 (*angry*). *Relationship impact* describes the interpersonal consequences: How did this disagreement affect your relationship? Participants rated each disagreement on a 5-point scale ranging from 1 (*made it better*) to 5 (*made it worse*). A final question addressed the conflict aftermath: What happened immediately after the disagreement? Participants selected one of three alternatives: (1) we stayed together and continued talking; (2) we stayed together but stopped talking; and (3) we were not together. Two variables were drawn from this question. *Post-conflict social interaction* describes the proportion of disagreements in which friends stayed together and continued talking after the conflict. *Post-conflict separation* describes the proportion of disagreements in which friends were no longer together after the conflict. Previous studies with this measure have yielded moderately stable reports of conflict over a 2-week interval (Laursen & Koplas, 1995).

Youth Self-Report and Child Behavior Checklist. Participants completed the Youth Self-Report and mothers completed the Child Behavior Checklist. Each describes participant behavior problems on eight narrowband indices of adjustment, from which two broadband indices were derived. Self- and mother reports of *externalising problems* each included 30 items concerning delinquency and aggression. Self- and mother reports of *internalising problems* each included 30 items concerning withdrawal, somatic complaints, and anxiety/depression. Items were rated on a 3-point scale ranging from 0 (*never*) to 2 (*often*). These subscales have demonstrated high levels of internal consistency (Achenbach, 1991a, 1991b). Raw scores were used for all statistical analyses; percentile scores are presented in tables.

School grades. School officials provided the grade point average for each participant. School grades represent the mean of all grades received during the semester in which the data were collected. The potential range of school grades is from F (0.00) to A (4.00).

Procedure

Participants were recruited from classrooms selected by school personnel as representative of the entire school population. Research teams that included at least one Hispanic American research assistant described the project to students in predominantly Hispanic American schools. Research teams that consisted of at least one African American and one Anglo American research assistant described the project to students in other schools. Research teams answered questions and distributed parental consent forms and demographic surveys (in English and Spanish).

Participant assent forms were accompanied by a questionnaire requesting the names and contact information of three same-sex best friends, listed in rank order of preference. Friends were contacted by telephone, in rank order, to confirm friendship with the participant. The first to acknowledge a friendship with the target adolescent was solicited for involvement in the study. In no case was the same best friend nominated by more than one participant. Friend participation was limited to those who returned signed assent and parental consent forms. Of the 450 qualifying adolescents who returned parental consent forms, 168 completed surveys but were omitted from this investigation because reports were not available from their friends. Chi-squares and *t*-tests compared the 282 adolescents with friend reports to the 168 adolescents without friend reports in terms of demographic characteristics, participant reports of friendship qualities and conflict, participant reports of externalising and internalising problems, and school grades. Differences between adolescents with friend reports and those without friend reports did not occur at levels greater than chance. Similar analyses failed to reveal differences between the 103 adolescents with mother reports and the 347 adolescents without mother reports. Of the friends participating in this study, 249 (88.3%) were ranked first, 25 (8.9%) were ranked second, and 8 (2.8%) were ranked third. *T*-tests failed to reveal differences between adolescents paired with first-choice friends and those paired with other friends on reports of relationship quality, conflict, behaviour problems, and school grades.

Participants and friends completed the surveys separately. All but 19 friends attended the same schools as the participant. Of this total, 9 completed the surveys at home and returned them by mail and 10 completed the surveys during telephone interviews. For the remainder, surveys were administered in a quiet school setting in small group sessions that lasted approximately one hour for participants and 30 minutes for friends. Every effort was made to ensure that the ethnic background of at least one research assistant matched that of the adolescent. The name of the target friend was listed on each survey; participants and friends were instructed to describe their relationship with this target individual. Friends in 36 dyads completed their surveys on the same day, friends in 200 dyads completed their surveys within 2 weeks of each other, and friends in 46 dyads completed their surveys from 2 weeks to 3 months apart (*Mdn* = 7.50 days, *M* = 17.37, *SD* = 21.3). One-way ANOVAs failed to reveal statistically significant differences between friendship quality and conflict reports collected on the same day, reports collected within 2 weeks, and reports collected more than 2 weeks apart.

Plan of analysis

The analyses address three questions. Do participants and friends have interdependent perceptions of friendship negativity and friendship positivity? Dyadic similarity is assessed with intraclass correlations that partition between-dyad and within-dyad variance in a three-step procedure (Kashy & Kenny, 2000). First, two composite scores are calculated for negativity and positivity. The first composite is a between-dyad score (participant and friend reports are averaged and summed) and the second composite is a within-dyad score (friend reports are subtracted from participant reports and summed). Second, intraclass correlations are separately calculated for each variable, dividing the between-dyad scores by the within-dyad scores. Finally, statistical significance is tested with a standard F-ratio. Additional analyses determine whether patterns of interdependence are unique to friendships. To this end, participant scores of relationship quality are randomly paired with friend scores from different dyads. Intraclass correlations for random sets of pairings are followed by modified z-score contrasts (Meng, Rosenthal, & Rubin, 1992) to identify differences between friends and randomly selected peers in patterns of association. The number of contrasts for these analyses is arbitrary; 100 were conducted to minimise chance findings. Similar analyses were also conducted on reports of conflict management.

Are perceptions of friendship negativity and positivity linked to self-perceptions and partner perceptions of conflict? Actor effects describe two sets of associations: (1) self-perceptions of friendship negativity with self-perceptions of conflict, and (2) self-perceptions of friendship positivity with self-perceptions of conflict. Partner effects also describe two sets of associations: (1) self-perceptions of friendship negativity with partner perceptions of conflict, and (2) self-perceptions of friendship positivity with partner perceptions of conflict. To calculate actor and partner effects, pairs of between-dyad and within-dyad regressions are independently conducted (Kashy & Kenny, 2000). Between-dyad regressions utilise between-dyad scores (averaged scores from each dyad); within-dyad regressions utilise within-dyad scores (difference scores from each dyad). Four between-dyad regressions are performed. Between-dyad regressions include age group, ethnicity, and gender on the first step as control variables. Between-dyad scores of friendship negativity and friendship positivity are included on the second step. Between-dyad scores for one of the four conflict variables (i.e., affective intensity, relationship impact, post-conflict social interaction, and post-conflict separation) are the outcome. Four within-dyad regressions are also conducted. Within-dyad scores of friendship negativity and friendship positivity are entered on the first step. Within-dyad scores for one of the four conflict variables are the outcome. Unlike the between-dyad analyses, the within-dyad regressions do not include an intercept in the statistical model because of the arbitrary nature of the difference score sign (Kenny, 1996). Actor effects and partner effects are calculated by pooling the unstandardised between-dyad and within-dyad regression coefficients. Statistical significance is determined by a t-test, dividing the pooled coefficients by a pooled standard error (Kashy & Kenny, 2000).

To examine the moderating effects of age group, four regressions are performed. In each, the between-dyad scores of friendship negativity, friendship positivity, and age group are entered on the first step as control variables. Interaction terms are entered on the second step. One of the four between-dyad conflict scores is the outcome variable. Interaction terms are calculated by separately multiplying the between-dyad score of friendship negativity and the between-dyad score of friendship positivity by age group, which is dummy coded. Predictor variables are centred and interaction terms are computed from centred between-dyad scores (Aiken & West, 1991). Identical procedures examine the moderating effects of ethnicity and gender.

Are perceptions of friendship negativity and positivity linked to perceptions of behaviour problems and school grades? Three sets of analyses address this question. In the first set of analyses, participant and friend reports of relationship qualities are linked to measures of participant adjustment. Pearson correlations describe associations between friendship negativity and participant reports of externalising and internalising problems, mother reports of externalising and internalising problems, and school grades. Similar analyses were conducted for participant and friend reports of positivity. In the second set of analyses, within-dyad friendship quality scores (the absolute difference between friend and participant reports) are linked to measures of participant adjustment (Griffin et al., 1999). Pearson correlations describe associations between friendship negativity difference scores and participant reports of externalising and internalising problems, mother reports of externalising and internalising problems, and school grades. Similar analyses are conducted for friendship positivity difference scores. Partial correlations that include age group, ethnicity, and gender as covariates are also conducted.

The third set of analyses concern differences in adolescent adjustment as a function of discrepancies in participant and friend reports of friendship negativity and positivity. Dyads are classified into one of three groups on the basis of participant reports of negativity: low negativity (-0.5 SD and lower), medium negativity (between $+0.5$ SD and -0.5 SD), and high negativity ($+0.5$ SD and higher). Dyads are similarly classified on the basis of friend reports of negativity. This procedure yields nine friendship negativity groups. Three categories described friends with similar views of negativity: (1) consistent low negativity (both friends report low negativity, $n = 54$); (2) consistent medium negativity (both friends report medium negativity, $n = 46$); (3) consistent high negativity (both friends report high negativity, $n = 39$). Six categories described friends with disparate views of negativity. Because same-sex friends are considered exchangeable cases (Griffin & Gonzalez, 1995), redundant pairs of categories (e.g., self high, partner low and partner high, self low) were collapsed, leaving three categories of friends with dissimilar views of negativity: (1) low and medium negativity (one friend reports low negativity and the other friend reports medium negativity, $n = 61$); (2) medium and high negativity (one friend reports medium negativity and the other friend reports high negativity, $n = 48$); and (3) low and high negativity (one friend reports low negativity and the other friend reports high negativity, $n = 34$). Identical procedures yielded six friendship positivity groups: (1) consistent low positivity (both friends report low positivity, $n = 30$); (2) consistent medium positivity (both friends report medium positivity, $n = 41$); (3) consistent high positivity (both friends report high positivity, $n = 59$); (4) low and medium positivity (one friend reports low positivity and the other friend reports medium positivity, $n = 59$); (5) medium and high positivity (one friend reports medium positivity and the other friend reports high positivity, $n = 60$); and (6) low and high

Table 1

Interclass and intraclass correlations between participant reports and friend reports of friendship quality and conflict

	(1)	(2)	(3)	(4)	(5)	(6)	M	(SD)
Friendship quality								
(1) Negativity	.37**	−.19**	.42**	.31**	−.39**	.23**	2.11	(0.9)
(2) Positivity	−.13*	.26*	−.21**	−.28**	.37**	−.24**	3.77	(0.8)
Friendship conflict								
(3) Affective intensity	.04	.05	.30**	.60**	−.47*	.15*	2.01	(0.9)
(4) Relationship impact	.14	−.07	.64**	.18*	−.32**	.19**	2.12	(0.8)
(5) Post-conflict interaction	.01	−.02	−.39**	−.37**	.24*	−.73**	0.81	(0.3)
(6) Post-conflict separation	.04	−.08	.36**	.29**	−.66**	.32**	0.07	(0.2)
M	2.21	3.90	2.21	2.16	0.70	0.14		
(SD)	(0.9)	(0.8)	(0.9)	(0.9)	(0.4)	(0.3)		

Participant scores are presented below the diagonal; friend scores are presented above the diagonal. Intraclass correlations ($N = 112$) are presented on the diagonal in italic. Interclass correlations ($N = 146$ for participant reports of conflict, $N = 200$ for friend reports of conflict, and N = 282 for participant and friend reports of friendship quality) are presented in normal typeface. Friendship negativity and friendship positivity scores range from 1 (*little or none*) to 5 (*the most*). Affective intensity scores range from 1 (*friendly*) to 5 (*angry*). Relationship impact scores range from 1 (*made it better*) to 5 (*made it worse*). Post-conflict interaction and post-conflict separation proportion scores range from 0 to 1.00.
* $p < .05$; ** $p < .01$.

positivity (one friend reports low positivity and the other friend reports high positivity, $n = 33$). Chi-square analyses failed to reveal statistically significant differences in the distribution of negativity and positivity groups as a function of age group or ethnicity. Negativity groups also did not vary by gender, but differences emerged in the distribution of positivity groups, $\chi^2(5, N = 282) = 33.73$, $p < .001$. Post hoc binomial tests revealed more females ($n = 51$) than males ($n = 8$) in the consistent high positivity group.

Group differences in adjustment are determined by ANOVAs with 2 (age group) × 3 (ethnicity) × 2 (gender) × 6 (friendship quality group) independent variables. One of the five participant adjustment measures (self-reports of externalising problems, self-reports of internalising problems, mother reports of externalising problems, mother reports of internalising problems, and school grades) is the dependent variable. Limited statistical power precludes the examination of three-way and four-way interactions. Follow-up t-tests explore whether shared reporter variance contributes to statistically significant differences between friendship quality groups in adolescent adjustment. Specifically, analyses contrast outcomes of dyads with dissimilar views of the relationship to determine whether self-perceptions of adverse outcomes are a function of self-perceptions of poor friendship quality (e.g., the self low, partner high relationship negativity group with the self high, partner low relationship negativity group on self-reports of externalising problems).

Results

Participants reported a total of 653 disagreements ($M = 2.47$, $SD = 3.63$, range: 0 to 17 conflicts) and friends reported a total of 762 disagreements ($M = 3.24$, $SD = 4.04$, range: 0 to 19 conflicts) from the previous weekday. Many adolescents reported no disagreements, but 200 friends and 146 participants described at least one conflict. There were 112 dyads in which both the participant and the friend reported at least one disagreement during the previous weekday. Tables 1 and 2 provide means and standard deviations for all friendship quality, conflict, and adolescent adjustment variables.

Do participants and friends have interdependent percep-

tions of friendship negativity and positivity? Intraclass correlations (presented on the diagonal in italic in Table 1) provide an estimate of dyadic similarity. Similar analyses employing pairwise correlational procedures for exchangeable cases (Griffin & Gonzalez, 1995) revealed the same pattern of statistically significant associations. Intraclass correlations represent the total amount of the variance (in contrast to interclass correlations, which represent the square root of the variance). This suggests considerable interdependence in participant and friend reports of friendship quality and daily conflict. One-way ANOVAs failed to reveal statistically significant differences between data from dyads collected on the same day, reports collected within 2 weeks, and reports collected more than 2 weeks apart.

Table 2

Interclass correlations between participant and friend reports of friendship quality and indices of adolescent adjustment

	Self-reports		Mother reports		
Friendship quality	Externalising problems	Internalising problems	Externalising problems	Internalising problems	School grades
Self-reports					
Negativity	.23**	.14*	.14	.24**	−.20**
Positivity	.06	.05	.15	−.09	.04
Friend reports					
Negativity	.10	.04	.12	.01	−.15*
Positivity	.01	−.15*	.07	.07	.12
Difference scores					
Negativity	.13*	.10	−.10	.16	−.18**
Positivity	−.04	−.05	−.04	−.02	−.09
M	49.98	49.32	48.74	48.94	2.73
(SD)	(10.4)	(10.1)	(10.4)	(10.1)	(0.8)

$N = 103$ for interclass correlations involving mother reports, $N = 282$ for all other interclass correlations. Externalising problems and internalising problems percentile scores range from 25 to 100. School grades range from 0.00 (F) to 4.00 (A).
* $p < .05$; ** $p < .01$.

To determine whether these interdependent patterns of association were unique to friends, 100 sets of intraclass correlations were calculated between samples of randomly paired participant and friend reports of friendship negativity (Mean $r = .01$, $SD = .08$, range $= -.19$ to .18), friendship positivity (Mean $r = -.01$, $SD = .07$, range $= -.18$ to .16), affective intensity (Mean $r = .00$, $SD = .10$, range $= -.24$ to .25), relationship impact (Mean $r = .00$, $SD = .09$, range $= -.22$ to .16), post-conflict social interaction (Mean $r = -.02$, $SD = .09$, range $= -.33$ to .23), and post-conflict separation (Mean $r = .01$, $SD = .11$, range $= -.17$ to .30). Modified z-score contrasts (Meng et al., 1992) compared the results of these 100 sets of random pairings with the correlations presented in Table 2. Statistically significant differences between friends and random pairings of peers were found in 94 to 97 of the 100 contrasts for each friendship quality and conflict variable. In each case, intraclass correlations between friend reports explained more variance than those between randomly paired dyads, suggesting that friend reports reflect unique perceptions of a particular relationship rather than generic views of peer affiliations.

Are perceptions of friendship negativity and friendship positivity linked to self-perceptions and partner perceptions of conflict? Table 3 presents the results of actor analyses (links between a participant's or friend's perceptions of friendship qualities and his or her own perceptions of conflict) and partner analyses (links between a participant's or friend's perceptions of friendship qualities and his or her partner's perceptions of conflict). Demographic variables entered on step 1 of these analyses revealed only one association between participant characteristics and conflict: Males reported that conflicts were more apt to have a detrimental impact on the relationship than females. Step 2 of these analyses included negativity and positivity as predictor variables. Actor effects indicated that friendship negativity was linked to higher affective intensity, detrimental relationship impact, less post-conflict social interaction, and more post-conflict separation. Actor effects also indicated that friendship positivity was linked to improved relationship impact. Partner effects indicated that friendship negativity was linked to less post-conflict social interaction and more post-conflict separation. No statistically significant partner effects emerged for friendship positivity. Additional actor and partner analyses controlling for the number of days between participant and friend reports of conflict revealed a similar pattern of statistically significant results. A final set of analyses, to determine whether associations between friendship qualities and conflict are moderated by demographic variables, failed to identify any statistically significant two-way interactions involving age group, ethnicity, or gender.

Are perceptions of friendship negativity and friendship positivity linked to participant behaviour problems and school grades? Interclass correlations (see Table 2) indicated associations between participant reports of negativity and participant reports of externalising and internalising problems, mother reports of internalising problems, and school grades. Additional associations emerged between friend reports of positivity and participant reports of internalising problems, and between friend reports of negativity and school grades. Table 2 also includes interclass correlations of associations between friendship quality difference scores and adolescent adjustment. Friendship negativity difference scores were associated with participant reports of externalising problems and school

Table 3

Actor effects, partner effects, and unstandardised regression coefficients for associations between friendship quality and conflict

Predictor variable	Actor effects	Partner effects	Between-dyad		Within-dyad	
			B	(SE)	B	(SE)
Affective intensity						
Step 1						
Age group			0.00	(.08)		
Ethnicity			0.02	(.10)		
Gender			0.03	(.08)		
Step 2						
Negativity	2.92**	0.44	0.24*	(.10)	0.18	(.10)
Positivity	0.22	−1.55	−0.12	(.12)	0.16	(.13)
Relationship impact						
Step 1						
Age group			0.00	(.07)		
Ethnicity			−0.04	(.08)		
Gender			0.15*	(.07)		
Step 2						
Negativity	1.91*	0.54	0.16	(.08)	0.09	(.10)
Positivity	−1.71*	−0.98	−0.22*	(.10)	−0.06	(.13)
Post-conflict interaction						
Step 1						
Age group			−0.08	(.28)		
Ethnicity			−0.12	(.33)		
Gender			−0.34	(.28)		
Step 2						
Negativity	−3.38**	−1.83*	−1.31*	(.33)	−0.39	(.38)
Positivity	1.48	0.26	0.54	(.40)	0.38	(.48)
Post-conflict separation						
Step 1						
Age group			0.04	(.19)		
Ethnicity			−0.37	(.23)		
Gender			0.04	(.19)		
Step 2						
Negativity	2.34**	2.08*	0.73*	(.23)	0.04	(.24)
Positivity	−1.93	−0.50	−0.51	(.27)	−0.29	(.31)

Actor effects and partner effects are presented as *t*-values. Degrees of freedom range from 204 for affective intensity to 211 for post-conflict social interaction.
* $p < .05$; ** $p < .01$.

grades. Partial correlations controlling for age group, ethnicity, gender, and number of days between reports revealed a similar pattern of statistically significant results.

To identify group differences in individual adjustment, a series of 2 (age group) × 3 (ethnicity) × 2 (gender) × 6 (negativity group) ANOVAs were conducted (see Table 4). In the first ANOVA, participant reports of externalising problems were the dependent variable. Main effects emerged for age group $F(1, 247) = 5.77$, $p < .01$, and negativity group $F(5, 247) = 3.61$, $p < .01$. Adolescents in the consistent low negativity group reported fewer externalising problems than those in the consistent high negativity group and in the low and high negativity group. Mid-adolescents ($M = 52.72$, $SD = 9.5$) reported more externalising problems than early-adolescents ($M = 48.21$, $SD = 10.6$). In the second ANOVA, participant reports of internalising problems were the dependent variable. A main effect emerged for gender $F(1, 247) = 8.67$, $p < .01$. Females ($M = 51.46$, $SD = 9.5$) reported more internalising problems than males ($M = 46.74$, $SD = 11.2$). In the third

Table 4

Adolescent adjustment as a function of friendship negativity groups

| | Friendship negativity group | | | | | | | | | | | |
| | Consistent low | | Consistent medium | | Consistent high | | Low and medium | | Medium and high | | Low and high | |
Adjustment variable	M	(SD)	M	(SD)	M	(SD)	M	(SD)	M	(SD)	M	(SD)
Self-reports												
Externalising problems	45.83$_a$	(11.1)	49.24	(9.7)	53.21$_b$	(10.6)	49.83	(10.2)	50.09	(10.0)	53.09$_b$	(9.6)
Internalising problems	48.13	(9.7)	47.78	(9.5)	50.13	(9.3)	47.87	(10.5)	51.06	(10.2)	52.62	(10.5)
Mother reports												
Externalising problems	47.12$_a$	(10.2)	43.80$_a$	(10.6)	56.70$_a$	(8.9)	45.44$_a$	(10.8)	50.27	(10.6)	48.09	(7.2)
Internalising problems												
Early-adolescence	43.75	(10.8)	48.00	(13.8)	54.44	(12.6)	47.60	(8.5)	50.00	(12.0)	51.89	(9.0)
Mid-adolescence	47.08	(4.8)	38.00$_a$	(5.6)	52.33$_b$	(13.1)	46.83	(10.1)	50.83	(5.8)	58.00$_b$	(11.3)
School grades												
Early-adolescence	3.28$_a$	(0.5)	2.77$_b$	(0.7)	2.96$_b$	(0.7)	2.84$_b$	(1.0)	2.79$_b$	(0.8)	2.04$_b$	(0.8)
Mid-adolescence	3.16$_a$	(0.6)	2.76	(0.7)	2.07$_b$	(1.0)	2.67	(0.5)	2.46$_b$	(0.9)	2.49$_b$	(1.0)

$N = 103$ for contrasts involving mother reports; $N = 282$ for all other contrasts. Across rows, means with different subscripts differ significantly at $p < .05$ in Tukey's HSD comparisons. Externalising problems and internalising problems percentile scores range from 25 to 100. School grades range from 0.00 (F) to 4.00 (A).

ANOVA, mother reports of externalising problems were the dependent variable. A main effect emerged for negativity group, $F(5,70) = 4.38$, $p < .01$. Adolescents in the consistent high negativity group reported more externalising problems than adolescents in the consistent low negativity group, in the consistent medium negativity group, and in the low and medium negativity group. In the fourth ANOVA, mother reports of internalising problems were the dependent variable. A main effect emerged for negativity group, $F(5, 70) = 2.85$, $p < .05$, qualified by a two-way interaction between age group and negativity group, $F(5, 70) = 2.47$, $p < .05$. Follow-up analyses conducted separately by age group indicated that mothers of mid-adolescents in the consistent medium negativity group reported fewer externalising problems than mothers of mid-adolescents in the consistent high negativity group and mothers in the low and high negativity group. In the fifth ANOVA, school grades were the dependent variable. Main effects emerged for ethnicity, $F(2, 247) = 5.62$, $p < .01$, and negativity group, $F(5, 247) = 6.21$, $p < .01$, qualified by a two-way interaction between age group and negativity group, $F(5, 247) = 3.06$, $p < .05$. Anglo Americans ($M = 2.89$, $SD = 0.8$) had higher school grades than African Americans ($M = 2.54$, $SD = 1.0$) and Hispanic Americans ($M = 2.62$, $SD = 0.9$). Follow-up analyses conducted separately by age group indicated that early-adolescents in the low and high negativity group received lower school grades than those in all other negativity groups. Mid-adolescents in the consistent low negativity group received better school grades than those in the consistent high negativity group, the medium and high negativity group, and the low and high negativity group.

Five 2 (age group) × 3 (ethnicity) × 2 (gender) × 6 (positivity group) ANOVAs were also conducted. There were no statistically significant main effects or interactions involving positivity group for participant and mother reports of externalising and internalising problems. Analyses of school grades revealed a main effect for ethnicity, $F(2, 247) = 3.77$, $p < .05$, qualified by a two-way interaction between ethnicity and positivity group, $F(10, 247) = 2.29$, $p < .05$. Follow-up Tukey HSD comparisons failed to reveal statistically significant differences between positivity groups among Anglo

Americans and Hispanic Americans. Among African Americans, adolescents in the consistent high positivity group ($M = 3.17$, $SD = 0.7$) and in the consistent medium positivity group ($M = 3.03$, $SD = 0.6$) received better school grades than those in the low and medium positivity group ($M = 2.21$, $SD = 0.9$) and in the medium and high positivity group ($M = 2.29$, $SD = 0.9$).

For each statistically significant group effect, three sets of follow-up tests contrasted groups with dissimilar relationship views: (1) the self low negativity, friend high negativity group with the self high negativity, friend low negativity group; (2) the self low negativity, friend medium negativity group with the self medium negativity, friend low negativity group; and (3) the self medium negativity, friend high negativity group with the self high negativity, friend medium negativity group. No statistically significant differences emerged, indicating that outcomes in dyads with discrepant views of their relationship should not be attributed to shared reporter variance.

Discussion

Shared and unique views of friendship were associated with self- and partner perceptions of interpersonal conflict and with self- and mother perceptions of individual adjustment. Negative perceptions of relationship quality were more apt to be linked to outcomes than positive perceptions. Specifically, negativity was associated with self- and friend perceptions of conflict management, school grades, and self- and mother reports of behaviour problems. Individual differences emerged in adolescent adjustment such that the worst outcomes tended to be reserved for dyads in which either (1) both friends reported high levels of negativity or (2) friends reported discrepant levels of negativity.

As expected, friends' perceptions of relationship qualities were interdependent. Simply put, friends tended to share views concerning negative and positive relationship features. The results extend prior findings of similarity in adolescent perceptions of friendship in two noteworthy directions. First, there was considerable convergence in friends' perceptions of daily conflict, even though most participants did not report on events from the same day. Previous studies have documented interdependence in perceptions of global properties of friendship (Buhrmester, 1990; Furman, 1996); the present study suggests that shared views extend to daily interactions. Second, interdependent perceptions were found to be a distinctive feature of friend relationships. Comparisons with randomly paired peers indicated that shared perceptions are unique to friendships and are not a product of cognitive schemes that describe views toward peer relationships in general.

Perceptions of friendship negativity were more apt to be associated with conflict management, behaviour problems, and school grades than perceptions of friendship positivity. These findings are consistent with a growing body of evidence indicating that negative interactions are especially salient to friends. Negativity has previously been linked to a preference for coercive strategies in hypothetical disagreements (Rose & Asher, 1999), but to our knowledge this is the first study to tie friendship negativity to reports of actual conflict behaviour. Friendship negativity has also been linked to adolescent maladjustment (Loeber et al., 1998), a pattern of findings replicated in the present study. In contrast, friendship positivity demonstrated few reliable ties to either conflict management or individual adjustment. Although prior studies have implicated friendship positivity in improved academic performance (Berndt & Keefe, 1992), efforts to link perceived support from friends to adolescent behaviour problems have proven largely unsuccessful (Barrera, Chassin, & Rogosch, 1993; Hussong, 2000). Of course, null findings must be interpreted with caution, but it should be noted that evidence does not support the widely held view that positive friendship qualities buffer against adolescent maladjustment.

Unique to this study was the use of data analytic strategies that incorporated the views of both participants. Similar techniques have been applied to study peer relationships (Kenny & Kashy, 1999; Simpkins & Parke, 2002), but this is one of the first investigations to address perceptions of adolescent friends and to link these views to interpersonal and individual outcomes. The findings suggest that interdependent reports and shared reporter biases may have inflated some estimates of association described in previous studies of adolescent friendship quality. Two sets of results from the present study illustrate the problem. First, simple correlations indicated that friend reports of positivity and negativity were linked with friend reports of conflict management, but APIM analyses revised these estimates of association downward. Actor effects described associations between self-reports of friendship quality and self-reports of conflict management. After adjusting for bias due to interdependent self- and partner reports, these analyses indicated that negativity was linked to conflict management but, for the most part, positivity was not. Partner effects described associations between self-reports of friendship quality and partner reports of conflict management. After adjusting for shared reporter bias, negativity was linked only to post-conflict interaction and separation; positivity was unrelated to any feature of conflict management. Second, simple correlations indicated that self-reports of negativity were linked with self-reports of externalising and internalising, but these associations were not reliably corroborated by other reporters. Friend reports of negativity did not correlate with self- or mother reports of behaviour problems, and self-reports of negativity were correlated with mother reports of internalising but not externalising. In each example, analyses relying on reports from a single participant yielded stronger associations than those incorporating reports from different participants. These findings illustrate why developmental scholars must take to heart warnings about the limitations of applying traditional parametric statistics to the study of close relationships (Kashy & Kenny, 2000).

Of particular note are analyses examining dyadic views of friendship. In contrast to actor and partner analyses, which focus on the unique contributions of each participant, dyadic analyses reflect the extent to which friends agree about qualities of their relationship. The analyses revealed that discrepant views of friendship negativity were associated with lower levels of individual adjustment. Consistent with the assertion that disparate friendship perceptions are a marker of social maladjustment (Parker et al., 1995), difference score correlations indicated that as discrepancies between reports of negativity increased, behaviour problems and school grades worsened. The magnitude of these associations was modest, however, and findings were not consistent across outcome variables. More compelling results emerged in analyses contrasting friends grouped according to dyadic perceptions of friendship negativity. The best school grades and the fewest externalising problems were found among friends who agreed that their relationship was low in negativity. The worst school grades and the most externalising and internalising problems were found among friends who agreed their relationship was high in negativity and among friends with discrepant views of friendship negativity. Such results do not appear to be driven by shared reporter biases; outcomes in groups with dissimilar views did not differ as a function of whether the participant or the friend considered the relationship to be of lower quality. The risks associated with participation in poor-quality friendships are well documented (Rubin et al., 1998), but this is one of the first studies to demonstrate that these risks may extend to friendships in which participants disagree about the quality of their relationship. Taken together, the findings underscore the importance of gathering data from both participants in a relationship because discrepant views of negativity may provide a clue to identifying children who are insensitive to their friends and children who cannot distinguish better- from lesser-quality relationships.

A few caveats should be noted. First, the omission of participants who lacked data from friends and mothers reduced the sample size and limited our ability to consider higher-order interactions. Although we found no mean-level differences between adolescents whose friends and mothers participated in the study and those who did not, systematic differences in patterns of association may limit generalisations from this sample. Second, reports from most friends were not collected on the same day. There was no evidence that differences in the timing of data collection had a systematic influence on the results; if anything, reports from different days increased measurement error and reduced the magnitude of the effects. Nevertheless, future scholars should strive to minimise this potential source of error. Third, grouping dyads on the basis of continuous scores minimised differences between groups and reporters. A general linear model approach may be preferable for identifying interactions between self and friend perspectives, especially where effects are as small as they were for positivity. Finally, the concurrent nature of the data limits conclusions about influence processes. Longitudinal evidence suggests that friendship quality predicts subsequent individual adjustment (Berndt, 1996), but there is a good reason to suspect that friendship quality may be a product of participant characteristics that exert transactional influences over time.

We conclude that dyadic views of relationship quality hold the potential to extend our understanding of adolescent friendships in important directions. The findings illustrate the need to distinguish perceptions of negative relationship qualities from perceptions of positive relationship qualities. Conflict management and individual adjustment demonstrated more reliable links to negative views of friendship than to positive views. The findings also illustrate the importance of identifying discrepant perceptions of relationship quality. Adverse outcomes were found among friends who disagreed about the quality of their relationship as well as among those who agreed that it was of poor quality.

References

Achenbach, T. M. (1991a). *Manual for the Youth Self-Report and 1991 Profile.* Burlington, VT: University of Vermont, Department of Psychiatry.

Achenbach, T. M. (1991b). *Manual for the Child Behavior Checklist/4-18 and 1991 Profile.* Burlington, VT: University of Vermont, Department of Psychiatry.

Adams, R., & Laursen, B. (2001). The organization and dynamics of adolescent conflict with parents and friends. *Journal of Marriage and Family, 63,* 97–110.

Aiken, L. S., & West, S. G. (1991). *Multiple regression: Testing and interpreting interactions.* Newbury Park, CA: Sage.

Barrera, M., Jr, Chassin, L., & Rogosch, F. (1993). Effects of social support and conflict on adolescent children of alcoholic and nonalcoholic fathers. *Journal of Personality and Social Psychology, 64,* 602–612.

Berndt, T. J. (1996). Friendship quality affects adolescents' self-esteem and social behavior. In W. M. Bukowski, A. F. Newcomb, & W. W. Hartup (Eds.), *The company they keep: Friendship during childhood and adolescence* (pp. 346–365). New York: Cambridge University Press.

Berndt, T. J., & Keefe, K. (1992). Friends' influence on adolescents' perceptions of themselves at school. In D. H. Schunk & J. L. Meece (Eds.), *Student perceptions in the classroom* (pp. 51–73). Hillsdale, NJ: Lawrence Erlbaum Associates Inc.

Brendgen, M., Little, T. D., & Krappmann, L. (2000). Rejected children and their friends: A shared evaluation of friendship quality? *Merrill-Palmer Quarterly, 46,* 45–70.

Buhrmester, D. (1990). Intimacy of friendship, interpersonal competence, and adjustment during preadolescence and adolescence. *Child Development, 61,* 1101–1111.

Buhrmester, D., & Prager, K. (1995). Patterns of functions of self-disclosure during childhood and adolescence. In K. J. Rotenberg (Ed.), *Disclosure processes in children and adolescents* (pp. 10–56). New York: Cambridge University Press.

Furman, W. (1989). The development of children's social networks. In D. Belle (Eds.), *Children's social networks and social supports.* New York: Wiley.

Furman, W. (1996). The measurement of friendship perceptions: Conceptual and methodological issues. In W. M. Bukowski, A. F. Newcomb, & W. W.

Hartup (Eds.), *The company they keep: Friendship in childhood and adolescence* (pp. 41–65). New York: Cambridge University Press.

Furman, W., & Buhrmester, D. (1985). Children's perceptions of the personal relationships in their social networks. *Developmental Psychology, 21,* 1016–1024.

Gottman, J. M. (1979). *Marital interaction: Experimental investigations.* New York: Academic Press.

Griffin, D., & Gonzalez, R. (1995). The correlational analysis of dyad-level data: Models for the exchangeable case. *Psychological Bulletin, 118,* 430–439.

Griffin, D., Murray, S., & Gonzalez, R. (1999). Difference score correlations in relationship research: A conceptual primer. *Personal Relationships, 6,* 505–518.

Hollingshead, A. B. (1975). *Four Factor Index of Social Status.* Unpublished manuscript, Yale University.

Hussong, A. M. (2000). Perceived peer context and adolescent adjustment. *Journal of Research on Adolescence, 10,* 391–415.

Kashy, D. A., & Kenny, D. A. (2000). The analysis of data from dyads and groups. In H. Reis & C. M. Judd (Eds.), *Handbook of research methods in social and personality psychology* (pp. 451–477). New York: Cambridge University Press.

Kenny, D. A. (1996). Models of independence in dyadic research. *Journal of Social and Personal Relationships, 13,* 279–294.

Kenny, D. A., & Kashy, D. A. (1999). Enhanced co-orientation in the perceptions of friends: A social relations analysis. *Journal of Personality and Social Psychology, 67,* 1024–1033.

Laursen, B. (1993). The perceived impact of conflict on adolescent relationships. *Merrill-Palmer Quarterly, 39,* 535–550.

Laursen, B., & Collins, W. A. (1994). Interpersonal conflict during adolescence. *Psychological Bulletin, 115,* 197–209.

Laursen, B., Finkelstein, B. D., & Betts, N. T. (2001). A developmental meta-analysis of peer conflict resolution. *Developmental Review, 21,* 423–449.

Laursen, B., Hartup, W. W., & Koplas, A. L. (1996). Towards understanding peer conflict. *Merrill-Palmer Quarterly, 42,* 76–102.

Laursen, B., & Koplas, A. L. (1995). What's important about important conflicts? Adolescents' perceptions of significant daily disagreements. *Merrill-Palmer Quarterly, 41,* 536–553.

Loeber, R., Farrington, D., Stouthamer-Loeber, M., & Van Kammen, W. (1998). *Antisocial behavior and mental health problems: Explanatory factors in childhood and adolescence.* Mahwah, NJ: Lawrence Erlbaum Associates Inc.

Meng, X., Rosenthal, R., & Rubin, D. B. (1992). Comparing correlated correlation coefficients. *Psychological Bulletin, 111,* 172–175.

Parker, J. G., & Asher, S. R. (1993). Friendship and friendship quality in middle childhood: Links with peer group acceptance and feelings of loneliness and social dissatisfaction. *Developmental Psychology, 29,* 611–621.

Parker, J. G., Rubin, K. H., Price, J., & DeRosier, M. E. (1995). Peer relationships, child development, and adjustment: A developmental psychopathology perspective. In D. Cicchetti & D. Cohen (Eds.), *Developmental psychopathology: Vol. 2. Risk, disorder, and adaptation* (pp. 96–161). New York: Wiley.

Rose, A. J., & Asher, S. A. (1999). Children's goals and strategies in response to conflicts within a friendship. *Developmental Psychology, 35,* 69–79.

Rubin, K. H., Bukowski, W., & Parker, J. G. (1998). Peer interactions, relationships, and groups. In W. Damon (Ed.) & N. Eisenberg (Vol. Ed.), *Handbook of child psychology: Vol. 3. Social, emotional, and personality development* (pp. 619–700). New York: Wiley.

Simpkins, S. D., & Parke, R. D. (2002). Do friends and nonfriends behave differently? A social relations analysis of children's behavior. *Merrill-Palmer Quarterly, 48,* 263–283.

International Journal of Behavioral Development
2005, 29 (2), 165–172
http://www.tandf.co.uk/journals/pp/01650244.html

Ψ Psychology Press
Taylor & Francis Group

Predictors of dyadic friendship quality in adolescence

Antonius H. N. Cillessen
University of Connecticut, Storrs, USA

X. Lu Jiang
University of California at Los Angeles, USA

Tessa V. West and Dagmara K. Laszkowski
University of Connecticut, Storrs, USA

Five dimensions of friendship quality (conflict, closeness, companionship, helping, and security) were predicted from self-reports and peer reports of physical aggression, relational aggression, and prosocial behaviour, using the Actor-Partner Interdependence Model (Kenny & Acitelli, 2001). Participants were 224 adolescents aged 15–17 years (142 girls, 82 boys) who formed 112 unique same-sex best friend dyads. Significant actor and partner effects were found for both self-ratings and peer nominations of social behaviour and the five friendship qualities. Aggression was associated with self and partner perceptions of friendship conflict and low positive friendship qualities. Prosocial behaviour was associated with self and partner perceptions of positive friendship qualities and low conflict. The findings of this study were mostly consistent between male and female dyads. The importance of examining dependence due to dyads in peer relations research was discussed.

Researchers traditionally distinguish three levels of analysis in the study of peer relations in development: individual, dyad, and group (Rubin, Bukowski, & Parker, 1998). Important substantive phenomena have been investigated at each of these levels, resulting in a large body of knowledge on the developmental significance of peer relations. Methodologically and statistically, the study of dyads and groups must be considered separately from the study of individuals. In the past, however, peer relations researchers have often ignored the statistical dependence due to dyads and groups when analysing peer relations data. For example, in the majority of observational studies of peer group behaviour from the 1980s (see Rubin et al., 1998, for a review), the individual child was typically treated as the unit of analysis, and the effects of groups were not examined.

For data collected in dyads, similar dependencies exist. For example, in marital relations research, individuals are nested within couples that differ in their average levels of relationship satisfaction or conflict (Kashy & Kenny, 2000). While statistical solutions for group research have existed for some time (Kashy & Kenny, 2000), similar solutions for dyadic research are relatively new. The study of adolescent friendships is an area that may benefit from these new approaches. In the current study, we used the Actor-Partner Interdependence Model (APIM, Kashy & Kenny, 2000; Kenny & Acitelli, 2001; Kenny, Mannetti, Pierro, Livi, & Kashy, 2002) to study the predictors of dyadic friendship quality in adolescence.

Dyadic relationships such as friendships and enmities make unique contributions to social development over and beyond the effects of group status (Hartup & Abecassis, 2002). Hartup (1996) distinguished three aspects to the developmental significance of friendships: having friends, the identity of one's friends, and the quality of the friendships. Berndt (2002) argued that friendship quality is particularly important and that high-quality friendships contribute positively to developmental processes and outcomes even after individual characteristics are controlled. High-quality friendships may enhance self-esteem, adjustment, and the ability to cope with stress (Hartup & Stevens, 1999). The quality of a friendship may also moderate the influence of the friend, with positive or negative results. For example, a high-quality friendship with a delinquent peer may increase a child's own delinquency (Berndt, 2002).

Much is known about the predictors of having friends and the identity of one's friends. Previous research has shown that measures of social competence, prosocial behaviour, and liking predict having friends (Berndt, 2002), although this does not mean that individuals who score low on these characteristics are necessarily friendless (Hartup, 1996). Behavioural similarity is also an important predictor of the identity of one's friends. For example, Haselager, Hartup, Van Lieshout, and Riksen-Walraven (1998) have shown that friends are likely to be similar to one another in traits and behaviours. Although researchers have argued for the importance and consequences of friendship quality, less is known about the predictors of friendship quality. The goal of the current paper is to make a contribution to the friendship literature by examining how individual social behaviours may contribute to the quality of adolescent friendships.

How may individual social behaviours influence friendship quality? Research on interpersonal perception in nonoverlapping groups suggests that individuals behave similarly with different others (Malloy, Albright, Kenny, Agatstein, & Winquist, 1997). Based on the consistency of behaviour across contexts, we expected that adolescents who are prosocial and cooperative with peers in general behave similarly with their

---

Correspondence should be addressed to Antonius H. N. Cillessen, Department of Psychology, University of Connecticut, 406 Babbidge Rd., Unit 1020, Storrs, CT 06269-1020, USA; e-mail: antonius. cillessen@uconn.edu.

This research was supported by a grant from the University of Connecticut Research Foundation to the first author. The authors are grateful to the children, parents, teachers, and school administrators who participated in this study.

friends and therefore have high-quality friendships. Conversely, adolescents who are generally aggressive with others may also be aggressive with their friends, and therefore have friendships that are qualitatively more negative. We expect that prosocial adolescents have friendships that are rated high in quality by themselves and by their partners. We expect that aggressive adolescents have friendships that are rated low in quality by themselves and their friends (Dishion, Andrews, & Crosby, 1995).

When examining the association between friendship quality and aggression, forms of aggression should be considered, in particular physical and relational aggression (see, e.g., Crick & Grotpeter, 1995). While physical aggression consists of direct physical attacks against another person, relational aggression is defined as deliberate attempts to harm or hurt someone else through relationship manipulation (e.g., deliberately excluding someone from a group).

Different hypotheses are possible for the effects of physical and relational aggression on friendship quality. Physically aggressive adolescents may have poor relationships with everyone, including their friends. However, relational aggression is associated with certain positive outcomes such as perceived popularity and social prominence in adolescence (Cillessen & Mayeux, 2004). One way in which relational aggression may increase social prominence is through its effect on dyadic relationships. If two friends are relationally aggressive against a third person, their coalition may be strengthened (Grotpeter & Crick, 1996).

Thus, in contrast to the hypothesis for physical aggression, relationally aggressive friends may perceive their friendships as higher in quality rather than lower. This effect may not apply equally to all friendship qualities. For example, while relational aggression may strengthen the coalition between two friends, it may not necessarily increase their level of closeness or intimacy, if the partners believe that they themselves may also become the target of the other person's aggression. In this case, the relationship may actually suffer on the dimension of trust.

Positive associations between relational aggression and dyadic friendship qualities may explain why relational aggression is sometimes associated with high social prominence (Cillessen & Mayeux, 2004). Perhaps relationally aggressive adolescents build strong dyadic relationships and alliances with each other. Those alliances may then become the building blocks for high status in the peer group at large. Thus, high-quality dyadic relationships may mediate the empirically demonstrated connection between relational aggression and social prominence.

Several measures exist that assess overlapping as well as unique domains of friendship quality and that vary in the age group for which they are intended (Berndt & Perry, 1986; Bukowski, Hoza, & Boivin, 1994; Furman & Adler, 1982; Furman & Buhrmester, 1985; Parker & Asher, 1993; Sharabany, Gershoni, & Hofman, 1981). In the present study, we used the Friendship Qualities Scale (Bukowski et al., 1994) which assesses five dimensions of friendship considered important in adolescence (Bukowski et al., 1994): conflict, closeness, companionship, security, and helping.

The goal of this study, then, was to predict adolescents' friendship quality in terms of these five dimensions from measures of physical aggression, relational aggression, and prosocial behaviour. By examining the association between individual behaviours and dyadic friendship qualities, this study may make a contribution to our understanding of the predictors of friendship quality, which has been examined only infrequently in the peer relations literature. We used the analytic framework of the APIM to address this research question.

Kenny and colleagues (Kashy & Kenny, 2000; Kenny et al., 2002) designed the Actor Partner Interdependence Model (APIM) for the analysis of dyadic data. APIM models can be estimated with SEM programs or with mixed-level models in SAS or SPSS. The APIM estimates two types of effects: the effect of each individual's behaviour on their own rating of the relationship ("actor coefficient"), and the effect of the individual's behaviour on their partner's rating of the relationship ("partner coefficient"). The model simultaneously estimates four paths: each member of the dyad has an actor path and a partner path. In Figure 1, the two actor paths are the horizontal paths labelled a, and the two partner paths are the diagonal paths labelled p.

The actor effect is the effect of an actor's behaviour on the actor's view of the relationship. For example, aggressive adolescents may rate their friendships as high in conflict, perhaps reflecting hostile attribution biases. The partner effect refers to the effect of an actor's behaviour on the partner's view of the relationship. For example, aggressive adolescents may have friends who rate their friendship as high in conflict, which may accurately reflect the actor's general aggressive tendencies. It does not matter in this context whether the actors' behaviour is assessed via self-, teacher, peer, or observer reports. The logic is identical in each case.

Thus, the goal of this study was to predict friendship quality (closeness, companionship, conflict, helping, and security) from social behaviour (physical aggression, relational aggression, and prosocial behaviour) using the analytic framework of the APIM. Data were collected in adolescence, during which friendships and friendship quality are particularly important (Bukowski et al., 1994). The data were derived from an ongoing study in which adolescents named their best friends and rated the quality of their relationship. Both self- and peer-report measures of the predictors were available. Since gender

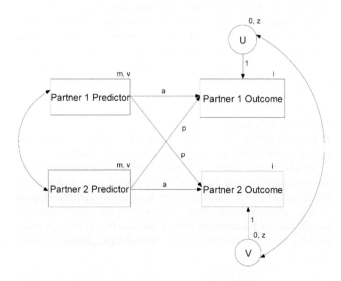

Figure 1. The Actor-Partner Interdependence Model (Kenny & Acitelli, 2001): a = actor effect; p = partner effect; m = predictor mean; v = predictor variance; i = outcome intercept (mean); U and V = outcome disturbances; z = disturbance variance.

may play a role in the associations of interest in this study, gender differences were explored in all analyses.

Method

Participants and design

Participants were 224 adolescents aged 15 to 17 years in a public high school in the Northeastern United States, selected from 797 students from 9th to 11th grade participating in a larger study on the social and academic development of youth. Participants in the larger study were recruited via a letter addressed to them and their parents that was sent to all students in their grade. Only students who obtained permission participated in the larger study. The sample of the current study was selected from the larger sample based on two criteria presented below. Participants were predominantly European American as indicated by self-reports of ethnicity and from lower to lower middle-class SES backgrounds as indicated by school records.

The 224 selected participants formed 112 friendship dyads (71 female and 41 male). Eleven mixed-sex dyads were identified but this number was too small for inclusion in the analyses. The selection criteria were: (1) dyad members named each other reciprocally as the one best friend for whom they completed a friendship qualities scale; (2) they also named each other as best friend on a separate sociometric measure. Because the sociometric measure was unlimited with grade as the reference group, 95% of the larger sample named more than one best friend on this measure (Criterion 2). However, because the friendship quality measure could be completed for only one best friend, the number of possible matches for Criterion 1 was restricted to 0 or 1. As a result, all 112 dyads that were identified by combining both criteria were unique, that is, no member of any dyad was also a member of another dyad.

The data for this study were collected in one 90-min class period at school in the spring of the school year. Participants first completed the sociometric measure that began with the best friend nomination question followed by a set of additional items, including peer nominations of physical aggression, relational aggression, and prosocial behaviour from which the peer reports of these behaviours were derived (see below). Following the sociometric instrument students completed a self-report measure that included the friendship qualities scale. The self-report measure also included ratings of physical aggression, relational aggression, and prosocial behaviour, from which the self-report scores for these behaviours were derived (see below).

Measures

Identification of best friendships. Best friendships were identified with two questions. First, before completing the FQS, participants indicated who their best friend was for whom they were going to complete the measure. Best friends were identified with a code number derived from a roster with names of all peers in the participants' grade. To corroborate the reciprocity of these friendships, best friend choices were examined that had been collected earlier in the testing session as part of a larger sociometric instrument. The sociometric instrument included 20 items in which participants were asked to name peers for a variety of criteria. Nominations were unlimited and across participants' entire grade. The best friend question was the first question on the sociometric measure. Participants were first asked to name all their best friends in their grade, and then ranked their top five choices. Members of the 112 dyads had all named each other within their list of top five best friends, thus validating the operationalisation of friendships in this study.

Friendship quality. Participants completed the Friendship Qualities Scale (FQS, Bukowski et al., 1994), a 23-item self-report measure with the following five subscales: conflict (4 items, $\alpha = .76$), closeness (5 items, $\alpha = .91$), companionship (4 items, $\alpha = .69$), receiving help (5 items, $\alpha = .80$), and security (5 items, $\alpha = .71$). Example items are: "My friend and I argue a lot" (conflict), "If my friend had to move away, I would miss him/her" (closeness), "My friend and I spend all our free time together" (companionship), "My friend helps me when I am having trouble with something" (receiving help), and "If there is something bothering me, I can tell my friend about it" (security). Participants rated on a 7-point scale (1 = *not true*, 7 = *really true*) how true each statement was for their best friendship.

Self-reports of social behaviour. Participants rated how frequently they engaged in two forms of aggression and prosocial behaviour on a 5-point scale (1 = *never*, 5 = *a few times a week*) using items from the Peer Experiences Questionnaire (PEQ, Prinstein, Boergers, & Vernberg, 2001; Vernberg, Jacobs, & Hershberger, 1999). Example items are: "I threatened to hurt another student" (physical aggression, 4 items, $\alpha = .86$), "I tried to damage another student's social reputation by spreading rumors about them" (relational aggression, 9 items, $\alpha = .87$), and "I helped another student when they were having a problem" (prosocial, 5 items, $\alpha = .83$).

Peer reports of social behaviour. Unlimited peer nominations were used within the entire grade, allowing both same- and cross-sex nominations. Three sociometric questions were used to assess *physical aggression* ("the people in your grade who start fights, say mean things, and tease others"), *relational aggression* ("the people who ignore others, spread rumors, and exclude other people in order to get their way"), and *prosocial behaviour* ("the people who cooperate, share, and help others"). Nominations received were counted and standardised within grade.

Results

Analysis strategy

The estimation of APIM was conducted using structural equation modelling. Figure 1 presents the model that estimates the effects. In APIM, paths are estimated with dyad as the unit of analysis. Because the dyads in this study consisted of either two females or two males, there is no role distinction between dyad members (as opposed to distinguishable dyads such as married couples). The estimation of actor and partner effects for indistinguishable dyads in SEM requires that the following parameters are set equal for both members of the dyad: the variance and mean for the predictor variables, the actor paths, partner paths, intercepts, and the mean and variance of the disturbances. These constraints are indicated in Figure 1. Olsen (2004, personal communication) first proposed this extension of Kenny and Acitelli's (2001) SEM model for APIM with distinguishable dyads to the case of indistinguishable dyads.

Separate analyses were conducted for all combinations of predictor variables (physical aggression, relational aggression, and prosocial behaviour, according to self and peers) and outcome variables (closeness, conflict, receiving help, security, and companionship). These analyses were conducted in AMOS 5.0 (structural equation modelling program), but the identical results can be obtained in SPSS 12.0 or SAS 9.0 using a linear mixed model. For each predictor–outcome combination, the analysis was conducted in three steps. First, we ran a two-group model in which all parameters were allowed to vary between gender (fully unconstrained model, $df = 14$). Second, to test whether actor or partner effects were moderated by gender, we ran the same two-group model in which the actor and partner paths were forced to be equal between gender (constrained model, $df = 12$). Third, we conducted a χ^2 difference test ($df = 2$) between the constrained and unconstrained models. If the fit of the constrained model was not significantly worse than the unconstrained model, there was no evidence for moderation by gender for either actor or partner effects. If the model fit was significantly worse, follow-up tests were conducted to determine whether moderation was due to actor, partner, or both.

Intercorrelations between main study variables

Table 1 shows the zero-order correlations between the main study variables, computed with individual as the unit of analysis. Because these correlations are inflated due to dependency, they are presented for comparison purposes only. The results are interpreted below, and should be compared to the exogenous correlations that follow.

As can be seen in Table 1, physical and relational aggression were positively correlated both according to self ($r = .69$) and peers ($r = .61$). The two types of aggression were not significantly correlated with prosocial behaviour for either self or peer measures. There was agreement between self and peer measures of physical aggression ($r = .25$) and prosocial behaviour ($r = .19$), but not for relational aggression. Physical

aggression and prosocial behaviour were negatively correlated across methods ($rs = -.21$ and $-.16$, respectively).

The positive friendship qualities closeness, companionship, helping, and security correlated positively with one another ($.57 < r < .76$), and negatively with conflict ($-.34 < r < -.18$). The correlations of these five friendship qualities with behaviour self-ratings followed a clear pattern. Friendship conflict was positively correlated with self-ratings of physical and relational aggression. The four positive friendship qualities were positively correlated with self-ratings of prosocial behaviour, and significantly and negatively correlated with self-ratings of physical and relational aggression, with one exception (companionship and physical aggression).

There were fewer significant correlations between friendship qualities and peer nominations of behaviour. Closeness and helping were negatively correlated with physical aggression. All four positive friendship qualities were significantly and positively correlated with peer nominations of prosocial behaviour.

The correlations of Table 1 were also computed for boys and girls separately, and tested for significance between gender using Fisher's r-to-Z transformations. Only 3 of the 55 comparisons were significant, and in only 1 of the 3 cases was one of the two correlations involved significantly different from zero. The correlation between self- and peer reports of relational aggression was significantly larger for girls ($r = .25$, $p = .003$) than for boys ($r = -.04$, $p > .05$), $Z = 2.047$, $p = .020$. It is interesting that there was larger cross-method consistency for relational aggression for girls than for boys.

Assessment of dyadic dependence

To assess the degree of dependence due to dyads, two methods were followed. First, we computed for each variable the intraclass correlation (ICC) that expresses the degree of dyadic dependence in a variable (Kashy & Kenny, 2000). An ICC close to zero indicates the absence of dyadic dependence, a positive ICC means positive dependence or similarity within dyads, and a negative ICC means negative dependence or dissimilarity within dyads. All ICCs were different from zero with large effect sizes (range .59–.82, $M = .68$, see Table 2). Because the ICC for any variable is computed by dividing the between-dyad variance by the total variance, it can also be interpreted as the proportion of variance due to dyads. Thus,

Table 1

Intercorrelations between main study variables (n = 224 participants)

	2.	3.	4.	5.	6.	7.	8.	9.	10.	11.
1. Physical ag. (self)	.69*	.03	.25*	.06	−.21*	.27*	−.22*	−.09	−.20*	−.19*
2. Relational ag. (self)		.10	.12	.13	−.11	.29*	−.25*	−.15*	−.28*	−.19*
3. Prosocial (self)			−.16*	.02	.19*	−.10	.42*	.30*	.33*	.44*
4. Physical ag. (peer)				.61*	−.12	−.01	−.22*	−.05	−.14*	−.13
5. Relational ag. (peer)					−.01	.01	.03	.11	.10	.05
6. Prosocial (peer)						−.06	.15*	.16*	.17*	.15*
7. Conflict							−.34*	−.18*	−.25*	−.29*
8. Closeness								.58*	.75*	.74*
9. Companionship									.57*	.61*
10. Helping										.76*
11. Security										

* $p < .05$.

Table 2

Intraclass correlations for main study variables (k = 112 dyads)

	ICC
1. Physical aggression (self)	.67★
2. Relational aggression (self)	.63★
3. Prosocial (self)	.64★
4. Physical aggression (peer)	.62★
5. Relational aggression (peer)	.59★
6. Prosocial (peer)	.73★
7. Conflict	.59★
8. Closeness	.82★
9. Companionship	.66★
10. Helping	.74★
11. Security	.75★

★ $p < .05$.

68% of the variance in our study variables was due to dyads (range 59% to 82%), further emphasising the importance of considering the effect of dyads in the analyses. The ICCs were also computed by gender and compared (see Donner & Bull, 1983). There were no significant gender differences.

In addition to the ICC, a separate estimate of the similarity between dyad partners is provided by the correlation between the two exogenous variables in the APIM model (the curved line on the left in Figure 1). These are presented in the first column of Table 3. APIM does not estimate a similar correlation for the dependent variables (see Figure 1), only the correlation between their disturbances, which are of lesser interest. As can be seen, five of the six exogenous correlations were significant indicating similarity between friends on these variables. The exogenous correlations were also compared by gender. No significant gender differences were found. (The test for moderation by gender in APIM is described below.)

Effects of social behaviour on dyadic friendship quality

For the 30 models, the initial test for gender differences yielded no evidence for moderation by gender except in two cases. Because of the general absence of gender differences, we first present the results of all APIM model tests in the total sample of 112 dyads. The parameter estimates for all models in the total sample are presented in Table 3. Follow-up tests for the

two cases where moderation occurred are presented at the end of this section.

Model fit was excellent for all 30 models in the total sample, with $\chi^2(12)$ ranging from 1.7 to 13.9, all $ps > .307$. As can be seen in Table 3, there were significant actor effects of self-reported physical and relational aggression on conflict. Adolescents who rated themselves as more aggressive (both physically and relationally) rated their dyadic friendships higher on conflict. Adolescents who rated themselves as more physically aggressive also rated their friendships as lower in closeness, helping, and security. Adolescents who rated themselves as more relationally aggressive rated their friendships lower on all four positive friendship qualities (closeness, companionship, helping, and security). Conversely, adolescents who rated themselves as more prosocial rated their friendships higher on all four positive friendship qualities.

Significant partner effects were found for self-ratings of physical aggression and prosocial behaviour. Participants who rated themselves as physically aggressive had friends who rated their relationship low in closeness, helping, and security. Participants who rated themselves as prosocial had friends who rated their relationship high on closeness, helping, and security. No significant partner effects were found for self-ratings of relational aggression.

For the peer-based measures, significant actor and partner effects were found for physical aggression. Adolescents who were physically aggressive according to peers rated their friendships low on closeness, and had friends who rated their relationship high on conflict. Adolescents who were seen as prosocial by their peers rated their friendships high on companionship and helping, and had friends who rated their relationship low on conflict and high on closeness. No significant effects were found for relational aggression.

For two models, there was significant moderation by gender. For the association between self-rated prosocial behaviour and security, the χ^2 difference test was significant, $\chi^2(2) = 6.8$, $p = .033$. Follow-up test indicated that model fit significantly worsened if the actor effect was constrained between genders, $\chi^2(1) = 5.6$, $p = .018$, but not when the partner effect was constrained, $\chi^2(1) = 0.1$, $p = .752$. Thus, moderation was due to gender differences for the actor effect. The actor effects were .19 ($p < .05$) for girls and .38 ($p < .05$) for boys. Thus, for both genders self-ratings of prosocial behaviour positively predicted self-ratings of friendship

Table 3

Estimates of exogenous correlations and actor and partner effects for the prediction of five friendship qualities from physical aggression, relational aggression, and prosocial behaviour according to self and peers

	r	Conflict		Closeness		Companionship		Helping		Security	
		Actor	Partner	Actor	Partner	Actor	Partner	Actor	Partner	Actor	Partner
Self-report											
Physical	.36★	.26★	.06	−.19★	−.16★	−.05	−.12	−.13★	−.19★	−.14★	−.15★
Relational	.26★	.27★	.09	−.24★	−.09	−.14★	−.02	−.25★	−.10	−.16★	−.12
Prosocial	.30★	−.06	−.16★	.38★	.23★	.30★	.02	.28★	.18★	.40★	.14★
Peer report											
Physical	.24★	−.06	.22★	−.18★	−.15	−.02	−.12	−.12	−.09	−.11	−.10
Relational	.18	−.02	.07	.03	−.02	.11	−.01	.10	−.04	.05	.02
Prosocial	.46★	.03	−.20★	.08	.14★	.14★	.06	.13★	.08	.10	.12

★ $p < .05$.

security, but this effect was significantly stronger (and twice as strong) for boys as it was for girls.

For the association between peer-nominated relational aggression and conflict, the χ^2 difference test was significant, $\chi^2(2) = 8.3$, $p = .016$. Follow-up test again indicated that moderation was due to the actor effect, $\chi^2(1) = 7.4$, $p = .007$, and not the partner effect, $\chi^2(1) = 0.7$, $p = .403$. The actor effects for boys and girls separately were .12 ($p > .05$) for girls and $-.25$ ($p < .05$) for boys. For boys, relational aggression negatively predicted self-ratings of friendship conflict. For girls, however, relational aggression did not predict ratings of friendship conflict.

Discussion

The goal of this study was to expand existing knowledge of adolescent friendships by examining predictors of friendship quality. While researchers have argued for the importance of friendship quality (see, e.g., Berndt, 2002), relatively little is known about the variables that predict high or low friendship quality in this age group. Specifically, we examined the predictive effects of physical aggression, relational aggression, and prosocial behaviour on conflict, closeness, companionship, helping, and security. Collins (2002) argued that the dyad is an essential unit of analysis in modern social development research. Consistent with this trend, we used the Actor-Partner Independence Model (Kenny & Acitelli, 2001) as our analytic framework.

Correlational analyses among the variables of this study indicated that physical and relational aggression were positively correlated, but independent from, prosocial behaviour. The correlations between peer and self evaluations of the three behaviours ranged from .13 to .25, indicating modest agreement. The correlation for relational aggression (.13) did not reach significance. There are three possible reasons for this modest agreement between peer and self constructs. First, the wording of the questions in both cases was not identical (see Method). Second, self-perceptions are subject to biases that do not influence peer evaluations. For example, individuals are less likely to rate themselves as aggressive than their peers are. Third, peer evaluations are aggregated across multiple informants reflecting the perspective of the peer group at large, whereas self-ratings only reflect the target person's own perspective. For these reasons, it makes sense to analyse the contributions of peer and self-perceptions separately.

Moreover, examining scores derived from peer nominations in APIM makes a new contribution to the use of this analytic model. Typically, on the predictor side are variables that measure self-perceptions. In this case, the APIM tests how individuals' own perceptions (e.g., perceptions of conflict) are related to ratings of the relationship by self and partner (e.g., satisfaction). In the current study, we have added peer-based variables to the predictor side, allowing us to examine the associations between how individuals are seen by their peers and their own and their partners' views of the relationship. This application may be of use in other dyadic studies in the peer relations domain where peer nomination variables are available and their predictive effects are of interest.

The initial correlations validated the structure of the Friendship Qualities Scale as consisting of a negative conflict dimension and four nonoverlapping positive dimensions that measure separate domains of adolescent friendship. The friendship qualities correlated quite consistently with the behaviour self-ratings. Positive correlations were found between self-perceived physical and relational aggression and friendship conflict, and between self-perceived prosocial behaviour and the four positive friendship qualities. Negative correlations were found between self-perceived physical and relational aggression and the four positive qualities. This pattern of results validated the questions of the Peer Experiences Questionnaire, from which the self-report scores were derived.

The correlations between peer measures of prosocial behaviour and positive friendship qualities confirmed what was found for the self measures, although the effects were smaller in size, possibly due to the above-mentioned reasons. As for the self measures, peer nominations of physical aggression correlated negatively with closeness and receiving help. Thus, across the two sources of information, consistent evidence was found that individual tendencies to be prosocial are associated with positive friendship qualities, whereas individual tendencies to be antisocial (physically aggressive) are correlated negatively with the same positive friendship qualities. These findings confirm at the correlational level the cross-contextual consistency between individual behaviours and dimensions of friendship quality.

Unlike the findings for self-ratings, peer nominations of physical aggression did not correlate with measures of friendship conflict. Adolescents who were seen as physically aggressive by the peer group at large did not necessarily report more conflict in their friendships. This fits with the idea that adolescents who have an aggressive reputation and may be rejected and/or disliked in the peer group at large may still have good-quality friendships. Although their friendships were lower in closeness and receiving help, other dimensions were not affected.

Interestingly, peer nominations of relational aggression did not correlate with any of the friendship qualities whereas self-ratings correlated with all of them. One possible explanation for this finding is that it is entirely due to the lack of shared variance between peer nominations and friendship quality ratings. If this were the case, however, other significant correlations such as those for prosocial behaviour would not have emerged either. Thus, there may also be substantive reasons for the lack of association. Relational aggression may function as a double-edged sword. While relationally aggressive behaviour is clearly disliked by peers, it can function at the same time to forge coalitions and alliances with others, which may lead to greater social network centrality, especially for girls (Cillessen & Mayeux, 2004). Thus, positive and negative correlations may cancel each other out, yielding zero-level correlations. The current findings suggest that the Janusian nature of relational aggression is also reflected at the dyadic level.

The intraclass correlations indicated that two thirds of the variance in the study variables was dyadic. Estimates of the exogenous associations indicated dyadic similarity for the independent variables. Thus, friends in general were similar to one another in self-reported physical aggression, relational aggression, and prosocial behaviour, and peer-reported physical aggression and prosocial behaviour. These findings confirm the well-established similarity-friendship hypothesis (e.g., Haselager et al., 1998). The consistent findings for physical aggression confirm the homophily hypothesis (Cairns, Cairns,

Neckerman, Gest, & Gariépy, 1988); that aggressive adolescents gravitate towards one another and begin to form deviant social networks. Interestingly, our results did not confirm these hypotheses for one of the relational aggression variables. Thus, while friendship dyads may be similar in physical aggression and prosocial behaviour, they are less likely to be symmetrical in terms of relational aggression.

Comparison of the APIM estimates in Table 3 with the zero-order correlations in Table 1 shows similar findings, but more attenuated and conservative effect sizes for APIM results than for individual level correlations. Together, these findings highlight the importance of taking the dyad into account when conducting dyadic research, and illustrate the amount of bias that may exist in the results when the dyadic level is not accounted for. Future research on dyads in the peer relations field needs to build in controls such as those provided by the APIM, in the same way that the group level of analysis needs to be controlled for in studies of groups with models such as the SRM (Kenny, 1994) or other multilevel models. At a minimum, researchers need to estimate the degree of dependence due to dyads or groups, as illustrated in this paper with the ICC. (See Green, Cillessen, Berthelsen, Irving, & Catherwood, 2003, for an example of using the ICC for behaviour in small groups.)

The main results of the present study are the significant actor and partner effects between social behaviours and friendship qualities. Adolescents who saw themselves as physically aggressive perceived their friendships as high in conflict. These adolescents themselves and their friends perceived their relationship as low in closeness, receiving help, and security. Adolescents who were physically aggressive according to their peers saw their friendships as low in closeness and had partners who rated their friendship high on conflict.

Adolescents who rated themselves as relationally aggressive perceived their friendships as high in conflict, and low on each positive friendship quality. Interestingly, the friends of these relationally aggressive adolescents did not confirm any of these negative relationship perceptions. Being perceived as relationally aggressive by one's peers also had no implications for perceived friendship quality by either member of the friendship dyad.

Adolescents who saw themselves as prosocial had friends who rated their relationship low in conflict. These adolescents themselves and their friends rated their friendship high on all four positive friendship qualities with one exception. The partners did not necessarily see the friendship as high in companionship. Adolescents who were prosocial according to peers rated their friendships high on companionship and helping, and their friends rated their relationships as low in conflict and high on closeness.

Together, these findings indicate that there is a substantial degree of consistency between individual behaviour tendencies, whether self-rated or determined by peers, and friendship quality as seen by both members of the dyad. These findings therefore confirm earlier findings of the cross-contextual consistency of behaviour (Malloy et al., 1997) and suggest that this consistency also extends itself to the domain of friendships in general and friendship quality specifically. The findings also suggest that behaviours and friendship quality are not entirely orthogonal. It has been suggested (Parker & Asher, 1993; Renshaw & Brown, 1993) that friendships may form a buffer against the negative consequences of rejected status in

the peer group. The current findings suggest that this may not be the case for students who are rejected and aggressive. Their friendships may not be optimal in quality, thus reducing the possibility that they can override the negative effects of poor status in the peer group at large.

Remarkably few gender differences were found in this general pattern of results. Only two gender differences emerged. Adolescents who saw themselves as prosocial rated their friendships positively on security, and this effect was stronger for boys than for girls. One possible interpretation of this finding may be that friendship security for girls is more dependent on other relationship characteristics, rather than just being prosocial. Boys who were relationally aggressive according to peers rated their friendships low in conflict, but for girls being seen as relationally aggressive was again not related to friendship quality. This finding may suggest that the meaning of relational aggression is different for boys than for girls, and that perhaps relational aggression in adolescent males is seen more as playful or teasing rather than mean behaviour. Such an interpretation, however, is speculative in the absence of a more consistent pattern of gender differences for this behaviour.

It is interesting that it was more difficult to identify dyads of adolescent boys than girls that met the criteria for study inclusion, to a ratio of almost 2 to 1 in favour of girls, even though the proportion of boys and girls in the study at large was about equal. Assuming that meeting the criteria for inclusion (reciprocal nominations on two best friend peer nominations) is an indication of stability or cohesion of a friendship relationship, this finding could suggest that there were fewer stable or cohesive best friend relations among adolescent boys in this study than among girls. Alternatively, the differential rate of meeting the best friend criteria may be due to the fact that girls are more exclusive in their friendships than boys are (Eder & Hallinan, 1978). It is also possible that the differential rate of identified friends is a methodological artifact of the questions that were asked. Perhaps a larger number of male dyads would be found if the criteria were relaxed or changed. It is possible, for example, that adolescent males are more likely to think of best friends as people they "hang around with", and that the use of such criteria for adolescent males might reveal frequencies of reciprocal dyads that are similar to those for girls based on the "best friend" question.

The current study relied on self-report measures of friendship quality and self- and peer-report measures of aggression. Observational data of friends' actual interactions with one another would provide an important way to extend this research. Important examples exist of observational research on friendship dyads, and the study of friendship quality would benefit from determining observationally which aspect of dyadic interaction might yield reliable actor and partner effects for the prediction of friendship quality.

The current study considered gender as a between-dyad variable. Given the importance of gender differences in social developmental research, the consideration of gender makes sense. However, other between-dyad factors are worthy of consideration in future research. Friendship dyads may differ in cohesiveness, degree of behavioural similarity, and ethnic composition, for example. Age and developmental differences may be considered as well. Variables such as these, considered either categorically or continuously, may serve as important moderators of the associations between individual social behaviours and friendship quality, and are important to be considered in future research.

References

Agnew, R. (1991). The interactive effects of peer variables on delinquency. *Criminology*, 29, 47–72.

Asher, S. R., & Parker, J. G. (1989). Significance of peer relationship problems in childhood. In B. H. Schneider, G. Attili, J. Nadel, & R. P. Weissberg (Eds.), *Social competence in developmental perspective* (pp. 5–23). Boston: Kluwer Academic.

Berndt, T. J. (2002). Friendship quality and social development. *Current Directions in Psychological Science*, 11, 7–10.

Berndt, T. J., & Perry, T. B. (1986). Children's perceptions of friendship as supportive relationships. *Developmental Psychology*, 22, 640–648.

Bukowski, W. M., Hoza, B., & Boivin, M. (1994). Measuring friendship quality during pre- and early adolescence: The development and psychometric properties of the Friendship Qualities Scale. *Journal of Social and Personal Relationships*, 11, 471–784.

Cairns, R. B., Cairns, B. D., Neckerman, H. J., Gest, S. D., & Gariépy, J. (1988). Social networks and aggressive behavior: Peer support or peer rejection. *Developmental Psychology*, 24, 815–823.

Cillessen, A. H. N., & Mayeux, L. (2004). From censure to reinforcement: Developmental changes in the association between aggression and social status. *Child Development*, 75, 147–163.

Coie, J. D., Cillessen, A. H. N., Dodge, K. A., Hubbard, J. A., Schwartz, D., Lemerise, E. D., & Bateman, H. (1999). It takes two to fight: A test of relational factors and a method for assessing aggressive dyads. *Developmental Psychology*, 35, 1179–1188.

Collins, W. A. (2002). Historical perspectives on contemporary research in social development. In P. K. Smith & C. H. Hart (Eds.), *Blackwell handbook of childhood social development* (pp. 3–23). Malden, MA: Blackwell.

Crick, N. R., & Grotpeter, J. K. (1995). Relational aggression, gender, and social-psychological adjustment. *Child Development*, 66, 710–722.

Dishion, T. J., Andrews, D. W., & Crosby, L. (1995). Antisocial boys and their friends in early adolescence: Relationship characteristics, quality, and interactional process. *Child Development*, 66, 139–151.

Donner, A., & Bull, S. (1983). Inferences concerning a common intraclass correlation coefficient. *Biometrics*, 39, 771–775.

Eder, D., & Hallinan, M. T. (1978). Sex differences in children's friendships. *American Sociological Review*, 43, 237–250.

Erwin, P. (1993). *Friendship and peer relations in children*. Manchester, UK: Wiley.

Furman, W., & Adler, T. (1982). *The Friendship Questionnaire*. Unpublished manuscript, University of Denver.

Furman, W., & Buhrmester, D. (1985). Children's perceptions of the personal relationships in their social networks. *Developmental Psychology*, 21, 1016–1024.

Green, V. A., Cillessen, A. H. N., Berthelsen, D., Irving, K., & Catherwood, D. (2003). The effect of gender context on children's social behavior in a limited resource situation: An observational study. *Social Development*, 12, 586–604.

Grotpeter, J. K., & Crick, N. R. (1996). Relational aggression, overt aggression, and friendship. *Child Development*, 67, 2328–2338.

Hartup, W. W. (1996). The company they keep: Friendships and their developmental significance. *Child Development*, 67, 1–13.

Hartup, W. W., & Abecassis, M. (2002). Friends and enemies. In P. K. Smith & C. H. Hart (Eds.), *Blackwell handbook of childhood social development* (pp. 285–306). Malden, MA: Blackwell.

Hartup, W. W., & Stevens, N. (1999). Friendships and adaptation in the life course. *Psychological Bulletin*, 121, 355–370.

Haselager, G. J. T., Hartup, W. W., Van Lieshout, C. F. M., & Riksen-Walraven, J. M. A. (1998). Similarities between friends and nonfriends in middle childhood. *Child Development*, 69, 1198–1208.

Hubbard, J. A., Dodge, K. A., Cillessen, A. H. N., Coie, J. D., & Schwartz, D. (2001). The dyadic nature of social information processing in boys' reactive and proactive aggression. *Journal of Personality and Social Psychology*, 80, 268–280.

Kashy, D. A., & Kenny, D. A. (2000). The analysis of data from dyads and groups. In H. T. Reis & C. M. Judd (Eds.), *Handbook of research methods in social and personality psychology* (pp. 451–477). New York: Cambridge University Press.

Kenny, D. A. (1994). *Interpersonal perception. A social relations analysis*. New York: Guilford Press.

Kenny, D. A., & Acitelli, L. K. (2001). Accuracy and bias in the perception of the partner in a close relationship. *Journal of Personality and Social Psychology*, 80, 439–448.

Kenny, D. A., Mannetti, L., Pierro, A., Livi, S., & Kashy, D. A. (2002). The statistical analysis of data from small groups. *Journal of Personality and Social Psychology*, 83, 126–137.

Malloy, T. E., Albright, L., Kenny, D. A., Agatstein, F., & Winquist, L. (1997). Interpersonal perception and meta-perception in non-overlapping social groups. *Journal of Personality and Social Psychology*, 72, 390–398.

Parker, J. G., & Asher, S. R. (1993). Friendship and friendship quality in middle childhood: Links with peer group acceptance and feelings of loneliness and social dissatisfaction. *Developmental Psychology*, 29, 611–621.

Prinstein, M. J., Boergers, J., & Vernberg, E. M. (2001). Overt and relational aggression in adolescents: Social-psychological adjustment of aggressors and victims. *Journal of Clinical Child Psychology*, 30, 479–491.

Renshaw, P. D., & Brown, P. J. (1993). Loneliness in middle childhood: Concurrent and longitudinal predictors. *Child Development*, 64, 1271–1284.

Rubin, K. H., Bukowski, W. M., & Parker, J. G. (1998). Peer interactions, relationships, and groups. In W. Damon (Series Ed.) & N. Eisenberg (Vol. Ed.). *Handbook of child psychology: Vol. 3. Social, emotional and personality development* (5th ed., pp. 619–700). New York: Wiley.

Sharabany, R., Gershoni, R., & Hofman, J. E. (1981). Girlfriend, boyfriend: Age and sex differences in intimate friendship. *Developmental Psychology*, 17, 800–808.

Vernberg, E. M., Jacobs, A. K., & Hershberger, S. L. (1999). Peer victimization and attitudes about violence during early adolescence. *Journal of Clinical Child Psychology*, 28, 386–395.

Wright, J. C., Giammarino, M., & Parad, H. W. (1986). Social status in small groups: Individual-group similarity and the social "misfit." *Journal of Personality and Social Psychology*, 50, 523–536.

Zakriski, A. L., & Coie, J. D. (1996). A comparison of aggressive-rejected versus nonaggressive-rejected children's interpretation of self-directed and other-directed rejection. *Child Development*, 67, 1048–1070.

International Journal of Behavioral Development
2005, 29 (2), 173–179

http://www.tandf.co.uk/journals/pp/01650244.html

Ψ Psychology Press
Taylor & Francis Group

© 2005 The International Society for the
Study of Behavioural Development

DOI: 10.1080/01650250444000388

On the use of Social Relations and Actor–Partner Interdependence Models in developmental research

Todd D. Little and Noel A. Card

University of Kansas, Lawrence, USA

We offer comments on the eight works contained in the Special Issue, all of which use advanced methods for analysing interdependencies using variants of the Social Relations Model (SRM) or the Actor–Partner Interdependence Model (APIM). After critically discussing the SRM and APIM as used in these works, we describe similarities and differences between these two approaches. We also discuss the substantive contributions of this collection and then offer our suggestions for future development of the two models.

Developmental research is inherently a study of interpersonal interactions, yet researchers have too long been hampered by traditional analytic techniques that make assumptions about independence of cases. Fortunately, techniques that accurately model the interdependencies of group and dyadic contexts have been developed, including the Social Relations Model (SRM) and the Actor–Partner Interdependence Model (APIM). The collection of eight articles in this Special Issue offer a rich representation of the manner in which interdependencies can be conceptualised and analysed in developmental research.

In the following, we review and comment upon the analytic application of the SRM and APIM in the articles of this Special Issue. We then compare and contrast these two techniques. We will also comment on the substantive contribution of these articles, including how the conceptual focus on interdependencies have allowed these researchers to answer questions that could not be considered using traditional individual-oriented approaches. Finally, we will offer our suggestions for future substantive and analytic work.

As we begin our commentary, we note that there is no necessarily "right" way to analyse interdependent data; and the papers of this Special Issue present a range of analytic options, each with different advantages and foci. Although we address strengths and potential weaknesses, our aim is to highlight the exemplary nature and substantial advances represented by these works.

The Social Relations Model (SRM)

The SRM represents a powerful conceptual and analytic approach to examining interdependencies within groups. This approach has been applied for quite some time in research with adults (for reviews see Kenny, 1994; Kenny, Albright, Malloy, & Kashy, 1994; Kenny, Mohr, & Levesque, 2001; Malloy & Kenny, 1986), but has not enjoyed widespread usage with children or adolescents. Perhaps the earliest application of the SRM in developmental psychology was Ross and Lollis' (1989) analysis of observations of toddlers' (20- and 30-month-olds) social behaviour in dyadic play settings. SRM analysis of play groups of unacquainted third-grade boys has shed light on the interpersonal nature of aggressive behaviour (Coie et al., 1999) and aggression-encouraging cognitions (Hubbard, Dodge, Cillessen, Coie, & Schwartz, 2001). Using the SRM in naturalistic settings is even less common, with only two prior studies to our knowledge that used this approach in classroom settings: Malloy and colleagues (Malloy, Sugarman, Montvilo, & Ben-Zeev, 1995; see also Malloy, Yarlas, Montvilo, & Sugarman, 1996) performed SRM analysis of first- through sixth-graders' interpersonal perceptions to determine the relative amount of actor and partner variances; and Scarpati, Malloy, and Fleming (1996) examined the perceptions of adolescents in special education classes of both their special education and mainstream peers. In the context of the family, however, Cook (1993, 1994, 2000, 2001; Cook & Kenny, 2004), Branje (Branje, Van Aken, & Van Lieshout, 2002; Branje, Van Aken, Van Lieshout, & Mathijssen, 2003), and others (e.g., Delsing, Oud, De Bruyn, & van Acken, 2003) have used the SRM, typically represented as structural equation models, in examining interpersonal perceptions and behaviours among different family members.

The four studies of this Special Issue that used the SRM build upon this small foundation, and, in our opinion, significantly advance the application of the SRM in developmental psychology. Specifically, the works advance prior applications through theory-driven partitioning of the sociomatrix, sophisticated modelling of social relations in families

---

Correspondence should be addressed to Todd Little or Noel Card at Schiefelbusch Institute for Life Span Studies, University of Kansas, 1000 Sunnyside Avenue, Lawrence, KS 66045-7555, USA; e-mail: yhat@ku.edu or ncard@ku.edu

Author contribution was equivalent. This work was supported in part by grants from the NIH to the University of Kansas through the Mental Retardation and Developmental Disabilities Research Center, (5 P30 HD002528), the Center for Biobehavioral Neurosciences in Communication Disorders (5 P30 DC005803), and an NRSA fellowship to the second author (1 F32 MH072005). Its contents are solely the responsibility of the authors and do not necessarily represent the official views of the NIH.

as structural equation models, and applying a little-used ANOVA-based approach for analysing dyadic interactions between siblings and parents and children. We will discuss these four works in order of their emphasis on group to dyadic levels of analysis.

Card, Hodges, Little, and Hawley (2005) conducted traditional SRM analysis of interpersonal perceptions within children's naturally occurring classroom groups to elucidate the degree of actor and partner variances (and degrees of generalised and dyadic reciprocity) in sixth-graders' perceptions of various aspects of aggression and social status. This study is similar to prior work applying the SRM to children's interpersonal perceptions (e.g., Malloy et al., 1995). A unique aspect of this study, however, was the division of the round robin sociomatrix by gender, thereby allowing comparisons of both within- and between-sex perceptions. Although Card and colleagues examined only the influence of gender, the logic of their approach could be applied to other features that might be central to group identification, such as children's ethnicity. A second feature of their study is the application of the SRM model to peer nomination data, challenging typical usage that considers only partner effects.

Ross, Stein, Trabasso, Woody, and Ross (2005) present an interesting application of the social relations model to study the quality of relationships within four-person families. They assessed each individual's self-reported behaviour toward others and their reports of others' behaviours toward themselves. Ross et al. provide a good example of how to analyse the SRM through structural equation modelling procedures. Representing the SRM as a structural equation model is made possible by the fact that individual's within these families can be assigned to meaningful roles (i.e., father, mother, older child, or younger child). The meaningful roles provide multiple indicators such that sources of shared and unique variance can be partitioned according to the SRM model (e.g., actor and partner variance).

Branje, Van Lieshout, and Van Aken (2005) expand upon their previous univariate social relations models of interpersonal support (Branje et al., 2002) and personality judgments within families (Branje et al., 2003) to present a multivariate social relations model of both agreeableness and support within families. Like Ross and colleagues, each family consisted of four individuals having distinct roles, here fathers, mothers, older adolescents, and younger adolescents, and the SRM was again represented as a structural equation model. In contrast to Ross and colleagues, however, this paper models the SRM decomposition for two variables in a multivariate manner in which social relations analysis for two variables are modelled simultaneously, rather than as two separate univariate models. The advantage of this approach is demonstrated by Branje and colleagues' ability to explore unattenuated latent associations across constructs. This multivariate approach (whether performed within traditional SRM approaches or within structural equation representations) exponentially expands the range of covariances that can be explored from within-construct generalised and dyadic covariances to both within- and between-construct generalised and dyadic covariances, as well as between-construct covariances of actor, partner, and relationship effects.

We believe that modelling the SRM within structural equation models, as demonstrated by the two papers by Ross and colleagues and Branje and colleagues, represents an important advancement in the field. The study by Branje and colleagues highlights the utility of modelling multiple variables of interest simultaneously. A useful aspect of SRM is its ability to meaningfully analyse multivariate data. With multivariate data unbiased estimates of actor, partner, and relationship effects are obtained for each construct, and the interrelations of these effects across constructs can be modelled. Simultaneous analysis of multivariate data within a single structural equation model allows for the estimation of disattenuated correlations between the self- and other-report actor, partner, and relationship constructs (as well as cross-construct generalised and dyadic reciprocity covariances). The advantage to such a modelling approach, as opposed to examining the manifest correlations among these constructs, is that it provides more accurate estimates of cross-construct covariances because they are corrected for measurement error.

A second advantage of modelling the SRM within structural equation models is the ability to include mean-level information in the model (i.e., Means and Covariance Structures, or MACS, analysis; see Little, 1997; Little & Slegers, in press). By including a constant in the model, one could make comparisons of the *latent* mean levels across roles (e.g., do mothers provide more support than fathers, both in general or toward specific children?) or constructs (e.g., is self-reported support greater than others' reports for each actor, partner, or relationship?). Again, the greater accuracy and power in comparing means, variances, and covariances among latent variables, as opposed to manifest variables, is a key advantage of modelling the SRM within MACS modelling framework.

Martin and Ross (2005) also examined four-person families, here consisting of fathers, mothers, older siblings (M ages = 4.4 years and 6.3 years at Times 1 and 2), and younger siblings (M ages = 2.4 years and 4.4 years at Times 1 and 2), observing families six times at each of two waves separated by approximately 2 years. The current report goes beyond previous reports from these data by examining the interdependency among siblings and between parents and children and by placing an emphasis on gender differences. The authors present data in which the four combinations of brother / sister with age-of-siblings is balanced (i.e., 10 each of brother-brother, brother-sister, sister-brother, and sister-sister as older-younger sibling pairs). Despite studying similar family structures (i.e., four-person families) as Ross and colleagues and Branje and colleagues did, Martin and Ross take a somewhat different analytic approach. Specifically, they used a form of Kraemer and Jacklin's (1979) method of analysing interdependent data described by Seay and Kay (1983), which is based more on an analysis of variance framework than the regression framework utilised by Ross and colleagues and Branje and colleagues. This method could also be analysed as a structural equation model. This observation should come as no surprise to readers familiar with parallelism between ANOVA and regression, although the complexity of the variance partitioning procedures shown in the Appendix of Martin and Ross makes this translation more subtle. Interested readers should consult Kenny (1996).

Although each of the four studies discussed in this section report using the SRM approach, it is important to distinguish between analysing group interdependency versus dyadic interdependency. The need for this distinction is not a negative quality, but rather, as discussed later, illustrates the flexibility and similarities of the SRM and APIM. Card and colleagues most strictly apply the random-effects *group-based* SRM, though they then subdivide the sociometric data to perform fixed-effects comparisons of interpersonal perception between boys and girls. Ross and colleagues and Branje and colleagues examine four-person families in which each individual has a specific role in the family, and thus model *small groups* as composed of distinguishable dyadic combinations. Martin and Ross also examine interactions within families, but here the analytic focus is primarily *dyadic* (i.e., inter-sibling aggression, parents' responses to child's aggression).

The Actor–Partner Interdependence Model (APIM)

Relative to the SRM, the APIM is a new development in the analysis of interdependent data. In contrast to the SRM, the APIM explicitly examines the potential mutual influence within dyadic (rather than group) contexts. Four articles of this Special Issue utilise this approach. Cook and Kenny (2005) provide a clear and accessible overview of the APIM, in which characteristics of individuals in dyads are examined in terms of actor and partner effects. As Cook and Kenny explain, the APIM can be analysed within the framework of multiple regression, structural equation modelling, or multilevel modelling. Before discussing this and related approaches in more detail, we briefly summarise the analytic approach taken in these four articles using the APIM. In this summary, we will emphasise the difference between distinguishable and exchangeable case dyads: With distinguishable dyads there is some meaningful manner by which to distinguish the two individuals across dyads (e.g., relationships between parents and children, relationships between older and younger siblings, or mixed-sex romantic relationships); whereas with exchangeable case dyads there is no relevant characteristic by which the individuals in the dyads can be consistently distinguished (e.g., same-sex friendships).

Cook and Kenny provided an example of the APIM by analysing data on interpersonal comfort, interpreted as attachment security, among mother-adolescent dyads. These dyads can be considered distinguishable cases, and were analysed in a straightforward manner using structural equation modeling.

Cillessen, Jiang, Laszkowski, and West (2005) apply the APIM to the study of adolescent same-sex friendships, examining actor and partner effects of social behaviour (physical and relational forms of aggression and prosocial behaviour) on friendship qualities. Because these are same-sex friendships, and the dyads are not distinguished on any other characteristic, these dyads can be considered exchangeable. The authors present bivariate correlations between individual's characteristics and the characteristics of their friendships. In contrast to common misconceptions, such correlations are unbiased estimates of the association—only the standard errors and resultant inferential tests are biased by dependency (e.g., Cohen, Cohen, West, & Aiken, 2003). In other words, the association between individuals within dyads, averaged across dyads, is an unbiased estimate of the population association; but the sample estimates of the population variance (and hence standard errors and significance tests) are biased by dependency (either underestimated or overestimated, depending on the direction and magnitude of correlation and dependency).

Cillessen and colleagues also present the intra-class correlation of similarity within friendship dyads and path analysis (i.e., structural equation modelling with manifest variables) testing the APIM of the social behaviour of both individuals in the friendship predicting individuals' reports of the friendship quality. Because the dyads are exchangeable, Cillessen and colleagues appropriately modify the APIM by equating the means and variances of the exogenous variables and endogenous residuals and the actor and partner paths across dyad members.

Burk and Laursen (2005) also examine friendships using the APIM, specifically evaluating several questions related to friends' agreement of friendship qualities, the contributions of actor and partner perceptions of friendship qualities to conflict, and the contributions of actor and partner perceptions of friendship qualities to several individual indices of adjustment. As with Cillessen and colleagues, Burk and Laursen examine same-sex friendships, which are exchangeable case dyads. Burk and Laursen, however, adapt an analytic approach quite different from Cillessen and colleagues: They analyse dyad average (between-dyad variance) and difference (within-dyad variance) scores. The reason that this approach is useful in the analysis of exchangeable case dyads is that relations among means and differences of different variables are not affected by which individual is considered in which position (as long as the position is consistent within the dyad in computation of difference scores for different variables). This approach was recommended by Kenny (1996) as an extension to the strategy of Kraemer and Jacklin (1979), represented in the paper by Martin and Ross. Although the approach of Martin and Ross was appropriate for the evaluation of gender (a dichotomous variable), it would have been inappropriate for the analyses of Burk and Laursen because their predictors were continuous (see Kenny, 1996). We note that, although Burk and Laursen chose to perform a series of univariate analyses rather than a more complex multivariate analysis, Kenny's (1996) more generalised extension can also be applied to multivariate analyses.

Adams, Bukowski, and Bagwell (2005) examine how children's aggression (an actor effect) and their friends' aggression (a partner effect) predict aggression 6-months later. Thus, this study applies the APIM to the study of friends' influence on aggressiveness. Adams and colleagues analysed 149 dyads (with no overlapping individuals) comprised of reciprocated (66 dyads) and unreciprocated (83) friendships. Such a data set creates difficulties in the analyses because the reciprocated friends can be considered exchangeable case dyads whereas the unreciprocated friends should be considered distinguishable case dyads. To manage this analytic difficulty, Adams and colleagues randomly assigned reciprocated friends to either the first or second position and analysed these data as if they were distinguishable cases. This approach represents a reasonable approach to managing a difficult analytic situation, given that they wanted to examine reciprocated friends (exchangeable cases) and unreciprocated friends (distinguishable cases) within the same set of analyses. Asymptotically, we expect that such an approach probably would not bias estimates of actor and partner effects; however, such an approach certainly does lead to lower power than would be obtained if these data from reciprocated friendships had been analysed using exchangeable case procedures. Nevertheless, this approach highlights the important fact that unique research questions regarding interdependency are going to lead to unique analytic problems, for many of which clear answers are not available. Through the creative application of extant approaches, however, the researcher can still address these questions in a reasonable manner.

Together these four papers provide examples of the complexity of dyadic data as well as sophisticated approaches to the analysis of dyadic data in either the distinguishable or exchangeable case. Cook and Kenny explain methods by which distinguishable case dyads can be analysed within the APIM framework using either regression analysis, structural equation modelling, or multilevel modelling. We view the regression approach as the least sophisticated because (1) separate (rather than simultaneous) analyses must be performed, and (2) there is no potential for modelling latent variables (i.e., correction for unreliability). However, this approach may be useful to those who want to reconceptualise previously published data (e.g., in meta-analytic work) within the framework of the APIM. We view the use of structural equation or multilevel modelling as preferable, and it is likely that similar results are obtained using either approach. Another advantage of the structural equation approach (either with manifest or latent variables) is that it provides a graphical presentation format that is very intuitive and easily accessible for readers.

The three papers in this Special Issue examining exchangeable case dyads (i.e., same-sex friendships) present three different approaches to the APIM, each with advantages and disadvantages. The simultaneous analysis of distinguishable and exchangeable dyads by Adams and colleagues presented difficult analytic choices; these authors ultimately chose to perform analyses appropriate to distinguishable case dyads and asymptotically unbiased (but low in power) with exchangeable cases. The approach of Burk and Laursen utilises a variance partitioning approach; although providing accurate results, extending this approach to latent variable modelling is complicated (see Kenny, 1996). Cillessen and colleagues' modification of the distinguishable case APIM by equating parameters across individuals in the dyad has the advantages of being easily comprehensible and easily modified to model latent interrelations.

We would also like to note an approach to analysing dyadic data not represented among these articles, which represents a reasonable alternative in both the distinguishable and exchangeable cases: the correlation procedures described by Gonzalez and Griffin (e.g., 1997). This approach involves analysing a data set in which data from each dyad are entered twice, once for each of the two positions of the dyad members. In the exchangeable case (Griffin & Gonzalez, 1995), similarities among dyad members and relations among variables of each member (i.e., actor and partner effects) are calculated using Pearson correlations within the doubly entered data arrangement (with the N* used for the computation of standard errors adjusted depending on the degree of dependence, ranging from N* = number of dyads for complete dependence to N* = number of individuals for complete independence). With distinguishable cases (Gonzalez & Griffen, 1999), similar analyses are performed, but a dichotomous variable representing the order of the distinguishable cases is covaried from the correlations. While we see no apparent reason why this approach would be more (or less) appropriate than those used in this Special Issue, it does represent yet another alternative for researchers analysing either exchangeable or distinguishable case dyadic data.

Similarities and differences between the SRM and the APIM

In some ways, the SRM and the APIM can be viewed as similar variants of one another. Before discussing similarities between the two models, however, we would like to emphasise the necessity of precision in terminology. Cook and Kenny point out in a footnote, and we wish to emphasise here, the distinction between the terms actor and partner effects in SRM and in the APIM. In the SRM, actor effects refer to the unbiased estimates of an individual's perception or behaviour toward others in general, and partner effects refer to the unbiased estimates of an individual's tendency to be perceived or behaved toward by others in general. Unfortunately, researchers using the SRM sometimes refer to actor and partner variances, or degrees of individual differences among individual's estimated actor and partner effects, as effects.

We wish to reiterate this distinction between effects and variances in the SRM; the former refers to individuals' estimates and the latter refers to the variability within a group (often averaged across multiple groups). In the APIM the terms actor and partner effects have an entirely different meaning. Here, these effects refer to regression paths (or comparable measures of association) between a characteristic of one individual in the dyad with either another characteristic of that same individual (an actor effect) or with a characteristic of the other individual in the dyad (a partner effect). To summarise, actor and partner effects in the SRM refer to estimated means of individuals, actor and partner variances in the SRM refer to the degree of individual differences among individuals, and actor and partner effects in the APIM refer to associations between variables either within an individual or across individuals in a dyadic relationship.

Keeping these terminological distinctions in mind, it is possible to envision the APIM of dyadic contexts demonstrated in this Special Issue being generalised to group-level analyses. Here, actor effects would be interpreted in the same manner—as relations among characteristics of one individual (between either different characteristics or across time). However, partner effects could be extended by interpreting them not as specific to one partner but rather as generalised across interaction partners (see Kashy & Kenny, 2000). In other words, whereas analysis in the dyadic context views partner effects as the relation of a *specific* partner's characteristics of the individuals, a group extension would view partner effects as the relation of the *average* of the other members of the group on a variable with the individual's dependent variable.

Dyadic data could also be considered a special case of the SRM in which there is insufficient information to determine the mean levels of dyadic behaviour for both the actor and partner. Such consideration is useful conceptually, if not analytically. The minimum number of individuals per group in the SRM is four, which can be reduced to three if reciprocity is not estimated (i.e., fixed at zero; see Kenny & La Voie, 1984). With dyadic data, one can not disentangle actor and partner mean tendencies (i.e., actor and partner effects in SRM terminology); for example, if child A aggresses against child B, it is impossible to determine if this is because child A is aggressive in general, child B is likely to be victimised in general, or if there is a unique aggressor–victim relationship between child A and child B.

If children interact with multiple partners, consistencies in their actor effects across partners (e.g., tendencies to aggress against others) and partner effects across actors (e.g., tendencies to be victimised) can be identified (as can relationship effects with multiple indicators, and reciprocity correlations). Considering the structural equation model representations of the SRM, dyads within families would be under-identified (i.e., one could not estimate actor and partner variances for two family members based on two observed variables representing the directional behaviours between the two individuals); three-person families (with roles) could be identified (with assumptions of equal loadings between dyadic interaction variables and latent actor and partner constructs); and four- (or more) person families are identified as demonstrated in these two papers.[1] If we consider the APIM conceptually as a special case of the SRM, we must remember that correlations in the APIM are computed across groups (dyads), whereas actor-actor, partner-partner, and actor-partner cross-construct correlations in the SRM are computed within each group and then averaged across groups.

Substantive advances of these works

Although we have focused much of our attention in this Commentary on the analytic details of the works of this Special Issue, we would be remiss if we did not comment on the important substantive advances made by these works. Here, we comment on the contributions of these works in understanding the family and peer group environments.

Four of these works provide insight into the interpersonal dynamics of family relations, each focusing on a specific aspect of the family. Branje and colleagues and Ross and colleagues each examine exchanges among fathers, mothers, and children in four-person families. The example provided by Cook and Kenny focused on dyadic mother-adolescent interactions. The study of Martin and Ross focused both on dyadic sibling interactions as well as triadic parental involvement in these interactions. We will briefly discuss each of these in turn.

Branje and colleagues examined perceptions of agreeableness and the receipt of support among parents and adolescent children; their application of the SRM allowed them to detect associations both in general (e.g., fathers who are seen as agreeable are reported to provide more support) and within specific relationships (e.g., fathers who are seen as agreeable by older children are reported to provide more support to older children). Interestingly, the findings showed that being perceived as agreeable in general does not translate into the receipt of more support in general; instead, being perceived as agreeable by a specific family member translates into support only from that family member. Together, these findings suggest both generality and specificity in the interpersonal perceptions within families, but only specificity in the elicitation of support from other family members.

Ross and colleagues examined family members' appraisals of the quality of their relationships with one another. Their findings suggest differences in mean levels of quality between different roles (e.g., parent–child relationships are seen more positively than sibling relationships). The inclusion of both self and other report provides information on the degree of bias within intra-family relationship quality. These results indicated that some family members tended to exhibit biases across relationships (e.g., younger children exhibited positive self bias across relationships with all family members), whereas others varied in their biases across relationship partners (e.g., mothers exhibited positive self bias with their children and negative self bias with their husbands). These findings, as well as those of Branje and colleagues, highlight the importance of considering the specific dyadic relationships that are present within the larger family system.

Although Cook and Kenny presented data primarily to demonstrate analysis using the APIM, this work adds to prior contributions by Cook (2000, 2001) by demonstrating the mutual influence[2] between mothers' and adolescents' comfort with one another. The authors also examine how the child's age might moderate these effects. This example provides further demonstration of the interpersonal family processes demonstrated by Ross and colleagues and Branje and colleagues.

Martin and Ross examined various forms of aggression among siblings, with a focus on gender differences in acts of aggression and in parents' responses to sibling aggression. Relative to the study of aggression in the peer group, inter-sibling aggression has received little empirical attention. The results of this study reveal important differences in rates of aggression depending on the sex of both the aggressor and target. Although gender differences in parents' responses to aggression were rather inconsistent, this direction of research has potentially important implications for the socialisation of gender differences in aggression. If a larger sample were available (which might also clarify the noted inconsistencies), it would be interesting to test whether the gender differences in parents' responses fully or partially account for gender differences in behaviour (ideally in longitudinal studies).

The other four papers of this Special Issue focus on the peer context. Three of these examine friendships, whereas Card and colleagues look at interpersonal perception within the peer group. Specifically, this latter study examined interpersonal perception of various aspects of aggression and social status both in general and among boys and girls, testing two theoretically driven hypotheses about gender differences in interpersonal perception. The translation and testing of existing theories within the emergent interpersonal models such as the SRM and APIM represents an important direction for future work.

Cillessen and colleagues considered the impact of individual's social behaviour (aggression and prosocial) on the

---

[1] As a technical note, one should be aware that the actor and partner effects in the SRM in which individuals are exchangeable approximate the row and column means, respectively, of the sociomatrix only in very large groups; there is a correction in the calculation of actor and partner effects, which becomes increasingly substantial in smaller groups because individuals do not interact with a peer identical to themselves in terms of their partner or actor effects, respectively (see Appendix B of Kenny, 1994).

[2] We use the phrase "mutual influence" somewhat loosely here. According to the more precise definitions provided by Kenny (1996), the process modelled in the example of Cook and Kenny should specifically be termed partner effects. The term mutual influence would refer to a different model in which only intra-individual paths between the independent and dependent variables are modelled, and the only inter-individual influence is the modelling of reciprocal causal paths between the two individual's dependent variables (see Kenny, 1996).

quality of their friendships, and Burk and Laursen examined the contributions of friendship qualities on the qualities of conflict within the friendships, as well as on the individual's adjustment. An important advancement of both of these studies is the consideration of friends' agreement on relational qualities (i.e., friendship and conflict qualities) and the contributions of both friends' characteristics and perceptions to the quality of the friendship. Although results generally indicated greater actor effects than partner effects, there was some evidence that partner effects provided additional predictive power. An important detail of these studies was the reliance on multireporter assessments; studies relying only on self-reports would be expected to contaminate actor effects with shared rater variance, yet these authors use multiple reporters (e.g., peers, teachers) to avoid this confound in many of their analyses.

The study by Adams and colleagues is unique in examining both reciprocated and unreciprocated friends within the same set of analyses. This represents a significant substantive advancement in our understanding of the influence of friendships. Too often in studies of childhood friendships, individuals without reciprocated friends are excluded from analysis. Moreover, there is little prior work distinguishing the impact of unreciprocated and reciprocated friends. This study considers young people with and without reciprocated best friendships, and finds that the socialising influence on aggression is modestly greater within reciprocated than unreciprocated friendships.

We would like to note that although three of the papers examining the peer context focused on friendships, the APIM is in no way limited to these types of relationships. Further work applying this conceptual and analytic approach to the study of romantic relationships, antipathetic relationships, and aggressor-victim dyads all are potentially fruitful avenues for research. The application of the SRM as applied to family systems by Ross and colleagues and Branje and colleagues might also be used to study peer relations; there exist numerous role classifications within the peer relations literature (e.g., sociometric classifications) that could meaningfully be used as a framework to explore interpersonal perception, affect, and behaviours.

Future directions in analytic strategies

Although the papers of this Special Issue represent substantial advances in the analysis of interpendent data in developmental research, they also point to the need for further advancement in analytic techniques. We note three limitations that warrant discussion.

As seen among the works by Cook and Kenny, Adams and colleagues, Burk and Laursen, Cillessen and colleagues, and Martin and Ross, there exist multiple approaches to analysing dyadic data, all of which are perfectly valid. We also pointed out the correlational approaches advocated by Gonzalez and Griffin (1997, 1999; Griffen & Gonzalez, 1995) as another alternative. Given these multiple options, further work is needed in comparing these approaches. Opinions could be offered regarding the relative transparencies of the different approaches, adaptability to both distinguishable and exchangeable dyad situations, and ability to model latent constructs, and we have hinted at our preferences earlier. However, simulation work is needed regarding how well these approaches perform

given various sample sizes, degrees of dyadic interdependence, and distribution properties (e.g., violations of normality, noninterval measurement) before solid recommendations among these alternatives can be offered.

Another important future direction is the development of appropriate methods of handling missing data. A common approach is simply to drop individuals or families with missing data; however, this practice is well known to bias parameter estimates and decisions of inference. Another approach to missing data is to impute using algorithms developed under assumptions of interdependence. Although this approach is certainly preferable to deletion of cases (individuals, dyads, or families) with missing data, we believe that further advances in missing data estimation are needed. Specifically, if we know that interdependence is evident within our data, then this interdependence should be part of the imputation model. The development of techniques considering this interdependence in the imputing of missing data represents an important future direction.

Developmental research is inherently dependent on longitudinal results, yet methods of modelling longitudinal research in the SRM and APIM are lacking. Cook and Kenny noted that the APIM is adaptable to longitudinal designs, including analysis of longitudinal trajectories of individuals within dyads or time-series analysis of dyads over numerous time points. However, the methods of analysing these longitudinal patterns within the other dyadic analytic approaches are unclear. Moreover, modelling of longitudinal processes in the SRM is a topic that is virtually unexplored. We believe that appropriate techniques for modelling longitudinal processes within interdependent data represents one of the most critical future directions for applying the SRM and APIM in developmental research.

Conclusions

As mentioned, developmental research is inherently a study of interpersonal interactions, yet the field has generally relied on traditional analytic techniques that assume independence of cases. The papers presented in this Special Issue provide us with a variety of ways in which the interdependence of interpersonal interactions can be analysed accurately. More importantly, however, these papers offer us terrific examples of how the various analytic models also function as informative conceptual models. That is, the various modelable aspects of interpersonal interactions become grist for theorising about their basic nature, their developmental unfolding, and their mediating and moderating functions.

References

Adams, R. E., Bukowski, W. M., & Bagwell, C. (2005). Stability of aggression during early adolescence as moderated by reciprocated friendship status and friend's aggression. *International Journal of Behavioral Development*, 29, 139–145.

Branje, S. J. T., Van Aken, M. A. G., & Van Lieshout, C. F. M. (2002). Relational support in families with adolescents. *Journal of Family Psychology*, 16, 351–362.

Branje, S. J. T., Van Aken, M. A. G., Van Lieshout, C. F. M., & Mathijssen, J. J. J. P. (2003). Personality judgments in adolescents' families: The perceiver, the target, their relationship, and the family. *Journal of Personality*, 71, 49–81.

Branje, S. J. T., Van Lieshout, C. F. M., & Van Aken, M. A. G. (2005). Relations between Agreeableness and perceived support in family relationships: Why nice people are not always supportive. *International Journal of Behavioral Development, 29,* 120–128.

Burk, W. J., & Laursen, B. (2005). Adolescent perceptions of friendship and their associations with individual adjustment. *International Journal of Behavioral Development, 29,* 156–164.

Card, N. A., Hodges, E. V. E., Little, T. D., & Hawley, P. H. (2005). Gender effects in peer nominations for aggression and social status. *International Journal of Behavioral Development, 29,* 146–155.

Cillessen, A. H. N., Jiang, X. West, T. V., & L., Laszkowski, D. K. (2005). Predictors of dyadic friendship quality in adolescence. *International Journal of Behavioral Development, 29,* 165–172.

Cohen, J., Cohen, P., West, S. G., & Aiken, L. S. (2003). *Applied multiple regression / correlation analysis for the behavioral sciences* (3rd ed.). Mahwah, NJ: Lawrence Erlbaum Associates Inc.

Coie, J. D., Cillessen, A. H. N., Dodge, K. A., Hubbard, J. A., Schwartz, D., Lemerise, E. A., & Bateman, H. (1999). It takes two to fight: A test of relational factors and a method of assessing aggressive dyads. *Developmental Psychology, 35,* 1179–1188.

Cook, W. L. (1993). Interdependence and the interpersonal sense of control: An analysis of family relationships. *Journal of Personality and Social Psychology, 64,* 587–601.

Cook, W. L. (1994). A structural equation model of dyadic relationships within the family system. *Journal of Consulting and Clinical Psychology, 62,* 500–509.

Cook, W. L. (2000). Understanding attachment security in family context. *Journal of Personality and Social Psychology, 78,* 285–294.

Cook, W. L. (2001). Interpersonal influence in family systems: A social relations model analysis. *Child Development, 72,* 1179–1197.

Cook, W. L., & Kenny, D. A. (2004). Application of the social relations model to family assessment. *Journal of Family Psychology, 18,* 361–371.

Cook, W. L., & Kenny, D. A. (2005). The Actor-Partner Interdependence Model: A model of bidirectional effects in developmental studies. *International Journal of Behavioral Development, 29,* 101–109.

Delsing, M. J. M. H., Oud, J. H. L., De Bruyn, E. E., & Van Aken, M. A. G. (2003). Current and recollected perceptions of family relationships: The Social Relations Model approach applied to members of three generations. *Journal of Family Psychology, 17,* 445–459.

Gonzalez, R., & Griffin, D. (1997). On the statistics of interdependence: Treating dyadic data with respect. In S. Duck (Ed.), *Handbook of personal relationships* (2nd ed., pp. 271–302). New York: Wiley.

Gonzalez, R., & Griffin, D. (1999). The correlational analysis of dyad-level data in the distinguishable case. *Personal Relationships, 6,* 449–469.

Griffin, D., & Gonzalez, R. (1995). Correlational analysis of dyad-level data in the exchangeable case. *Psychological Bulletin, 118,* 430–439.

Hubbard, J. A., Dodge, K. A., Cillessen, A. H. N., Coie, J. D., & Schwartz, D. (2001). The dyadic nature of social information processing in boys' reactive and proactive aggression. *Journal of Personality and Social Psychology, 80,* 268–280.

Kashy, D. A., & Kenny, D. A. (2000). The analysis of data from dyads and groups. In H. T. Reis & C. M. Judd (Eds.), *Handbook of research methods in social and personality psychology* (pp. 451–477). New York: Cambridge University Press.

Kenny, D. A. (1994). *Interpersonal perception: A social relations analysis.* New York: Guilford.

Kenny, D. A. (1996). Models of non-independence in dyadic research. *Journal of Social and Personal Relationships, 13,* 279–294.

Kenny, D. A., Albright, L., Malloy, T. E., & Kashy, D. A. (1994). Consensus in interpersonal perceptions: Acquaintance and the big five. *Psychological Bulletin, 116,* 245–258.

Kenny, D. A., & La Voie, L. (1984). The social relations model. In L. Berkowitz (Ed.), *Advances in experimental social psychology, Vol. 18* (pp. 141–182). Orlando, FL: Academic Press.

Kenny, D. A., Mohr, C. D., & Levesque, M. J. (2001). A social relations variance partitioning of dyadic behavior. *Psychological Bulletin, 127,* 128–141.

Kraemer, H. C., & Jacklin, C. N. (1979). Statistical analysis of dyadic social behavior. *Psychological Bulletin, 86,* 217–224.

Little, T. D. (1997). Mean and covariance structures (MACS) analyses of cross-cultural data: Practical and theoretical issues. *Multivariate Behavioral Research, 32,* 53–76.

Little, T. D., & Slegers, D. (in press). Factor analysis: Multiple groups with means. In D. Rindskopf (Section Ed.), *Encyclopedia of statistic in behavioral sciences.* Chichester, UK: Wiley.

Malloy, T. E., & Kenny, D. A. (1986). The social relations model: An integrative method for personality research. *Journal of Personality, 54,* 199–225.

Malloy, T. E., Sugarman, D. B., Montvilo, R. K., & Ben-Zeev, T. (1995). Children's interpersonal perceptions: A social relations analysis of perceiver and target effects. *Journal of Personality and Social Psychology, 68,* 418–426.

Malloy, T. E., Yarlas, A., Montvilo, R. K., & Sugarman, D. B. (1996). Agreement and accuracy in children's interpersonal perceptions: A social relations analysis. *Journal of Personality and Social Psychology, 71,* 692–702.

Martin, J. L., & Ross, H. S. (2005). Sibling aggression: Sex differences and parents' reactions. *International Journal of Behavioral Development, 29,* 129–138.

Ross, H. S., & Lollis, S. P. (1989). A social relations analysis of toddler peer relations. *Child Development, 60,* 1082–1091.

Ross, H., Stein, N., Trabasso, T., Woody, E., & Ross, M. (2005). The quality of family relationships within and across generations: A social relations analysis. *International Journal of Behavioral Development, 29,* 110–119.

Scarpati, S., Malloy, T. E., & Fleming, R. (1996). Interpersonal perception of skill efficacy and behavioral control of adolescents with learning disabilities: A social relations approach. *Learning Disability Quarterly, 19,* 15–22.

Seay, M. B., & Kay, E. J. (1983). Three-way analysis of dyadic social interactions. *Developmental Psychology, 19,* 868–872.

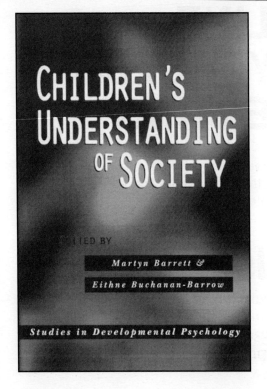

IDENTITY IN ADOLESCENCE

The Balance Between Self and Other

Third Edition

Jane Kroger

Fully updated to include the most recent research and theoretical developments in the field, the third edition of *Identity in Adolescence* examines the two-way interaction of individual and social context in the process of identity formation. Setting the developmental tradition in context, Jane Kroger begins by providing a brief overview of the theoretical approaches to adolescent identity formation currently in use. This is followed by a discussion of five developmental models which reflect a range of attempts from the oldest to among the most recent efforts to describe this process and include the work of Erik Erikson, Peter Blos, Lawrence Kohlberg, Jane Loevinger, and Robert Kegan. Although focusing on each theorist in turn, this volume also goes on to compare and integrate the varied theoretical models and research findings and sets out some of the practical implications for social response to adolescents. Different social and cultural conditions and their effect on the identity formation process are also covered as are contemporary contextual, narrative, and post-modern approaches to understanding and researching Identity issues.

SERIES: ADOLESCENCE AND SOCIETY

HARDBACK: 0-415-28106-7: 2004: 256PP: 216X138: **£39.95 / $70.00**
PAPERBACK: 0-415-28107-5: 2004: 256PP: 216X138: **£16.95 / $29.95**

Prices are subject to change; please check our website for current information: **www.psypress.co.uk**

For titles and resources on this and related topics, or to order this title, visit:

www.developmentalpsychologyarena.com